O_l
C_i

A CASEBOOK

ORSON WELLES'S
Citizen Kane

◆ ◆ ◆

A CASEBOOK

Edited by
James Naremore

OXFORD
UNIVERSITY PRESS

2004

OXFORD

UNIVERSITY PRESS

Oxford   New York

Auckland   Bangkok   Buenos Aires   Cape Town   Chennai
Dar es Salaam   Delhi   Hong Kong   Istanbul   Karachi   Kolkata
Kuala Lumpur   Madrid   Melbourne   Mexico City   Mumbai   Nairobi
São Paulo   Shanghai   Taipei   Tokyo   Toronto

Copyright © 2004 by Oxford University Press, Inc.

Published by Oxford University Press, Inc.
198 Madison Avenue, New York, New York 10016

www.oup.com

Library of Congress Cataloging-in-Publication Data
Orson Welles's Citizen Kane: a casebook / edited by James Naremore.
p. cm. — (Casebooks in criticism)
Includes bibliographical references.
ISBN 0-19-515891-1; 0-19-515892-X (pbk.)
1. Citizen Kane (Motion picture) I. Naremore, James. II. Series.
PN1997.C5117 C36 2004
791.43'72—dc22   2003018676
Rev.

1 3 5 7 9 8 6 4 2

Printed in the United States of America
on acid-free paper

I wish to express my thanks to William Andrews for inviting me to compile this anthology.

I dedicate the volume to Ronald Gottesman and Jonathan Rosenbaum, in appreciation for their indispensable scholarship on Orson Welles.

Credits

✦ ✦ ✦

Paul Arthur, "Out of the Depths: *Citizen Kane*, Modernism, and the Avant-Garde Impulse," in *Perspectives on* Citizen Kane, edited by Ronald Gottesman (Hall, 1996).

Peter Bogdanovich, "Interview with Orson Welles," and "Editor's Notes on the Welles Interview" by Jonathan Rosenbaum, in *This Is Orson Welles*, edited by Jonathan Rosenbaum (HarperCollins, 1992).

Robert L. Carringer, "The Scripts of *Citizen Kane*," *Critical Inquiry* 5 (1978): 369–400.

Michael Denning, "The Politics of Magic: Orson Welles's Allegories of Anti-Fascism," in *The Cultural Front: The Laboring of American Culture in the Twentieth Century* (Verso, 1996).

Laura Mulvey, "*Citizen Kane*: From Log Cabin to Xanadu," in *Perspectives on Orson Welles*, edited by Morris Beja (Hall, 1996).

James Naremore, "Style and Meaning in *Citizen Kane*," in *The Magic World of Orson Welles* (Oxford University Press, 1978; rev. ed., Southern Methodist University Press, 1989).

François Thomas, "*Citizen Kane*: The Sound Track," in *Citizen Kane*, by Jean-Pierre Berthomé and François Thomas (Flammarion, 1992).

Peter Wollen, "*Citizen Kane*," in *Readings and Writings* (Verso, 1982).

Contents

✦ ✦ ✦

Orson Welles's
Citizen Kane

A CASEBOOK

Introduction

JAMES NAREMORE

❖ ❖ ❖

I

WHEN IT WAS FIRST RELEASED by RKO Pictures in 1941, *Citizen Kane* enjoyed a spectacular critical reception. American novelist John O'Hara, writing for *Time* magazine, said quite simply that it was the best motion picture he had ever seen.[1] Other serious reviewers in this country didn't debate whether or not it was unusually good, but whether or not it was a great, even revolutionary, achievement. Meanwhile, *Kane* was the subject of considerable controversy in Hollywood; it was nominated for nine Academy Awards but received only one, for best original screenplay by Herman Mankiewicz and Orson Welles, who were booed by detractors at the award ceremony.

After World War II, when *Kane* became available for international distribution, it prompted widespread discussion among intellectuals and filmmakers. In Argentina, modernist author Jorge Luis Borges described it as a brilliantly constructed "labyrinth without a center"—a bit too heavily "Germanic," perhaps, but

worthy of comparison with the novels of Franz Kafka.² Philoso-
pher Jean-Paul Sartre wrote that the entire world of French cinema was abuzz with excitement over *Kane*, although he himself
thought it too much the work of American intellectuals who
were "cut off from the masses."³ Sartre predicted that sophisticated Europeans would find the film less innovative and important than had the inexperienced American reviewers. As things
turned out, he could not have been more wrong. *Kane* was a
crucially important picture for Sartre's contemporary, French film
theorist André Bazin, and for the younger generation of critics
at the influential journal *Cahiers du Cinema* during the 1950s; indeed
its director, Orson Welles, became one of the chief inspirations
for the French New Wave and for international art cinema as a
whole.

Citizen Kane was also an important influence on Hollywood
style in the 1940s, on the American avant-garde cinema in the
same period, and on American auteurs Peter Bogdanovich, Martin
Scorsese, and Francis Coppola in the 1970s. Its overall reputation
has continued to grow. Each decade since 1952, the British Film
Institute and its leading journal, *Sight and Sound*, has conducted an
international poll of critics to name the ten best films of all time.
In every decade from 1962 until 2002, when *Sight and Sound* broad-
ened the poll to include the votes of 145 critics and academics
and 108 film directors, *Kane* has been voted number one. The
results were the same in 2000, when the American Film Institute
conducted a more populist and less informed survey of U.S. ce-
lebrities, newspaper critics, and Hollywood directors, who chose
Kane number one among the "100 best films" ever made. Even if
we regard such rankings, which are seldom explicitly applied to
books, music, or paintings, as unreliable guides to artistic value,
they have considerable sociological interest, giving solid evidence
that during the past sixty years *Kane* has become emblematic of
the cinema itself. Predictably, no movie has been more written
about in academic anthologies like the one you are now reading.
(The first article about a film ever published in the august journal
PMLA, which is subscribed to by virtually every literature teacher

in U.S. universities, was devoted to *Kane*.) If any film is canonical, it is this one.

Canonicity is a mixed blessing. It assures that *Kane* will be preserved for posterity, but at the same time it makes the film seem overly respectable and serious, something to be studied rather than thoughtfully enjoyed and experienced. It also creates expectations in the mind of a first-time viewer that probably cannot be fulfilled, enshrouding the revered cultural object with so much critical judgment that we may have difficulty seeing it clearly. For Orson Welles, who was only twenty-six when he produced, cowrote, directed, and starred in *Kane*, the picture ultimately became something of an albatross, or at least a benchmark against which everything he did afterward was measured and found wanting by critics who seemed to relish his fall from grace. Given this phenomenon, plus my own admiration for Welles's work as a whole, I usually avoid naming it as his best film. Sure, *Kane* is brilliant, I usually say, but have you seen, just for starters, *The Magnificent Ambersons*, *The Lady from Shanghai*, *Othello*, *Touch of Evil*, or *Chimes at Midnight*? Some of these productions are marred by studio re-editing and others are relatively difficult to find in good prints, but all of them are remarkable, worth viewing again and again.

Interestingly, although *Kane* has a unique reputation among Welles's films, critics and historians have disagreed about the nature of its importance. Especially in America, there is a certain tendency to view the film as a happy accident, born of the so-called collaborative nature of the Hollywood system. In a famous essay published in 1971, *New Yorker* critic Pauline Kael helped to fuel this notion by arguing that *Kane* belonged squarely in the tradition of well-made 1930s theater and movie satire, and that the person most responsible for its script was not Orson Welles (who, Kael charged, tried to take all the credit), but veteran Hollywood screenwriter Herman Mankiewicz, a former New York newspaperman who was celebrated for his cynical wit. A somewhat similar thesis was propounded in the memoirs of Welles's former associate John Houseman, who had assisted in the writing of the screenplay but declined credit. In the next decade, Robert L. Carringer's extremely useful production history of the film contended that *Kane* was essentially a collaboration among its writers, its photographer, and the various set designers and technicians at RKO. Even some of the historians who have written entire books about Welles—including Charles Higham, Simon Callow, and David Thomson—view the film as a special case in which the director's artistic ego was mediated by the contributions of others. The fact that Welles never again made a film that provoked such widespread discussion is usually offered as proof of the argument.

In response to these writings, let me say immediately that *Citizen Kane* is the product of a particular movie director and a group of his associates working at a specific studio at a specific historical moment. The credits as they appear on screen at the beginning and end of the picture are reasonably accurate: *Kane* is a "Mercury Production by Orson Welles," but it is also the work of others, including Welles's cowriters, an ensemble of actors, and a large technical staff. Certainly it would not look the same had it been photographed by someone other than Gregg Toland, who had previously done most of his work with the Samuel Goldwyn company, or if it had been made at any other studio than RKO, which was famous for the black-and-white set designs of the early Fred Astaire–Ginger Rogers musicals, for the matte photography and special effects in *King Kong* (1933), and for Walt Disney's animated production of *Snow White and the Seven Dwarfs* (1937). And yet a great deal is at stake when we choose to emphasize Hollywood over Welles. To do so is to promote the myth of a "golden age" of studio production and to transform *Kane* into an official classic of American pop culture—all the while forgetting or repressing its controversial politics and artistic differences.

It would appear that Orson Welles represents what his most articulate and knowledgeable critic, Jonathan Rosenbaum, has described as an "ideological challenge" to the American media's normal way of evaluating the movie industry, and for that reason alone his importance cannot be underemphasized.[4] We should understand that, far from being a typical studio production, *Kane* is a direct outgrowth of Welles's work during the late 1930s and early 1940s as a prodigious director in the New York Federal Theater Project (the Harlem *Macbeth, Dr. Faustus, The Cradle Will Rock*) and in his own Mercury Theater organization (the modern-dress *Julius Caesar, Heartbreak House, Native Son*), both of which espoused progressive, New Deal politics and reflected the Popular Front alliance between socialists, communists, and liberal democrats against the spread of fascism. His dazzling success on the New York stage and in network radio, where the Mercury Theater engaged in a series of experimental dramas, was closely connected to major political events of the day—the economic depression, the rise of Hitler, and the impending world war. Initially he resisted offers from Hollywood, but the infamous "War of the Worlds" broadcast (1938), which appeared just after the Munich crisis and caused a national panic, transformed him overnight into a household name and led to a generous contract at RKO, where he was given a remarkable degree of control over his first movie. As a result, he brought the entire Mercury Theater organization to California—including music composer Bernard Herrmann and virtually every actor who appears in *Kane*—in an attempt to create a production unit comparable to the one he and John Houseman had established in New York.

Welles's radio dramas were distinguished by the way they employed various types of first-person narration, and, perhaps because of the Mars panic, he was drawn to stories about demagogues who manipulate the public. For his first project in Hollywood, he tried to adapt Joseph Conrad's *Heart of Darkness*, updating the story to comment on present-day fascism and using a gyroscopic camera (a forerunner of today's steadicam) to represent the subjective point of view of Marlow, Conrad's first-person narrator. (He also wrote scripts for a couple of political thrillers, *The Smiler with a Knife* and *The Way to Santiago*, which were never put into production.) When the Conrad project proved too complicated and expensive, he became attracted to the idea of a thinly disguised story about a famous American, which would be told from the "prismatic" perspective of several characters who had known him. Various figures, among them John Dillinger and

Howard Hughes, were floated as possible subjects for this new film, until Herman Mankiewicz proposed the perfect candidate: William Randolph Hearst, the multimillionaire publisher who was one of the creators of "yellow journalism."

An American imperialist, Hearst had used his newspapers to promote the Spanish-American War and to back various jingoistic causes. Despite his populist approach to the news, he was a life-long opponent of organized labor and a staunch opponent of Franklin Roosevelt's New Deal. When his own attempts at a political career failed, he gradually retreated to his magnificent California estate, San Simeon, where he lived openly with his mistress, movie star Marion Davies, and gave fabulous parties for the Hollywood elite. (Mankiewicz had been a guest at some of those parties.) From the moment when the motion-picture camera was invented, he had shown a strong interest in the propagandistic possibilities of movies, and in the 1920s and 1930s he established his own film production unit at MGM, where he sponsored the proto-fascistic *Gabriel over the White House* (1933) and sometimes burdened Davies, a charming comedienne, with leaden, elaborately mounted costume pictures. All the while, his newspapers continued to support reactionary politicians, including, for a time, Hitler and Mussolini.

Part of the impact of *Citizen Kane* for its original audience lay in the exhilarating sense it gave of a bright, iconoclastic young director using the means of production against one of America's most wealthy media moguls. But *Kane* would have been of merely topical interest had it not also been a powerful example of film art. At the most obvious level, it represents a strikingly modernist intervention into Hollywood narrative; thus its gothic atmosphere has reminded some viewers of Kafka, and its manipulations of time, memory, and point of view have evoked critical comparisons with such novelists as Proust, Conrad, Faulkner, and Fitzgerald. *Kane* also makes us aware of almost fifty years in the development of the film medium. Its movie-within-the-movie, "News on the March," cleverly encapsulates the entire history of newsreels, and its dramatic episodes synthesize the major schools of film making prior to 1941: Soviet montage, French surrealism,

German expressionism, and the Hollywood biopic. At the same time, *Kane* introduces a new style, forever afterward associated with Welles, based on deep-focus photography, wide-angle lenses, and shots of unusually long duration.

The film's achievement is not merely technical or stylistic. *Kane* tells us something about American politics, and its central images keep returning in the national life: Richard Nixon secluding himself at San Clemente, or Howard Hughes, just before his death, living in a Bahamas retreat he called the "Hotel Xanadu." But even though *Kane* gives us the definitive satire of a certain American type, it also depicts that type with a fascinating ambivalence, using Freud as much as Marx in order to understand him. In this regard, we should note that the film's complex treatment of its central character is not shared by the two biographies of Hearst written in the 1930s, which are in as much disagreement as Walter Parks Thatcher and the anonymous labor spokesman in the *Kane* newsreel. The authorized portrait, Mrs. Freemont Older's *William Randolph Hearst, American* (1936), makes Hearst seem a paragon of civic virtue, a sort of philosopher-king; in contrast, Ferdinand Lundberg's *Imperial Hearst* (1937), which was later cited in an absurd plagiarism case against Mankiewicz and Welles, is a muckraking journalist's exposé of a tycoon's crimes against society. Both books are valuable to students of the film because they show how much *Kane* delights in making references to Hearst's life; but they also show that Kane and Hearst are not identical. In turning the yellow journalist into a creature of fiction, Mankiewicz and Welles borrowed freely from other lives and departed from biographical fact in ways that are crucially important to the dramatic and perhaps also to the ideological effects of the film. Unlike the biographers, they chose to concentrate on a private life rather than the public structuring of an empire. They also gave Kane a humble birth, which was not true of any of his possible models. Last, and in some ways most significant because more than anything else it roused the ire of the Hearst press, they made Kane's second wife, Susan Alexander, into a tormented creature who walks out on her supposed benefactor—this in contrast to the Hearst-Davies relationship, which was generally happy. Indeed when death finally came to William Randolph Hearst, some years after the controversy provoked by the film, he was not living alone in the caverns of his estate; he had moved to the less resplendent Beverly Hills mansion of his mistress, and he died with her close at hand. His last words went unrecorded.

To some viewers, these changes have suggested that Mankiewicz and Welles allowed their sense of melodrama to undercut their politics. As a poor boy suddenly given wealth, Kane becomes less representative of his class, and as a lonely old man he seems to embody a sentimentalized, money-can't-buy-happiness mythology that has long been promulgated by the movies. Furthermore, as reviewer Joy Davidman wrote in the *New Masses* when the film was first released, "Welles has not escaped one Hollywood convention: the smirking thesis that the important thing about a public figure is not how he treats his country but how he treats his women."[5] In response to such criticism, it might be noted that Hearst's life *was* in some sense melodramatic, and that left-wing writers during the 1930s had taken relish in depicting his biography as a kind of morality play. In the *Big Money* (1935), novelist John Dos Passos had described Hearst as a "spent Caesar grown old with spending," and Professor Charles Beard, in his introduction to the Lundberg biography, had predicted that the old man would die lonely and unloved. By showing Kane as a tragicomic failure, Mankiewicz and Welles were doing the same thing that these writers had done, and in concentrating on a tyrant's psyche, they were simply popularizing their critique and trying to create an engaging fiction.

In any case, the film clearly does satirize Kane's public life. It exposes his manipulative interest in the Spanish-American War; it reveals his exploitative "philosophy" of journalism; and it makes several references to his attacks on organized labor. In the election scenes, it depicts the corruptions of big-money politics with the force of a great editorial cartoon; moreover, it links the press to the politicians themselves and ultimately shows Kane being hoist on his own petard. Kane's democratic aspirations are seen as a cover for his desire for power, a means to extend paternalistic benevolence to the "people." In the newsreel, we even see him standing on a balcony with Hitler. What is even more radical and at least equally interesting, however, is that *Kane* brings its own workings under scrutiny, questioning the whole process of "image making" in the movies. From the beginning, when "Rosebud" is used as a means of spicing up a newsreel, until the end, when the reporter Thompson confesses the futility of searching out the meaning of a single word, the film casts doubts on its own conclusions. Along the way, Welles's superb direction keeps reminding us that we are watching a movie, an exceedingly clever and entertaining manipulation of reality, rather than reality itself.

Doubtless one of the more important reasons that *Kane* takes a somewhat psychological rather than a purely didactic approach to its central character is that from the time of his 1937 production of *Julius Caesar* on the New York stage, Welles had wanted to avoid a major problem of left-wing drama, which, he once observed, was a tendency to create cardboard, Simon Legree villains. Another reason is that *Kane* often seems to be about Orson Welles himself. It was Welles, after all, who was known as an *enfant terrible*, and this may account for the film's emphasis on infantile rage; it was Welles, not Hearst, who was raised by a guardian, and the guardian's name has been given to a character in the film; and it was the young Welles who had made a famous comment comparing the movies to his own personal electric train set, almost like Kane saying that it would be "fun" to run a newspaper. According to several people who worked on the film, including John Houseman and Bernard Herrmann, Welles deliberately filled the screenplay with in-jokes and autobiographical references (a practice he had already established in his script for *Heart of Darkness*). Even Raymond the butler, the last witness to Kane's life, is modeled on a suspicious servant who used to lurk around Welles's big Hollywood house.

It would nevertheless be quite wrong to equate Kane with Welles. In the last analysis, the film is a work of fiction, a social parable with psychological overtones, based on a recognizable type of wealthy and powerful American from the gilded age of U.S. capitalism. The original title for the film was *American* (a term Hearst repeatedly used to describe himself, while accusing his critics of being "anti-American"), and the indictment of Kane extends to an entire class of people who betrayed democracy. Welles himself summarized his aims in language that seems appropriate to what we see on the screen. "The protagonist of my 'failure story,' " he wrote,

> must retreat from a democracy which his money fails to buy and his power fails to control. There are two retreats possible: *death* and the *womb*. The house [Xanadu] was the womb. Here too was all the grandeur, all the despotism which my man had found lacking in the outside world. Such was his estate—such was the obvious repository for a collection large enough to include, without straining the credulity of the audience—a little toy from the dead past of a great man.[6]

Whatever Welles's intentions, the political and personal significance of his film was certainly not lost on the man who was the chief model for Charles Foster Kane. The most important fact about *Citizen Kane* is that it was a fundamentally dangerous project, loosely based on a live and kicking subject—a fascist sympathizer whose power in Hollywood was second only to his power over a newspaper and communications empire. The results were about what could have been expected. Hearst was rumored to have taken the film lightly, but his reprisals are a matter of record. His papers refused to allow advertising or even mention of *Kane*, and he sent a personal note to columnist John Chapman saying that anyone who admired the film was not a "loyal American." His minions approached J. Edgar Hoover, who launched a secret FBI investigation of Welles that lasted for more than a decade, at one point labeling the director of *Kane* a threat to the national security.[7] Meanwhile, Hearst's friend Louis B. Mayer, the production chief at MGM, tried to purchase *Kane* from RKO with the express intention of destroying it forever. *Kane* got sensational publicity from Hearst's rivals in the publishing world (as Welles probably expected it would), but Hearst used his influence to make sure it would not receive an all-important "circuit booking" in West Coast theater chains. Hence it never had an opportunity to show a strong profit in its initial release. *Kane* had been held to a relatively modest A-picture production budget (the negative cost was $749,000) and was praised by *Hollywood Reporter* for its frugality. Nevertheless, Hollywood bosses were beginning to perceive Welles as a left-wing ideologue and a menace to business. *Kane* may not have been a thoroughgoing anticapitalist attack, but it was close enough to ensure that Welles would never again be given such creative freedom in Hollywood.

II

This anthology represents only a small fraction of the literature on *Citizen Kane*. Those who wish to read more about the film are advised to find a good library and consult two previous, unfortunately out-of-print anthologies, both edited by Ronald Gottesman: *Focus on* Citizen Kane (1971) and *Perspectives on* Citizen Kane (1996). The second of these is especially important, not only because of the breadth of its selections and the strength of its bibliography, but also because of Gottesman's fine introduction, which surveys the entire history of criticism on the film. In making my own selections from the literature, I tried to avoid too much overlap with the items Gottesman chose to reprint, but it was impossible not to include several of them.

I have not tried to present a gallery of critical approaches, a technique that usually produces a sterile display of academic methodologies rather than a useful study of the object under discussion. I also avoided arranging the writings as a set of critical debates, in the belief that such an arrangement would sacrifice insight for the sake of a rhetorical gesture. (The attentive reader will nonetheless discover disagreements and differences among the essays.) I was guided instead by the desire to assemble a small group of previously published writings that would provide accurate production information, along with critical analyses of the film's aesthetics, politics, and cultural/historical context. Given the large amount of impressive commentary on *Kane*, I had to sacrifice many items for which I have the greatest respect. I can

only recommend that readers consult the footnotes at the end
of each essay and the selected bibliography at the conclusion of
the volume, which lists a number of influential books and essays
not represented here.

The collection begins with Peter Bogdanovich's 1970 interview
with Orson Welles, which was published as the second chapter of
This Is Orson Welles (1992), a large volume of interviews covering
most of Welles's career. I have also included bibliographic and
critical notes written by the volume's editor, Jonathan Rosenbaum, who provides essential background information. As Rosenbaum indicates, parts of Bogdanovich's conversation with Welles
appeared previously in an article ostensibly written by Bogdanovich, "The *Kane* Mutiny," published by *Esquire* magazine in 1972.[8]
Despite Welles's apparent reluctance to talk about *Kane*, he had
been deeply wounded by Pauline Kael's claim that he tried to
take all the credit for the film, and also by some of her patron-
izing critical judgments. In fact, much if not all of "The *Kane*
Mutiny" was actually written by Welles himself, who used his
friend Bogdanovich as a willing front to refute Kael, and who
provided documentary evidence from the Mercury Theater production files to substantiate his case. The definitive scholarly discussion of exactly who wrote what on *Citizen Kane* can be found
in the next item of the collection, Robert L. Carringer's "The
Scripts of *Citizen Kane*," which not only helps to settle a troublesome dispute, but also gives us intriguing insight into the development of the screenplay and the process of refinement it went
through both before and during filming.

All of the other essays in the volume deal with the completed
film. My own contribution, "Style and Meaning in *Citizen Kane*,"
is a condensation and slight revision of two chapters from *The
Magic World of Orson Welles*, the first full-scale academic book on
Welles, which was initially published by Oxford in 1978. (A few
paragraphs from that book were also used in the foregoing introduction.) This essay offers a commentary on the film's deep-
focus photography and narrative strategies, highlighting Welles's
work as a director. It is followed by François Thomas's "*Citizen
Kane*: The Sound Track," which has been translated from French

especially for this anthology. Here it might be noted in passing that some of the most important writings on *Kane* and on Welles in general have come from Paris, the capital of international film culture. André Bazin's post–World War II discussion of *Kane* was enormously influential in the reception of the film, and Youssef Ishaghpour has recently published *Orson Welles: Cinéaste Une Caméra Visible*, an impressively learned and intelligent three-volume study of Welles, a considerable portion of which is devoted to *Kane*. Among these French writings is Jean-Pierre Berthomé and François Thomas's excellent *Citizen Kane* (1992), which carefully analyzes every aspect of the film, including the screenplay, photography, editing, musical score, sound track, and the relationships between Kane, Hearst, and Welles. From this book I have selected Thomas's chapter on the sound track, which reminds us that film is an audiovisual medium and which offers the single most accurate description and analysis of the sound design for *Kane*.

The next two items in the anthology deal mainly with cultural politics. Michael Denning's "The Politics of Magic" is extracted from his chapters on Welles in *The Cultural Front*, a wide-ranging book about the American Popular Front in the 1930s and 1940s. Denning provides a cogent account of how *Citizen Kane* relates to the political project of Welles's antifascist theatrical productions, radio shows, and later work as a director of Hollywood *film noir*. Laura Mulvey's "*Citizen Kane*: From Log Cabin to Xanadu" (a condensation of her British Film Institute monograph on *Kane*) places equally strong emphasis on politics, viewing *Kane* from a European perspective and giving serious attention to its psychoanalytic themes. One of the most influential feminist theorists in the world, Mulvey has particularly interesting things to say about the way *Kane* elicits an active spectatorship "not founded on a polarization of gender."

The last two essays are concerned in different ways with the relationship between *Citizen Kane* and the non-Hollywood cinema. Peter Wollen's essay on *Kane* was initially published in *Film Reader* as an introduction to a structural analysis of the film by a group of his students at Northwestern University; in contrast to most previous commentators, Wollen views *Kane* in the context of international literary modernism, and he emphasizes the way the film's narrative and camera style (particularly its use of the long take) foreshadow the radical aesthetics of such European film-makers as Alain Robbe-Grillet and Margaret Duras. Paul Arthur's "Out of the Depths: *Citizen Kane*, Modernism, and the Avant-Garde Impulse" calls attention to the complex dialectic between illusionism and anti-illusionism in Welles's work, and shows how *Kane* anticipated and influenced an American avant-garde movement in the later 1940s, most notably in such pictures as Maya Deren and Alexander Hammid's *Meshes of the Afternoon*. As these and the other essays in the volume suggest, *Kane* is uniquely important for the way it attracts the interest of both realists and antirealists, both formalists and political activists, and both Hollywood and the avant-garde. Perhaps no other motion picture has meant so much to different theorists and directors from around the world, at different points in history.

III

To conclude this introduction, let me offer a note on what might be called the "texts" of *Citizen Kane*. Obviously, the best way to view the film would be to see a carefully restored 35-millimeter print in an actual movie theater. Unfortunately, the fiftieth-anniversary "restoration" of *Kane*, supervised by Robert Wise for theatrical release in 1991, was somewhat poorly done. Few 16-millimeter prints of the film available today are of truly superior quality, especially when they are copied from the 1991 theatrical version, and any videotape based on that version should also be avoided. The best American video copies of *Kane* are the 1992 Criterion edition and the more recent DVD edition produced by Warner Brothers in 2000. In general, the "timing" or control of light levels in the Warner DVD makes the film look somewhat brighter than it should; on the whole, however, everyone agrees that this is an extremely good copy of the film. The disk also contains useful commentary from both Peter Bogdanovich and

Roger Ebert. The one extra on the DVD that I cannot recommend is a documentary entitled "The Battle over *Citizen Kane*." I was consulted by the makers of this film, who used some of the material I had uncovered on the FBI investigations of Welles and who, at my own request, listed me in the credits. When I saw the completed documentary, however, I was quite disappointed. It contains valuable archival footage of Hearst and Davies at San Simeon, but its central argument, that Orson Welles and William Randolph Hearst were very much alike, strikes me as a tabloid trick worthy of "News on the March." This is not the place to enter into an extended rebuttal of the argument. I will only say that among the many things it ignores or obfuscates is the fact that Welles was a political progressive who used most of the money he earned in the movies to create some of the most important works of art of the twentieth century (including the films he directed after *Kane*). Hearst, on the other hand, was a political reactionary who used the vast fortune he had inherited to assemble a relatively unremarkable private art collection. The DVD of *Citizen Kane* deserves much better supplementary material, and we can only hope that someday a good documentary on the making of *Kane* will be available.

Notes

1. John O'Hara, "*Citizen Kane*," in *Perspectives on* Citizen Kane, ed. Ronald Gottesman (New York: Hall, 1996), pp. 28–29.
2. Jorge Luis Borges, "*Citizen Kane*," in Gottesman, ed., *Perspectives on* Citizen Kane, pp. 54–55.
3. Jean-Paul Sartre, "*Citizen Kane*," trans. Dana Polan, in Gottesman, ed., *Perspectives on* Citizen Kane, pp. 56–59.
4. Jonathan Rosenbaum, "Orson Welles as Ideological Challenge," in *Movie Wars: How Hollywood and the Media Conspire to Limit What Films We Can See* (Chicago, Ill.: A Capella Press, 2000), pp. 175–96. See also Rosenbaum, "The Battle over Orson Welles," *Cineaste* 22, no. 3 (1996): 6–10.
5. Joy Davidman, "*Citizen Kane*," in Gottesman, ed., *Perspectives on* Citizen Kane, p. 38.

6. Quoted in Frank Brady, *Citizen Welles: A Biography of Orson Welles* (New York: Scribner's, 1989), p. 285.

7. See James Naremore, "The Trial: Orson Welles vs. the FBI," *Film Comment* (January–February 1991): 22–27.

8. Peter Bogdanovich, "The *Kane* Mutiny," *Esquire*, October 1972, pp. 99–105, 180–90.

Interview with Orson Welles

PETER BOGDANOVICH

✦   ✦   ✦

PETER BOGDANOVICH: What was your initial reaction to the Hearst blacklist on *Citizen Kane*?

ORSON WELLES: We expected it before it happened. What we *didn't* expect was that the film might be destroyed. And that was nip and tuck; it was very close.

PB: To the negative being burned?

OW: Yes. It was only *not* burned because I dropped a rosary.

PB: What?

OW: There was a screening for Joe Breen, who was the head of censorship then, to decide whether it would be burned or not. Because there was tremendous payola from all the other studios to get it burned.

PB: All because of Hearst's people?

OW: Yes. Everybody said, "Don't make trouble, burn it up, who cares? Let them take their losses." And I got a rosary, put it in my pocket, and when the running was over, in front of Joe Breen, a good Irish Catholic, I stood up and dropped my rosary on the floor and said, "Oh, excuse me," and picked it up and put it back in my pocket. If I hadn't done that, there would be no *Citizen Kane*.

Guaymas, Mexico. Orson is there acting in Mike Nichols's movie of Catch-22, *and they've given him the day off, so we've settled ourselves outside a spacious hotel overlooking the bay. It's hot, and Orson has brought only winter clothes, so he is still wearing the lightweight army uniform that is his costume for the film. Yesterday we tried to talk about Citizen Kane and got sidetracked—I suppose purposely—so I'm trying again, and Orson isn't too happy about it.*

PB: You act as though it's painful for you to remember any of these things.

OW: Oh, everything. Just awful.

PB: Are you up to trying *Kane*?

OW: Oh Christ! All right—let's get it over with. I can't be awfully good on the subject, because I haven't seen the picture since I ran the last finished print in an empty theater in downtown Los Angeles, about six months before it was released.

PB: Wait a minute—you went to the premiere.

OW: I went to the premiere and went right out the side door when it started, the way I always do. Because it makes me nervous not to be able to *change* anything. It comes from being in the theater—you used to go to the opening, then go backstage and change things. When I've got a play running, I go on changing it until the last day of the show. And it's awful to have it all locked up in a can forever. That's why I don't go to see them.

PB: I guess it's like some painters. My father's like that. And Cézanne who kept going into people's houses after he sold the painting—

OW: Yes! They'd smell wet paint and know Cézanne had been in! That's just the way I feel. I'd like to go to the projection booth and start snipping away.

PB: Griffith did—all during the run of *Birth of a Nation*, he'd be up in the booth making changes.

OW: Well, it was easier then. Silent picture—no damn sound to worry about.

PB: So when Hearst intervened . . .

OW: Hearst didn't really intervene—they intervened on his behalf. It began badly, because Louella Parsons had been on the set and had written a wonderful article about this lovely picture I was making. And it was Hedda Hopper, her old enemy, who blew the whistle. Think of the weapon that gave to the competition! After that it was the Hearst hatchet men who were after me, more than the old man himself.

PB: But wasn't Hedda Hopper supposedly your friend?

OW: Sure—but what a break for her as a newspaperwoman. Couldn't blame her. Imagine what that did to Louella!

PB: After *Kane*, you once said, "Someday, if Mr. Hearst isn't frightfully careful, I'm going to make a film that's really based on his life."

OW: Well, you know, the real story of Hearst is quite different from Kane's. And Hearst himself—as a *man*, I man—was *very* different. There's all that stuff about [Robert] McCormick and the opera. I drew a lot from that, from my Chicago days. And Samuel Insull. As for Marion [Davies], she was an extraordinary woman—nothing like the character Dorothy Comingore played in the movie. I always felt he had the right to be upset about that.

PB: Davies was actually quite a good actress—

OW: And a fine woman. She pawned all her jewels for the old man when he was broke. Or broke enough to need a lot of cash. She gave him everything, stayed by him—just the opposite of Susan. *That* was the libel. In other words, Kane was better than Hearst, and Marion was much better than Susan— whom people wrongly equated with her.

PB: You once said that Kane would have enjoyed seeing a film based on his life, but not Hearst.

OW: Well, that's what I said to Hearst.

PB: When!?

OW: I found myself alone with him in an elevator in the Fairmont Hotel on the night *Kane* was opening in San Francisco. He and my father had been chums, so I introduced myself and asked him if he'd like to come to the opening of the picture.

He didn't answer. And as he was getting off at his floor, I said, "Charles Foster Kane would have *accepted*." No reply. . . . And Kane *would* have, you know. That was his style—just as he finished Jed Leland's bad review of Susan as an opera singer.

PB: Where did Kane's trait of acquiring possessions come from?

OW: *That* comes directly from Hearst. And it's very curious—a man who spends his entire life paying cash for objects he never looked at. I know of no other man in history exactly like that. This jackdaw kind of mind. Because he never made any money, you know; his great chain of newspapers basically lost money. He was in every sense a failure. He just acquired things, most of which were never opened, remained in boxes. It's really a quite accurate picture of Hearst to that extent.

PB: There's only one moment in *Kane* where I thought your acting was self-conscious—

OW: Tell me. I'll tell you the bad moment for me—in the first scene with Susan, the close-up when I had the mud on my face. That's a real phony movie moment. Look at it again—it really is. I haven't seen it since I made it, but—

PB: It's not so bad as—

OW: Not so bad, but it's a real movie actor with mud on his face. What's yours?

PB: The close-up smile in the newspaper office when Cotten asks to keep the Declaration of Principles you wrote—

OW: Oh, but that's *supposed* to be a forced smile. It's because I don't think the document should be kept—I don't believe in it.

PB: Really?

OW: Of course.

PB: You mean Kane didn't mean what he'd written even as he wrote it?

OW: No.

PB: I didn't realize that.

OW: No. You weren't supposed to believe that smile. He's horrified that somebody wants to keep that as a document. It's going too far.

PB: [*laughs*] All right, then I take it back—it's a great moment!

OW: [*laughing*] Anyway, it's not supposed to be a real smile, but the smile of somebody deeply embarrassed, being caught out. There's a point to that moment. Nobody signals it, but that's what I meant. Because I always believed that Kane doesn't mean all that. He only wants to convince the two fellows. He wants them to believe it because he wants them to be his slaves. But he doesn't believe in anything. He's a damned man, you know. He's one of those damned people that I like to play and make movies about.

PB: There's a film written by Preston Sturges called *The Power and the Glory* [1933] which has been said to have influenced you in the flashback style of *Kane*. Is that true?

OW: No. I never saw it. I've heard that it has strong similarities; it's one of those coincidences. I'm a great fan of Sturges and I'm grateful I didn't see it. He never accused me of it—we were great chums—but I just never saw it. I saw only his comedies. But I would be honored to lift anything from Sturges, because I have very high admiration for him.

PB: You were friends.

OW: Right up till the end of his life [in 1959]. And I knew him before I went to Hollywood; in fact, I first met him when I was about thirteen and going to school at Todd. Wonderful fellow, and I think a great filmmaker, as it turned out.

PB: Yes, and he wrote marvelous dialogue.

OW: Started in a hospital. He was a businessman until he was about forty. He got very sick and lay in the hospital and decided to write a play, *Strictly Dishonorable*, which ran eight years or something on Broadway. And that made him a writer. Then later he became a director. He had never thought of it before.

PB: What happened to him in Europe in the 1950s? He only made one film.

OW: He was just trying to raise money for a picture. Nobody would give him a job. Simple as that.

PB: The idea for the famous breakfast scene between Kane and his first wife [the nine-year deterioration of their marriage is told through one continuing conversation over five flash-pans]—

OW: —was stolen from *The Long Christmas Dinner* of Thornton Wilder! It's a one-act play, which is a long Christmas dinner that takes you through something like sixty years of a family's life—

PB: All at dinner—

OW: Yes, they're all sitting at dinner, and they get old—people wheel baby carriages by, and coffins and everything. That they never leave the table and that life goes on was the idea of this play. I did the breakfast scene thinking I'd invented it. It wasn't in the script originally. And when I was almost finished with it, I suddenly realized that I'd unconsciously stolen it from Thornton and I called him up and admitted to it.

PB: What was his reaction?

OW: He was pleased.

PB: Is he still a good friend?

OW: Yes. Wonderful writer. I haven't seen him in a long time, but his newest novel, *The Eighth Day*, is marvelous.

PB: Did the idea literally come to you on the set?

OW: Well, there were going to be several breakfast scenes—you can see how it would have been written in the script—many scenes with transitions. And my idea was simply to photograph it as a continuous breakfast scene without dissolves, just whipping back and forth. Some of the conversation was written before; a lot of it was invented on the set and two or three days before, during rehearsal.

PB: Just how important was [Herman J.] Mankiewicz in relation to the script?

OW: Mankiewicz's contribution? It was enormous.

PB: You want to talk about him?

OW: I'd love to. I loved *him*. People did. He was much admired, you know.

PB: Except for his part in the writing of *Kane*. . . . Well, I've read the list of his other credits. . . .

OW: Oh, the hell with lists—a lot of bad writers have wonderful credits.

PB: Can you explain that?

OW: Luck. The lucky bad writers got good directors who could write. Some of these, like Hawks and McCarey, wrote very well indeed. Screenwriters didn't like that at all. Think of those old pros in the film factories. They had to punch in every morning, and sit all day in front of their typewriters in those terrible "writers' buildings." The way they saw it, the director was even worse than the producer, because in the end what really mattered in moving pictures, of course, was the man actually making the pictures. The big-studio system often made writers feel like second-class citizens, no matter how good the money was. They laughed it off, of course, and provided a good deal of the best fun—when Hollywood, you understand, was still a funny place. But basically, you know, a lot of them were pretty bitter and miserable. And nobody was *more* miserable, *more* bitter, and *funnier* than Mank, . . . a perfect monument of self-destruction. But, you know, when the bitterness wasn't focused straight onto you, he was the best company in the world.

PB: How did the story of *Kane* begin?

OW: I'd been nursing an old notion—the idea of telling the same thing several times—and showing exactly the same scene from wholly different points of view. Basically, the idea *Rashomon* used later on. Mank liked it, so we started searching for the man it was going to be about. Some big American figure—couldn't be a politician, because you'd have to pinpoint him. Howard Hughes was the first idea. But we got pretty quickly to the press lords.

PB: The first drafts were in separate versions, so when was the whole construction of the script—the intricate flashback pattern—worked out between you?

OW: The actual writing came only after lots of talk, naturally, . . . just the two of us, yelling at each other—not too angrily.

PB: What about the *Rashomon* idea? It's still there to a degree.

OW: It withered away from what was originally intended. I wanted the man to seem a very different person depending on who was talking about him. "Rosebud" was Mank's, and the many-sided gimmick was mine. Rosebud remained, because it was the only way we could find to get off, as they used to say in vaudeville. It manages to work, but I'm still not too keen about it, and I don't think that he was, either. The whole shtick is the sort of thing that can finally date, in some funny way.

PB: Toward the close, you have the reporter say that it doesn't matter what it means—

OW: We did everything we could to take the mickey out of it.

PB: The reporter says at the end, "Charles Foster Kane was a man who got everything he wanted, and then lost it. Maybe Rosebud was something he couldn't get or something he lost, but it wouldn't have explained anything. . . ."

OW: I guess you might call that a disclaimer—a bit corny, too. More than a bit. And it's mine, I'm afraid.

PB: I read the script that went into production. . . . There were so many things you changed on the set, or, anyway, after you'd started shooting. From the point of view of Kane's character, one of the most interesting is the scene where you're remaking the front page for about the twentieth time. In the script, Kane is arrogant and rather nasty to the typesetter. In the movie, he's very nice, even rather sweet. How did that evolve?

OW: Well, all he *had* was charm—besides the money. He was one of those amiable, rather likable monsters who are able to command people's allegiance for a time without giving too much in return. Certainly not love; he was raised by a bank, remember. He uses charm the way such people often do. So when he changes the first page, of course it's done on the basis of a sort of charm rather than real conviction. . . . Charlie Kane was a man-eater.

PB: Well, why was it in the script the other way?

OW: I found out more about the character as I went along.

PB: And what were the reactions of Mankiewicz to these changes?

OW: Well, he only came once to the set for a visit. Or, just maybe, it was twice. . . .

Here is a memo, dated August 26, 1940, which I [PB] came across after this conversation, from Herbert Drake, Mercury Productions' press agent:

RE: ... TELEPHONE CONVERSATION WITH HER-
MAN J. MANKIEWICZ RE CUT STUFF HE SAW ...

1. In Bernstein's office with Bill Alland: Everett Sloane is
   an unsympathetic looking man, and anyway you
   shouldn't have two Jews in one scene.
2. Dorothy Comingore [as Susan Alexander Kane] looks
   much better now so Mr. M. suggests you re-shoot the
   Atlantic City cabaret scene. [Miss Comingore had been
   carefully made up to look as bad as possible.]
3. There are not enough standard movie conventions being observed including too few closeups and very little
   evidence of action. It is too much like a play, says
   Mr. M.

PB: Before shooting began, how were differences about the script
worked out between you?

OW: That's why I left him on his own finally, because we'd
started to waste too much time haggling. So, after mutual
agreements on story line and character, Mank went off with
Houseman and did his version, while I stayed in Hollywood
and wrote mine. At the end, naturally, I was the one who was
making the picture, after all—who had to make the decisions.
I used what I wanted of Mank's and, rightly or wrongly, kept
what I liked of my own.

PB: As you know, Houseman has repeatedly claimed that the
script, including the conception and structure, was essentially
Mankiewicz's.

OW: It's very funny that he does that, because he deserves some
credit himself. It's very perverse, because actually he was a
junior writer on it, and made some very important contributions. But for some curious reason he's never wanted to take
that bow. It gives him more pleasure just to say I didn't
write it.

PB: I have the impression, somehow—well, let's put it this way:
do you believe John Houseman is an enemy?

OW: To rewrite an old Hungarian joke: if you've got him for a friend, you don't *need* an enemy. . . . The truth is, you know, that I cling to the pathetic delusion that I don't have such things as enemies. But Jack is the one who makes this sort of Christian Science a bit difficult.

PB: How did your partnership work in the Mercury?

OW: For the radio shows, he acted as super editor over all the writers; he produced all the first drafts. And that, in a way, was his function with Mank for that six or eight weeks of their separate preparation for *Kane*. In the theater, he was the business, and also, you might say, the political, boss. That last was important, particularly in the WPA. Without his gifts as a bureaucratic finagler, the shows just wouldn't have got on. I owe him much. Leave it at that. . . . It's a story I don't think I want to tell.

PB [*after a pause*]: There's a scene in which Susan is singing for you the first time in her apartment, and that dissolves to her singing for you in an entirely different, much-better-decorated apartment—

OW: —which Kane set up for her, yes.

PB: And you applaud in that scene, which goes to a group of people applauding Cotten, who is making a speech saying that Kane "entered this campaign"—cut to you finishing the sentence, "with one purpose only," in another campaign speech. Was a thing like that done in the preparatory stages?

OW: Yes, but the last preparatory stages—we were already rehearsing.

PB: It has the beautiful economy of segue-ing on a radio show.

OW: Yes, in a way, except faster than you could on radio.

PB: What about something like the woman screaming offscreen during your fight with Susan in the picnic tent?

OW: That was invented after we shot it. I thought, looking at the rushes, that's what we needed.

PB: As a counterpoint?

OW: Yes, and the song that went with it ["This Can't Be Love"], I'd heard Nat King Cole and his trio do in a little bar. I kind of based the whole scene around that song.

PB: There's a shot of a black singer at one point—

OW: It isn't him, but the music is by Nat Cole—it's his trio. He doesn't sing it—he's too legitimate. We got some kind of low-down New Orleans voice—but it was his number and his trio.

PB: How did you work with Bernard Herrmann on the score?

OW: Very intimately, as I always did for many years on radio. Almost note for note. Benny Herrmann was an intimate member of the family. I think his score was marvelous for the opera in the film, *Salaambo*. It was a delightful pastiche.

From a telegram sent by Welles to Herrmann on July 18, 1940, just a few days before shooting began on Kane:

> Opera sequence is early in shooting, so must have fully orchestrated recorded track before shooting. Susie sings as curtain goes up in the first act, and I believe there is no opera of importance where soprano leads with chin like this. Therefore suggest it be original . . . by you—parody on typical Mary Garden vehicle. . . . Suggest *Salammbo* [*sic*] which gives us phony production scene of ancient Rome and Carthage, and Susie can dress like grand opera neoclassic courtesan. . . . Here is a chance for you to do something witty and amusing—and now is the time for you to do it. I love you dearly.

OW: There's some music in the film Herrmann didn't write, like that tune for "Oh, Mr. Kane." That's a Mexican march I heard once down here in the north someplace.

PB: When we go to Mrs. Kane's boardinghouse, the snow is falling, and the music is lovely, very lyrical; then the snowball hits the house and the music just stops, right in the middle of a phrase.

OW: Typical radio device. We used to do that all the time. That music is very good right there.

PB: What about the idea of the light bulb spluttering out when Susan's voice fails and fades? Was a thing like that in the script?

OW: No. It was worked out later, of course.

PB: How did that shot evolve where the camera went all the way from Susan singing to two stagehands in the flies—and then one holds his nose?

OW: The idea for the way it ended was contributed by our prop man. His name was Red. We were just going to go up to them looking disgusted or something. Anyway, it was a big contribution.

PB: You've told me that everyone felt free to contribute—that was part of the atmosphere on the set.

OW: That's true—it was wonderful. We had a couple of spies on the set, as I told you, but everyone else hated them, so they were completely in quarantine. Of course, the first two weeks of the film were done without the studio knowing we were shooting a picture. We said we were making tests, because I had never directed a picture. That began part of the big legend: "Imagine, he's been fourteen days on camera tests with extras and actors in costume!" But we were shooting the *picture*. Because we wanted to get started and be already into it before anybody knew about it.

PB: So there wouldn't be pressure on you.

OW: Yes, that's right. It was Perry Ferguson's idea, the art director.

PB: Do you agree with André Bazin that deep-focus camera set-ups increase the ambiguity of a movie, because the director doesn't make choices for the audience—they can decide who or what they want to look at in the frame?

OW: That's right. In fact, I did a lot of talking about that in the early days of my life as a filmmaker—when I was more shameless and used to sound off on theory. I talked a lot about that "giving the audience the choice" business. It strikes me as pretty obvious now; I don't know why I came on so strong about it.

PB: I don't think it's so obvious; and it certainly wasn't twenty-five years ago. What about a shot like the one after Susan has tried to commit suicide? There's a bottle in the foreground, and we see you break through the door in the background. Did you have to use an outsized bottle in order to hold focus?

OW: No, it was just an ordinary, standard size.

PB: It must have been very difficult to get a dark scene that still had enough light to hold focus.

OW: You bet. It was a very dark scene until the door opens and I come in—and *then* you see this ID bracelet I had on by accident because I had a girlfriend who made me wear it. Every time I think of that scene, I think of my reaching down and you see this awful love charm—nothing at all to do with Kane. That's all I really remember about that scene.

PB: I never noticed it. You must have cursed yourself watching the rushes.

OW: Yes, when I saw it I said, "Shall we go back, do it again?" "No." "Maybe he could have such—" "He never would have it." "They won't see it." And whenever I think of seeing this picture, the reason I don't want to is because I don't want to see that goddamn bracelet come down.

PB: I guess one always remembers the little things that nobody in the world would notice.

OW: Well, you'll notice it the next time you see it.

PB: That's true.

OW: It glitters on the screen!

PB: Some people have said that the look of *Kane* is a result of Gregg Toland's photography, but all your pictures have the same visual signature, and you only worked with Toland once.

OW: It's impossible to say how much I owe to Gregg. He was superb. You know how I happened to get to work with Gregg? He was, just then, the number-one cameraman in the world, and I found him sitting out in the waiting room of my office. "My name's Toland," he said, "and I want you to use me on your picture." I asked him why, and he said he'd seen some of our plays in New York. He asked me who did the lighting. I told him in the theater most directors have a lot to do with it (and they used to, back then), and he said, "Well, fine. I want to work with somebody who never made a movie." Now, partly because of that, I somehow assumed that movie lighting was supervised by movie *directors*. And, like a damned fool, for the first few days of *Kane* I "supervised" like crazy. Behind me, of course, Gregg was balancing the lights and telling everybody to shut their faces. He was angry when somebody finally came to me and said, "You know, that's really supposed to be Mr. Toland's job."

PB: You mean he was protecting you?

OW: Yes! He was quietly fixing it so as many of my notions as possible would work. Later he told me, "That's the only way to learn anything—from somebody who doesn't know anything." And, by the way, Gregg was also the *fastest* cameraman who ever lived, and used fewer lights. And he had this extraordinary crew—his own men. You never heard a sound on a Toland set, except what came from the actors or the director. There was never a voice raised, only signs given. Almost Germanic, it was so hushed. Everybody wore neckties. Sounds depressing, but we had a jazz combo to keep our spirits up.

PB: Toland didn't mind that?

OW: Not so you'd notice. With all his discipline, he was easygoing, and quite a swinger off the set.

PB: How did you get along with him after you found out that lighting was his job?

OW: Wonderfully. I started asking for lots of strange, new things—depth-of-focus and so on. . . .

PB: An elementary question: why did you *want* so much depth-of-focus?

OW: Well, in life you see everything in focus at the same time, so why not in the movies? We used split-screen sometimes, but mostly a wide-angle lens, lots of juice, and stopped way the hell down. We called it "pan focus" in some idiot interview—just for the fun of it—

PB: Didn't mean anything?

OW: Of course not. But for quite a while that word kept turning up in books and highbrow articles—as though there really *was* something you could do called "pan focusing!" . . . Christ, he was the greatest gift any director—young or old—could ever, ever have. And he never tried to impress us that he was doing any miracles. He just went ahead and performed them. *Fast.* I was calling for things only a beginner would have been ignorant enough to think anybody could ever do, and there he was, *doing* them. His whole point was, "There's no mystery to it." He said, "*You* can be a cameraman, too—in a couple of days I can teach you everything that matters." So we spent the next weekend together and he showed me the inside of that bag of tricks, and, like all good magic, the secrets are ridiculously simple. Well, that was Gregg for you—that was how big he was. Can you imagine somebody they now call a "director of photography" coming right out and admitting you can bone up on the basic technical side of it all in a weekend? Like magic again: the secret of the trick is nothing; what counts is not the mechanics, but how you can make 'em work.

PB: You gave Toland credit on the same card as yourself, which Ford had done, too, on *The Long Voyage Home*.

OW: Up till then, cameramen were listed with about eight other names. Nobody those days—only the stars, the director, and the producer—got separate cards. Gregg deserved it, didn't he?

PB: What made you put on so many ceilings?

OW: The simple thing is that movies still go on telling lies. First of all, they pretend there isn't a fourth wall—as in the theater—that *has* to be because the camera is there. But then they pretend there's no ceiling—a big lie in order to get all those terrible lights up there. You can hardly go into a room without seeing a ceiling, and I believe the camera ought to show what the eyes see normally looking at something. That's all it was. Not because I thought the ceiling in itself had anything beautiful to say. It just seemed to me it was clearly a bad theatrical convention to pretend it wasn't there.

PB: Well, you also used a lot of low-angle shots that couldn't avoid seeing the ceiling. In fact, you're still fond of shots like that.

OW: I don't know why. I suppose it's because I think the picture looks better down there. Just that. I suppose I had more low angles in *Kane* just because I became fascinated with the way it looked—and I do it less now because it's become less surprising. But there are an awful lot of dull interiors—*Kane* is full of them—which are by their nature not very interesting and which look better when the camera is low. I think I overdid it.

PB: In the big scene between Kane and Leland after Kane loses the election, the whole thing is from an extreme low angle.

OW: Well, there's a purpose in that one—that was deliberate and wasn't just because the set looked better.

PB: What was the purpose?

OW: Oh, I don't know—I think if it doesn't explain itself, I can't explain it. There's this fallen giant. . . . I think that really called for the camera being there. And, of course, it was very low. We had to dig a hole, and they had to drill into the concrete floor for us to get down that low. And I'd sprained my ankle, so if you look carefully in that scene, you can see the steel brace I was wearing on my heel. I had fallen down the stairs in the scene where I threw Gettys out, and I was limping around in a steel brace. It took nerve to shoot from down there, with that steel brace right in front of the camera, but I thought rightly that at that point they'd be looking at Leland and not at me. Anyway, I wanted it like a big, kind of mythical encounter between the two. And also I wanted it to look outsized, because what they're saying is so prosaic, yet has reverberations—I had some such highfalutin idea. It still seems justified to me as I look back on it. But I don't have a general theory about low angles.

PB: How do you decide where you're going to put the camera?

OW: I don't make a conscious decision—I know instantly where it goes. There's never a moment of doubt. And I never use a viewfinder any more.

PB: You look through the camera when it's set up?

OW: No. I place my hand where the camera goes and that's it. It never moves—I know exactly where it's going to be.

PB: But don't you then look at the set-up?

OW: Then. And that's where it should be, and I'm right. For my money. I don't fish for it—or very seldom, only when I'm in real trouble. And then the fishing leads me nowhere and it's

better if I go home or go to another scene. Because if I'm
fishing it means I don't know, something's wrong.

PB: It's really instinctive rather than—

OW: Oh, it always is. I think I share with Hitchcock the ability
to say what lens goes in the camera and where it stands without consulting a finder or looking through the camera. He
does that, too, I believe.

PB: He sometimes draws a little sketch for the cameraman.

OW: Oh, I don't do that. I just walk over and say, "There it is."
I may be dead wrong, but I'm so certain that nothing can
shake it. It's the only thing I'm certain of. I'm never certain
of a performance—my own or the other actors'—or the script
or anything. I'm ready to change, move anything. But to me
it seems there's only one place in the world the camera can
be, and the decision usually comes immediately. If it doesn't
come immediately, it's because I have no idea about the scene,
or I'm wrong about the scene to begin with. It's a good sign,
a kind of litmus paper for me. If I start to fish, something is
wrong.

PB: Then it must be inconceivable to you, the idea of covering
a scene from many different angles, as many directors do.

OW: That's right. Inconceivable. I don't know what they're fishing around for—they don't know what they're doing in the
scene. Though I think the absolutely solid camera sense is *not*
a sign of a great director. It's just something you have or you
don't have. I think you can be a very great director and have
only a very vague notion of what the camera does at all. I
happen to think I have total mastery of the camera. That may
be just megalomania, but I'm absolutely certain of that area.
And everything *else* is doubtful to me. I never consult the
operator or anything. There it is.

PB: Was it that way on *Kane*, too?

OW: Yes.

PB: Right away?

OW: Right away.

PB: It's instinctive.

OW: Yes, kind of instinctive, if you will—an arrogance that I have about where it's going to be seen from.

PB: I know it's difficult to dissect the creative process—

OW: Well, it's not even creative, because it *is* an instinctive thing, like a question of pitch for a singer. Where the camera goes. If you're absolutely sure, you may be wrong but at least it's one thing you can hang on to. Because I'm filled with doubts all the time about a movie: that the whole tone is wrong, that the level of it is wrong, that all the text, the performances, the emphasis, what they say, what it should be about—I'm constantly reaching and fishing and hoping and trying and improvising and changing. But the one thing I'm rocklike about is where it's seen from, by what lens and so on. That to me doesn't seem to be open to discussion. And it's something I must be grateful for: even if I'm wrong, I don't have that worry. But I always find scenes in a movie—I did in *Kane* and I have ever since—that I don't know how to photograph, and it's always because I haven't really conceived of it fully enough.

PB: Do you let those go until you're ready?

OW: Well, on *Kane*, I walked away once early in the morning— just quit for the day—and went home. Made a big scandal. I just had no idea what to do. Came back the next day.

PB: What was the scene?

OW: In Susan's apartment, the big confrontation, when Gettys [Ray Collins] comes in. He was named, by the way, after the father of the wife of Roger Hill, my teacher at Todd. That's another in-joke. But that was just a scene in a room, and it seemed to me so boring, I didn't know what to do. And I just went away.

PB: When you came back, it worked?

OW: Yeah. And I didn't figure it out on paper. But I think that scene is a little overstated, visually. It's a little overemphasized. It shows some kind of insecurity, I think, visually. I can see it now. It came from that moment of doubt. And I think it's like lion taming or being the conductor of an orchestra—you have to come in and know where the camera is, or there are all sorts of evil demons who will attack you, and the doubts will show on the screen and in everything. You have to be absolutely on top of it. Or pay no attention to it. One of the two.

PB: By the way, in shooting that drunk scene with Cotten, I understand he was so tired that he accidentally said the line "dramatic crimitism" that way, instead of "criticism," and you left it in.

OW: It happened that way in rehearsal and then it was performed. He was that tired because he had to go to New York to join the road tour of *The Philadelphia Story*, which he originated on the stage. And we all worked something like twenty-four hours, around the clock, with nobody going to bed, to get him finished.

PB: Would you agree, in general, that *Kane* is more self-conscious directorially than any of your other films?

OW: Yes. There are more conscious shots—for the sake of shots—in *Kane* than in anything I've done since. It has things like that shot where they're all posed around that trophy which is just a "let's see if we can make that shot" kind of shot. I'm not that pleased with it, looking back.

PB: No, it's studied.

OW: Yeah. I've tried to avoid that kind of thing since then.

PB: Well, *Ambersons* is much more relaxed.

OW: Much.

PB: Perhaps that's something one feels making one's first picture. A sort of inhibition—which you combated by being daring to the point of self-consciousness at the time. Whereas *Othello* is very second-nature—as is everything you've done since.

OW: I think that's absolutely true. I stopped trying after *Kane*. There's a kind of unjustified visual strain at times in *Kane*, which just came from the exuberance of discovering the medium. And once you get used to it and learn how to swim, then you don't have to flex so many muscles. Now let's talk about something else.

PB: Well, we've barely scratched the surface of *Kane*.

OW: I'm sure—but I'm expiring.

PB: Well, OK. Let's talk about your name. Why'd you choose to be called by your middle name, Orson, instead of your first name, George?

OW: There wasn't any choice involved. I've been Orson all my life. I first learned my name was George when I was nine years old. It came as a terrible shock. Children started screaming, "Georgie, Porgie, puddin' and pie, kissed the girls and made them cry." This enraged me. I kicked out at my little playmates and got black eyes for it. How wrong I was. What a name to be born with and not use—George Orson Welles!

PB: All of it? You trust people with three names.

OW: With a name like George Orson Welles I wouldn't need to be trusted—I'd be Emperor of the World!

PB: Were you named after someone?

OW: George Ade, the great American humorist. Orson is a family name—descending (so the legend goes) from the Orsinis. Also because, by a bewildering and rather tiresome coincidence, my mother and father were on holiday in Rio—with George Ade and a man whose name was Orson Wells, without the "e," but *with* $30 million. I'd have those millions now if only I'd gone to visit my godfather. I hesitated, fearing old Mr. Wells would suspect my motives. I'd go *now*—on my knees. But as a twelve-year-old I had my pride. And then the news came that he'd gone to dwell with the morning stars.

PB: Was your father a great influence in your life—being an inventor?

OW: He didn't do much inventing in the years I knew him. I admired and loved him, but he was bitterly opposed to my interest in music and painting and everything like that. As far as he was concerned, if I was going to be an artist, it'd be better to be a cartoonist, like his friend George McManus, who drew "Jiggs and Maggie," otherwise known as "Bringing Up Father"—that's where the money was.

PB: But your mother was—

OW: The artist—the musician. Because of her I was a sort of *Wunderkind* of music: a child conductor, violinist, pianist. Then, when I was nine, she died. I've never done anything in music since.

PB: What was the influence of your guardian, Dr. Bernstein? And why did you give that name to the character in *Kane*?

OW: You're sneaking in *Kane* again.

PB: Sorry.

OW: [*laughs*] That was a family joke. He was nothing like the character in the movie. I used to call people "Bernstein" on the radio all the time, too—just to make him laugh. . . . I sketched out the character in our preliminary sessions—Mank did all the best writing for Bernstein. I'd call that *the* most valuable thing he gave us. . . .

PB: Where did Jed Leland [Joseph Cotten] come from?

OW: Jed was really based on a close childhood friend of mine— George Stevens's uncle Ashton Stevens. He was practically my uncle, too.

PB: Did you tell Stevens the character was based on him?

OW: Oh God, he could see it—I didn't have to *tell* him. I sent him the script before we began, of course, and while he was visiting me on the coast, I brought him on the set during shooting. Later he saw the movie and thought the old man would be thrilled by it. As it turned out, after *Kane* was released, Ashton was forbidden by his Hearst editors to even mention my name. . . . What I knew about Hearst came even more from him than from my father—though my father did know him well: there was a long story about putting a chamber pot on a flagpole, things like that, but I didn't get too much from *that* source. My father and Hearst were only close as young swingers. But Ashton had taught Hearst to play the banjo, which is how he first got to be a drama critic, and, you know, Ashton really was one of the great ones. The last of the dandies—he worked for Hearst for some fifty years or so, and adored him. A gentleman . . . very much like Jed.

PB: Jed Leland is really not all that endearing a character—I mean, you like him, but one's sympathies somehow are with Kane in the scene where he attacks Kane so strongly.

OW: Well, you know—when a man takes a stand on some question of principle at the expense of a personal friendship, the sympathy has to go to the victim of the righteousness, now, doesn't it?

PB: Getting back to your guardian, Dr. Bernstein—did he have any influence on your creative life?

OW: Well, he was an enormously important *element* in my life. But we seldom had the same tastes in anything. I'd say the biggest influence was Roger Hill, who became headmaster of the school to which I went for three years, and with whom I later wrote four textbooks on Shakespeare. He's still a great, a valued, friend.

Roger Hill's introduction to Everybody's Shakespeare (*1934; later,* The Mercury Shakespeare, *1939*), *which he edited with Welles, begins like this*:

ON STUDYING SHAKESPEARE'S PLAYS

Don't!

Read them. Enjoy them. Act them.

Shakespeare might not be surprised to know that his plays are still bringing money to producers and fame to actors throughout the world. He would be greatly surprised, however, to know that they are studied (by compulsion) in the classroom; that they are conned by scholars, dissected by pedants, and fed in synthetic and minute and quite distasteful doses to students, much in the same manner as are capsules of Cicero's Letters and pellets of Euclid's Geometry. . . . Put Shakespeare where he belongs—on the stage.

OW: Roger is now eighty-something, runs a chartering service in Florida, and he helped me with the boats on *The Deep* when I shot in the Bahamas. He's always been a great boat fellow— he was called "Skipper" at school.

PB: Todd School?

OW: Yes. He was the son of the owner. When I was there, he was the athletics coach. He only became the headmaster after I left. But he was a great influence in that school.

PB: How old were you?

OW: Well, I went there three years, and my last year I was four-teen.

PB: And he?

OW: Must have been twenty-eight, thirty—I really don't know. I can't imagine life without him, and I go ten years without seeing him but it doesn't seem like ten years, because I think of him all the time. He was a great direct influence in my life—the biggest by all odds. I wanted to be *like* him. Everything he thought, I wanted to think, and that wasn't true of Dr. Bernstein.

PB: Or your father?

OW: Or my father. My father was a very strange man. Fascinating. Great wit and great raconteur.

PB: Did you take up painting right after—

OW: I painted, always, from the minute I could walk.

PB: Is it true that you still can't add or subtract very well?

OW: What would make you think I'd learn at this advanced age? I can't do it at all.

PB: Really?

OW: No. I got through school because I paid a boy called Guggenheim to take that sort of drudgery off my shoulders. For a fee, Guggenheim did most of the paperwork on Latin declensions and geometry. I graduated *magna cum laude*.

PB: I read in the Alva Johnston pieces in the *Saturday Evening Post* [January 20, 27, February 3, 1940] that you never wanted to be a child—that you wanted to escape childhood.

OW: That's true.

PB: Have you ever wanted to return?

OW: To childhood? I've been back there ever since I left.

PB: I read that you dislike *A Midsummer Night's Dream*.

OW: Because it was my reading primer. You'll have to try it—just read the first scene of *Midsummer Night's Dream* and imagine it's the first thing you've ever had to spell out.

PB: Well, since you were two years old, it's hard to imagine it anyway.

OW: Johnston wrote that I was. In fact, I believe I achieved literacy somewhat later on in life. He got that, I suppose, from

Dr. Bernstein, who gilded the lily pretty thickly. I don't think I was very advanced in that way. I was a musician, all right, but as to book learning, I think I was rather backward.

PB: Were you really a bad student in school?

OW: All three years of it. I attacked the textbooks rather than mastered them. I led student revolutions—comic ones.

PB: You acted in and directed some school plays. Did you have a particular love of makeup even then?

OW: Yes, I used to when I was younger, and it was impossible for me to play any part that didn't look like a juvenile killer. Getting older, I discover I don't have to paint those lines under my eyes, and it's nice.

PB: But *Kane* is a masterpiece of makeup.

OW: There you go again—you had that whole chain of thought planned. God, you're crafty. . . . *Kane* had to be. Look at all those ages.

PB: Well, movies that have somebody age in them are usually quite bad.

OW: Yes, but you have no idea what work there was to that, because it was long ago; we didn't have sophisticated things for makeup which made it easy. In those days—you don't know what it was—I came to work many days on *Kane* at two-thirty in the morning, to be made up to start work at nine. It took that long, with the spraying and building. Maurie Seiderman was one of the two or three great makeup men of our time, and he's never really been allowed to do anything in the industry.

PB: Because he's too good?

OW: Yeah. How he worked! Two-thirty in the morning was normal all the time. With the contact lenses I wore, which in those days drove you mad with pain. Because I was a baby; you know, it's very hard to be seventy years old and make it believable. But the thing that's never been printed is the truth about me as a young man in that film. I was then twenty-five, twenty-six—I've forgotten how old I was—but I had my face lifted up with fish skin and wore corsets for the scenes as a young man.

PB: Why? Were you heavier than you looked?

OW: Of course. Not only heavier, but I always had that terrible round moon face and it was all faked up with fish skins and tucked under the hair. Everything. Just as though I were some terrible old leading man at the end of his day. [*laughs*] So I was just as heavily made up as a young man as I was as an old man! I could hardly move for the corsets and the fish skin and everything else. I read once—Norman Mailer wrote something or other—that, when I was young, I was the most beautiful man anybody had ever seen. Yes! Made up for *Citizen Kane*! And only for five days!

PB: You mean you never looked like that?

OW: Never! I wish I had! On the other hand, Everett Sloane, who aged with me, never wore any makeup at all! We just shaved his head and put the white around it. And he couldn't have been more than twenty-one. It had a profound effect on him. Because he thought, "How can I represent a seventy-five-year-old man without makeup? It must be that my nose is too big." And he began bobbing it. He must have had twenty operations before he killed himself. He must have thought, "If I could ever bob my nose right, then I'll be a leading man."

PB: But that's incredible.

OW: Terrible story, yes.

PB: He was brilliant in *Kane*.

OW: Yes. Much better than in *The Lady from Shanghai*. He'd already begun to go to pieces. And he became a very bad actor in the last ten years of his life. But in *Kane* he was wonderful.

PB: Yes, that scene with the reporter [William Alland]—

OW: That was *all* Mank, by the way—it's my favorite scene.

PB: And the story about the girl: "One day, back in 1896, I was crossing over to Jersey on the ferry. . . . There was another ferry pulling in, and . . . a girl waiting to get off. A white dress she had on. . . . I only saw her for a second . . . but I'll bet a month hasn't gone by since, that I haven't thought of that girl."

OW: It goes longer than that.

PB: Yes, but who wrote it?

OW: Mankiewicz, and it's the best thing in the movie. "A month hasn't gone by that I haven't thought of that girl." That's Mankiewicz. I *wish* it was me.

PB: Great scene.

OW: If I were in hell and they gave me a day off and said, "What part of any movie you ever made do you want to see?" I'd see that scene of Mank's about Bernstein. All the rest could have been better, but that was just right.

PB: You wanted all the actors in *Kane* to be new faces, didn't you?

OW: That's true—but I was tricked. [*laughs*] My whole idea of having only new faces was ruined by the first day of shooting—which was, as I said, the first of several days when we pretended to be testing but were actually shooting the picture. The scene was in the nightclub with Susan when she's grown old. For the waiter in that nightclub, casting sent me a tubby little round-faced Italian [Gino Corrado] who is the waiter in every movie ever made! And I couldn't possibly send him away on the basis that he was too well known a face because I was claiming to be testing. So there he is—spoiling the whole master plan in one of the first shots that I made!

PB: And you couldn't even rationalize it as an *hommage* to Hollywood, since I know that's not the sort of thing you do.

OW: I don't believe in *hommage*. Of course, nobody knew about it in those days, thank Christ—in our innocence—and I am terribly against all forms of *hommage*.

PB: I'm beginning to agree with you.

OW: You don't have to say that.

PB: No, I am. What was the big advantage of having actors inexperienced in movies?

OW: They didn't have terrible movie habits.

PB: Was Dorothy Comingore really a discovery of Chaplin's?

OW: Yes, but he didn't use her.

PB: And you liked her—

OW: After testing a lot of strippers. I tested about ten, none of whom were any good. I tested a lot of people for that part.

PB: You wanted that kind of cheapness?

OW: Yeah.

PB: Had she ever acted before?

OW: I don't think so. And she was such a success in it. Everybody said she was so wonderful that she turned down every offer she got for three years. And then there were no more offers, and that was the end of it. She was waiting for another part like that one.

PB: Was she an intelligent actress?

OW: Yes. Of course, her old-age scenes were tremendously tricked up. We blew dangerous drugs in her eyes and sprayed her throat so she couldn't talk, and everything else. But she was still great. "Well, what do you know—it's morning already." That's another favorite moment.

PB: What's so uncanny is that she reminds me so much of performances Judy Holliday was to give years later.

OW: Yes. Judy began with our theater, you know. She was two years in the Mercury.

PB: I didn't know that. Perhaps she was influenced by Comingore—

OW: No, I don't think so.

PB: Well, there's a marked similarity.

OW: Yes, very much. She didn't have the humor or richness of Judy, but there's a great big similarity.

PB: Did she sing her own things?

OW: No.

PB: You had to get a singer who could make it sound bad.

OW: That's right. That was big work—very well done by the girl. Worked a long time on that.

PB: How did you find Fortunio Bonanova, who played her singing teacher?

OW: I saw him as the leading man with Katharine Cornell in *The Green Hat* when I was about eight years old. I never forgot him. He looked to me like a leading man in a dirty movie. Sent for him the minute I wrote that part. He was a great romantic leading man. When he was prompting her in the opera, he was so marvelous. God, he was funny.

PB: Had he ever done a picture before?

OW: Yes, I think so—he was living in Hollywood. But nothing much, you know. He was another one of the exceptions in the film.

PB: Why did you use that shrieking cockatoo?

OW: Wake 'em up.

PB: Literally?

OW: Yeah. Getting late in the evening, you know—time to brighten up anybody who might be nodding off. [*laughs*]

PB: It has no other purpose?

OW: Theatrical shock effect, if you want to be grand about it— you can say it's placed at a certain *musical* moment when I felt the need for something short and exclamatory. So it has a sort of purpose, but no *meaning*. What's fascinating, though, is that, because of some accident in the trick department, you can see right through the bird's eye into the scenery behind.

PB: I always thought that was intentional.

OW: We don't know why it happened. Some accident. . . . I'm very fond of parrots.

PB: There's one in *Mr. Arkadin*.

OW: Yeah. I have a wonderful one at home in Spain.

PB: How'd you do the scene just after the cockatoo, where Kane breaks up Susan's room?

OW: Just did it, with four cameras—broke up the whole set in one take. Tore my wrists and hands apart. I was bleeding like a pig when I was done with all that glass and everything.

PB: William Alland has been quoted as saying, "He came off exhilarated and said it was the first time he'd ever felt the emotion while acting a scene."

OW: Naw. I'm sure that's one of those memories after the event that are more creative than accurate. I came off with a bleeding wrist—that's what I came off with—and I don't enjoy bleeding, I'm not one of those. Five hours of makeup, and then get on and break it all up. Very rough. But the set was wonderfully done by Perry Ferguson. Marvelously dressed—made it very easy to play. My God, it was a wonderful set. I can see it now. He was just brilliant—I think Ferguson did a marvelous job.

PB: I agree. What did Van Nest Polglase do, who's also listed as art director?

OW: That shows your youth. In the days of the big studios, and the system of department heads, every picture carried a credit for art direction which went not to the man who really did the job, but to the head of the department. The man who actually did the work was always listed as assistant. Thus Cedric Gibbons was apparently the art director of every Metro picture, but he didn't even make a sketch. He and Van Polglase and the other art department chiefs were much too busy for any actual creative work.

PB: Then you had no contact with Van Polglase at all?

OW: Just in budget meetings, costing—that was the regulation set-up.

PB: Well, the set director, Darrell Silvera, told me that those ice sculptures of Leland and Bernstein in the party scene were a last-minute idea.

OW: Yes. We got them from the Brown Derby or someplace like that. It took a long time to shoot that sequence—five days. I threw all the girls out and waited till we got prettier ones— and they were marvelous girls, finally.

PB: Did you yourself design sketches on *Kane*?

OW: I do on everything, and I almost always design shows for the theater. Let's go get another drink—I see this is going to be endless. . . .

An article could be devoted just to the "News on the March" digest that comes at the start of Kane. Apart from its perfection as an imitation news short, it is at the same time one of the most devilish parodies of vintage Time-style ever made: the inverted sentences, the taut fact-filled portentous reportage, the standard clichés.

OW [*with a new drink*]: I showed it to Luce. He was one of the first people to see the movie—in New York. He and Clare Luce loved it and roared with laughter at the digest.

PB: They saw the parody?

OW: They saw it as a parody and enjoyed it very much as such—
I have to hand it to them. He saw it as a joke—or *she* saw it
as a joke and he had to because she did.

PB: There's a "March of Time" sequence indicated in *Smiler with a
Knife*.

OW: Yes, that's where the idea for it in *Kane* came from. Of
course, I'd been years on the "March of Time" radio program.
Every day. It was a marvelous show to do. Great fun, because,
half an hour after something happened, we'd be acting it out
with music and sound effects and actors. It was a super show—
terribly entertaining.

PB: Did you write some of them?

OW: Never. I only acted. I began as an occasional performer,
because they had a regular stock company, and then I was
finally let in—one of the inner circle. And then I had the
greatest thrill of my life—I don't know why it thrilled me
(it does still, to think of it now), I guess because I thought
"March of Time" was such a great thing to be on. One day
they did as a news item on "March of Time" the opening of
my production of the black *Macbeth*, and I played myself on
it. And that to me was the apotheosis of my career—that I
was on "March of Time" acting *and* as a news item. I've never
felt since that I've had it made as much as I did that one
afternoon.

PB: And did you use the *Time* announcer, Westbrook Van Voor-
hies, for *Kane*?

OW: Oh, no. That was William Alland who imitated him. Great
imitation, but he's pretty easy to imitate. [*doing it*] "This week,
as it must to all men—death came to Charles Foster Kane."
We used to do that every day—five days a week! And, of
course, there was a lot of "it must to all men" every week,
and I used to play all these people. I played Zaharoff—it was
one of my first parts on the show. As a matter of fact, I got
the idea for the hidden-camera sequence in the *Kane* "news
digest" from a scene I did on "March of Time" in which Zaharoff, this great munitions maker, was being moved around
in his rose garden, just talking about the roses, in the last days

before he died. It was a radio show, but I remember the idea of an old tycoon being pushed around a rose garden.

PB: There's a wonderfully real sound cut during Thatcher's news conference in the "News" digest. A long shot of Thatcher sitting at the table with all these people around, but when you cut to a close-up of him as he starts to read his statement, the sound cuts a moment late, the way it often does in newsreels. I've always loved that touch.

OW: Yes, a slight mistake in the sound cutting. I'm glad you noticed it. You know how it was in those days—there was no tape, all the sound was on film. You can't imagine what mixing the sound was in those days—and what a cost in effort it was to get that little effect.

PB: Is it true that that news conference was reminiscent of a real J. P. Morgan news conference?

OW: No, but there *was* a famous J. P. Morgan news conference where a midget was put on his lap. I just know vaguely about it.

PB: Did you feel the newsreel was necessary so the juggling of time was possible?

OW: It was expository—to tell more about him than could be told in other ways.

PB: Were the shots for the "News" digest made depending on what makeup you were in?

OW: Yes, end of the day or during the day. There was a big back lot, and as we were moving from one place to another, we'd say, "Well, let's get on the back of the train and make me with Teddy Roosevelt," or whoever it was. It was all kind of half improvised—all the newsreel stuff. It was tremendous fun doing it. And did I tell you the reaction that sequence had in Italy when the film opened?

PB: No.

OW: They all stood up and hissed and booed because the quality of the film was so bad.

PB: They missed the point entirely.

OW: Yes! [*laughs*] You know, the total run in Rome in the entire life of *Citizen Kane* is three days—since it was made!

PB: That's about rock bottom, isn't it?

OW: Yeah. But I'm rock bottom in Italy. I've only started to come up in the last five or six years.

PB: Even among intellectuals?

OW: Oh, always low. Very low.

PB: Really?

OW: Because I came and lived there. And, you don't know this, but in many countries you're only respected if you're not living there. They think there must be something wrong with you if you come and stay there. So I had a great week when I arrived for *Black Magic* with every intellectual in the world— and after that I became nobody because I lived there. "Who is he? Must be something wrong with him or he wouldn't be in Italy." [*PB laughs*] It's been true in an awful lot of countries— Ireland and Italy and Yugoslavia. I know a lot of smaller countries that never respect either their own countrymen until they leave, or a foreigner who lives there. In Yugoslavia, I'm beginning to lose a lot of face because I'm there too much. It's a very basic thing. I remember when we toured with Katharine Cornell—we were going to open up the theater again in America—a thrilling ten-month tour, playing all over in theaters where no play had been for twenty, thirty, forty years. There we were, bringing really good actors and a repertoire of three plays, and the people would say, "What's wrong with Katharine Cornell, that she's here? She must be slipping." In other words, if she's any good, she'd stay in New York. It's just like the Yugoslavs or the Italians. They want to know why you aren't back in Hollywood!

PB: That's similar to American critics putting down Westerns and other typically American films.

OW: Yes, it's only the foreigners who appreciate the Western as a serious form. And comedy. There are very few people anywhere who take comedy seriously.

PB: That's true.

OW: You know, not one serious film festival in the world has ever given a first prize to a comedy.

PB: The Oscars rarely do, either.

OW: It's so idiotic, because it's quite easy to show that maybe the best movies and plays *are* comedies—or certainly as good as any tragedy. It's so idiotic to think that it's some kind of second-class tourist kind of entertainment. But these solemn boobs who talk about movies or anything else just cannot believe that a comedy is serious.

PB: Yes. [*picking up notes*] Why did you do the projection-room scene in such darkness?

OW: Because most of the actors play different parts later on. They're all doubling, except the head fellow. We didn't *dare* turn on the lights.

PB: It's dramatic.

OW: Of course, you've got a big excuse for that strong single light. It was the first scene I shot in the movie.

PB: Really?

OW: Yes, and I was supposed to be testing, so in case it was good I wanted to save it, and I didn't want to hire a lot of actors if it wasn't good. So I used the whole Mercury cast, heavily disguised by darkness.

PB: And you shot it in a real projection room?

OW: Yes, because we didn't want to alert anybody to the fact that we were shooting. And there they all are—if you look carefully, you can see them. Everybody in the movie is in it.

PB: Not you, too?

OW: Yes, I'm there.

PB: Peter Noble's book indicates that the projection-room scene was influenced by a stage effect in a play you had acted in— Sidney Kingsley's *Ten Million Ghosts* [1936].

OW: That is one of the biggest pieces of *Schweinerei* I've ever heard in my life. In *Ten Million Ghosts*, there is a scene in which a home movie of war atrocities is run off in an apartment somewhere in Europe. I never saw the scene, because I was in my dressing room during it the six days the play ran, but the fact that a home movie is shown is the only possible connection with a projection room. Wow!

PB: Not having seen *Ten Million Ghosts,* I don't—

OW: Well, almost nobody did. I fell asleep on the stage on opening night, but that's another story. Next.

PB: Someone criticized the actor who did the editor, saying he
was hammy, but I liked that—he was an editor, aware of the
role he was playing.

OW: Yes, he's supposed to be a kind of a parody. That's the point.

PB: Is it true that Alan Ladd's in there somewhere?

OW: Not in that one. He's the leading reporter when all of them
gather at Xanadu at the end. And you can't miss him—it was
his first movie part, and there he is, wearing his hat the way
he wore it for thirty pictures afterward.

PB: How did you find him?

OW: He was brought in by his agent, who was later his wife. He
read for me and I thought he was very good.

PB: He had a good voice.

OW: Yes. And very effective and intelligent. He's one of the only
people I didn't know who's in the picture. There were very
few—only three or four. You know, you are boring me to
death—

PB: OK, I'll change the subject—

OW: No, *you* talk for a while—

PB: Well, OK. There's a good story I heard about John Ford.

OW: Tell it.

PB: The producer came down on the set, and Ford immediately
stopped shooting. He sat down and started talking to the producer. And the producer noticed that everybody else sort of
stopped working, and after a while he said, "Don't you think
you ought to, you know, go back to work, Jack? I mean—"
And Ford said, "Oh no! Gee, that would be rude. I mean, if *I*
came into *your* office you'd stop making phone calls, wouldn't
you, or whatever you do? You wouldn't keep making phone
calls and talking to people while I was in your office. You'd
sit and talk to me, wouldn't you? Well, I'm just doing the
same thing—"

OW: That's great.

PB: I heard you once did a similar thing by telling the cast on *Kane* to play baseball when—

OW: Yes, we did, but that was intended as a practical joke and was friendly. It was when George Schaefer [head of the studio] came with all the bankers from New York, and they'd all heard, you know, about crazy Welles. We thought it would be nice if they came down and found us hard at work—playing baseball.

PB: Did it go over as a joke?

OW: Yes—it was quite benevolent. Don't think I didn't notice how you sneaked *Kane* in again.

PB: [*laughs*] OK. You had a fifteen-week schedule.

OW: Yes, and that included all the trick shots and everything else. There were so many trick shots—it was a big fake, full of hanging miniatures and glass shots and everything. There was very little construction.

PB: Did you purposely work for economy in making the picture?

OW: Of course. I wanted to go on working in Hollywood. I'd spent a year there before I made it, and I'd found out how important economy was. More important in those days than now, because grosses weren't as big.

PB: The trick shots are very good—

OW: I hope so. My God, I was months and months and months turning down versions of them, day after day, until they got good enough. Trick work *can* be good enough, but you must be brutal about it. Just refuse it, refuse it, refuse it till it gets better.

PB: Trick work in color gets to be almost impossible; it immediately looks phony.

OW: Yes, it *is* impossible. You mustn't do it in color—color looks like trick work anyway. It's only for black-and-white.

PB: I like the way real night looks in color, if it's very black.

OW: I like fog and fire and smoke in color, and winter snow. But it's pretty limited.

PB: All the dissolves were very carefully designed, it seemed to me.

OW: They're done electrically instead of optically.

PB: Could you describe that?

OW: We actually dimmed down lights on the stage—leaving lit the one key thing you wanted to see longer—and brought up the lights the same way for the incoming scene. In other words, if the last thing you want to see is Susan, that's the last thing you see, because all the other lights are fading out around her by dimmer, just as you would do it in the theater. When you add the dissolve electrically, Susan lingers there, instead of the whole picture going out and another whole picture coming in. They were very carefully designed. All so that the dissolve would be more beautiful. And I still do it all the time.

PB: On the incoming shot, did you place the object you want to see in a different area on the screen?

OW: That's right, so it would complement the outgoing shot.

PB: I've never heard of anybody doing that before.

OW: No, nobody had. I thought that's the way they must do dissolves. After I had done several of them, Gregg broke it to me that it was not the way it's usually done. It just seemed to me from the theater that that's what you would do. Innocence led me to it. . . . And, of course, we sent *them* back to the lab over and over again until they were right.

PB: You once said about the editing of *Kane*, "There was nothing to cut." What did you mean?

OW: When I made *Kane*, I didn't know enough about movies, and I was constantly encouraged by Toland, who said, under the influence of Ford, "Carry everything in one shot—don't do anything else." In other words, play scenes through without cutting, and don't shoot any alternate version. That was Toland in my ear. And secondly, I didn't *know* how to have all kinds of choices. All I could think of to do was what was going to be on the screen in the final version. Also, I had a wonderful cast.

I only learned about cutting when I got to Europe and had people who didn't speak English—or people who weren't even actors in the roles, wearing wigs and standing with their backs to the cameras—so that I had to fake things, and learn how to cut in order to cover troubles I was in. Now I'm in love with cutting. Transitions, yes—I knew about those instinctively for *Kane*, and they were written into the way we shot it, not discovered during cutting. But nothing was covered from other angles; there was no alternate to the master scene. Whenever I have a good enough cast, I never cover myself. So, of course, there wasn't anything to cut. It was just put together. There were hardly any close-ups—I think there are four in the whole picture. And they were the only four close-ups we made. And the only thing we deleted was a two-minute scene of me in a whorehouse, which was cut in its entirety very early in the cutting by general agreement, because we knew the censors wouldn't let it get by. It originally followed the dancing scene; I go off to a whorehouse—

PB: With the same women?

OW: No, with some other women. And it wasn't that good, so there was no reason to have it. That was the only *cut*; the picture was never previewed. There was never any alternate version of anything—it was simply put together as shot.

PB: Why did you decide not to have credits at the beginning of *Kane*? No one had ever done that before.

OW: The script dictated that. Look at all the other things that go on at the beginning, before the story starts: that strange dreamlike prologue, then "News on the March," and then the projection-room scene—it's a long time before anything starts. Now, supposing you'd added titles to all that. It would have been one thing too much to sit through. You wouldn't have know where you were in the picture.

PB: In that prologue you just mentioned, why does the light in his bedroom suddenly go off—and then come on again after a moment?

OW: To interest the audience. We'd been going on quite a while there with nothing happening. You see a light in the window—you keep coming nearer—and it better go off, or a shadow had better cross, or something had better happen. So I turned the light off—that's all.

PB: Then you cut inside.

OW: That's right. Maybe the nurse turned it off because it was getting in his eyes. Who knows? Who cares? The other answer is that it symbolized death. Got that? All right.

PB: We can use both answers—in different chapters.

OW: [*laughs*] Yes—use 'em both. In fact, that's really what was in my mind. He was supposed to die when the light went off, and then you go back a few minutes and see him alive again— if you really want a reason. The other, low-class reason was to keep the audience interested. And they're both valid.

PB: What did you mean by the mirrors at the end, when Kane walks by and you see his image reflected many times?

OW: I don't think a moviemaker should explain what he means. About anything. Leave it to the customers. Why spoil things for people who enjoy finding their own meanings?

PB: But you just explained the light going off—

OW: Next.

PB: The black smoke at the end has been said to symbolize the futility of his life. . . .

OW: I don't know—I hate symbolism.

PB: Fritz Lang said he dropped the use of symbols when he came to America because somebody at MGM said to him, "Americans don't like symbols."

OW: I'm one of those Americans. I never use it. If anybody finds it, it's for them to find. I never sit down and say how we're going to have a symbol for some character. They happen automatically, because life is full of symbols. So is art. You can't avoid them; but if you *use* them, you get into Stanley Kramer Town.

PB: I know you hate to think up titles—

OW: No! I love to think 'em up, but can't! *Citizen Kane* came from George Schaefer—the head of the studio, imagine that! It's a great title. We'd sat around for months trying to think of a name for it. Mankiewicz couldn't, I couldn't, none of the actors—we had a contest on. A secretary came up with one that was so bad I'll never forget it: *A Sea of Upturned Faces.*

PB: Can we talk about Leland's betrayal of Kane?

OW: He didn't betray Kane. Kane betrayed him.

PB: Really?

OW: Because he was not the man he pretended to be.

PB: Yes, but, in a sense, didn't Leland—

OW: I don't think so.

PB: I was going to say something else. Didn't Leland imagine that Kane was one thing and then was disappointed when he wasn't?

OW: Well, it comes to the same thing. If there was any betrayal, it was on Kane's part, because he signed a Declaration of Principles which he never kept.

PB: Then why is there a feeling that Leland is petty and mean to Kane in the scene when he gets drunk?

OW: Because *there* he is—only there, because he's defensive. It's not the big moment. The big moment is when he types the bad notice afterward. That's when he's faithful to himself and to Kane and to everything.

PB: I wonder if that's as simple as your answer is now, because if you were put in a position like that—

OW: *I'm* not his character. I'm a totally different kind of person from Jed Leland. I'm not a friend of the hero. And he's a born friend of the hero, and the hero turned out not to be one. He's the loyal companion of the great man—and Kane wasn't great; that's the story. So of course he's mean and petty when he's discovered that his great man is empty inside.

PB: Well, maybe one feels that Leland could have afforded to write a good review.

OW: Not and been a man of principle. That Declaration of Principles Kane signed is the key to it. Leland couldn't—no critic can. He's an honest man. Kane is corrupt. I don't think he betrays Kane in any way.

PB: Well, one has an emotional response to Kane in the picture, and I certainly felt that Leland betrays him—I felt that emotionally.

OW: No, he doesn't. You're using the word "betrayal" wrong. He's cruel to him, but he doesn't betray him.

PB: Well, he betrays their friendship, then.

OW: He doesn't. It's Kane who betrayed the friendship. The friendship was based on basic assumptions that Kane hadn't lived up to. I strongly and violently disagree with that. There is no betrayal of Kane. The betrayal is *by* Kane.

PB: Then why do I somewhat dislike Leland?

OW: Because he likes principles more than the man, and he doesn't have the size as a person to love Kane for his faults.

PB: Well, then, there you are.

OW: But that's not betrayal. "Betrayal" is a dead wrong word. He simply doesn't have the humanity, the generosity of spirit, to have been able to endure Kane—

PB: OK, he had a certain meanness of spirit.

OW: That's right. At that moment. He doesn't later, when he talks about him.

PB: He's not very nice about Kane to the reporter.

OW: Not very terrible.

PB: There are certainly ambiguous moments even there.

OW: Not to me. It's very clear how he feels about him. There's no ambiguity in my mind about it. He has an affectionate memory of a man who turned out to be an empty box. That's it. And it's not as bad as you think. Or, if it is, the effect is not what I intended. As author of the film, I regard Leland with enormous affection. I don't see him as a mean person— he's much superior to Bernstein.

PB: Well . . .

OW: He's the only true aristocrat. . . .

PB: In the story?

OW: Yeah. He's talking my language. With all his meanness, you see, he's essentially an aristocrat. I have deep sympathy for him.

PB: Do you think that Thompson, the reporter, is changed by going through the Kane story? Is he altered?

OW: He's not a person. He's a piece of machinery—

PB: To lead you through.

OW: Yes.

PB: Was there any mystery before the Rosebud element? I mean, did you try anything else?

OW: Yes. And there was a scene in a mausoleum that I wrote—it was a quotation from a poem or something, I can't remember—and Mankiewicz made terrible fun of it. So I believed him and just said, "All right, it's no good." It *might* have been good—I don't remember it, because I was so ashamed from Mankiewicz's violent attack on it.

PB: Why did you begin and end with the No Trespassing sign?

OW: What do you think? Anybody's first guess has got to be right.

PB: A man's life is private.

OW: Is it? That should theoretically be the answer, but it turns out that maybe it is and maybe it isn't. . . .

PB: Is the name Kane a play on Cain?

OW: No, but Mankiewicz got furious when I used that name, because he said that's what people will think. We had a big fight about that.

PB: The original name was Craig.

OW: Yes. And I said I thought Kane was a better name—

PB: Just *because* it was a better name—

OW: Yes. And Mankiewicz made the other point: "They'll think you're punning on Cain" and all that, because we had a big murder scene in the original script. And I said they won't, and he said they will, and so on. I won.

The first report:

HEARST OBJECTS TO WELLES FILM
Mention of RKO in His Press Barred as the Withdrawal of "Citizen Kane" Is Demanded
Studio Head Unmoved
Schaefer Says "No Serious Consideration" Is Given—Actor Denies Biography Intent
—*New York Times*, January 11, 1941

The Hearst press is under strict orders to ignore Welles, except for a series of articles pointing out that he is a menace to American motherhood, freedom of speech and assembly, and the pursuit of happiness.
—*New Yorker*, May 10, 1941

OW: In the original script we had a scene based on a notorious thing Hearst had done which I still cannot repeat for publication. And I cut it out because I thought it hurt the film and wasn't in keeping with Kane's character. If I'd kept it in, I would have had no trouble from Hearst. He wouldn't have dared admit it was him.

PB: Did you shoot the scene?

OW: No, I didn't. I decided against it. If I'd kept it in, I would have bought silence for myself forever. They were really after me. Before *Kane* was released, I was lecturing—I think it was Pittsburgh, some town like that—and a detective came up to me as I was having supper with some friends after the lecture. He said, "Don't go back to your hotel. I'm from police headquarters. I won't give you my name." I said, "Why not?" He said, "I'm just giving you advice." I said, "What are you talking about?" He said, "They've got a fourteen-year-old girl in the closet and two cameramen waiting for you to come in." And of course I would have gone to jail. There would have been no way out of it.

I never went back to the hotel. I just waited till the train in the morning. I've often wondered what happened to the cameramen and the girl waiting all night for me to arrive. But that wasn't Hearst. That was a hatchet man from the local Hearst paper who thought he would advance himself by doing it.

PB: What was your personal reaction to the whole Hearst business?

OW: What do you mean, "personal reaction"?

PB: How did you feel?

OW: He was right! He was dead right. Why not fight? I expected that. I *didn't* expect that everyone would run as scared as they did. And, then, the mistake that Schaefer made was not to believe me when I made the best showmanship suggestion I've ever made, which was that *Citizen Kane* should be run in tents all over America, advertised as "This is the picture that can't run in your local movie house." If we'd done that, we would have made $5 million with it. But he couldn't—I can see why not. Still, I *know* that I would be a rich man today if they'd listened to me. Because it didn't play in any major movie houses. It never played in any chain. Ever. Anywhere. It was always in independent houses. And my idea was to make it sound worse and take it to big tents, and they would've come. It would have been great.

PB: Is it true you offered to buy *Kane* from RKO?

OW: Yes. When RKO wouldn't show it in tents, I was willing to. Because I could have made a fortune on it. If they'd only sold it to me—they would have got out from under, and I would have been independently wealthy for the rest of my life— everybody would have been happy. And they wouldn't do it. I could have raised the money easily to buy it. Everybody was willing to buy in on it.

PB: So you had reckoned on Hearst's anger, but you hadn't re- alized how effective it would be.

OW: Of course not. And I always thought that courageous show- manship could have turned it to good account. Also, I didn't conceal anything. RKO had read the script and they went ahead and put up the money for it. So they then should have been willing to go all the way, theoretically. Although I have no criticism of Schaefer, that's the basic situation. Nothing was slipped over on them.

PB: There was talk about reshooting some scenes, wasn't there?

OW: No, not that I ever heard of. Only to burn it.

PB: Was Schaefer really a partisan?

OW: Oh, he was great. Schaefer was a hero—an absolute hero. He was marvelous with me.

PB: But he got fired afterward.

OW: Not as a result of that. He was fired during *Ambersons*, but as a result of a whole program of pictures. He was basically a New York–based salesman and not a production head. Floyd Odlum bought control of RKO and took over. But Schaefer stood by the picture finally; if he hadn't, it might never have opened.

PB: Do you think it was because of Hearst that the picture didn't really do the business it should have?

OW: It *did* all the business it should have in the theaters it played in. It did capacity business. But it played in no chains, no major theaters.

PB: In other words, it just didn't get the exposure.

OW: That's right. But wherever it played it did tremendous business. Not in England, where it was a disaster. Not in Italy. But in America it did very well wherever it was shown, because of my reputation on radio.

PB: But it couldn't get the bookings because of Hearst.

OW: Nobody would book it—they were scared. Nobody would put it in.

That fear often took devious shapes. Theaters would pay for the film to avoid blacklist suits, but refused actually to play it. This item appeared in the New York Times, *September 7, 1941, over three months after* Kane's *premiere:*

The controversial *Citizen Kane* . . . has been sold to the Fox–West Coast chain, a segment of the National Theatre organization, but it will not be displayed in any of the circuit's 515 theatres on the Pacific Coast, the Mountain States and through the Midwest although they will pay for it. The reason for National's generosity is obscure but whatever the motive, the deal has aroused Orson Welles to new heights of fury. . . .

This week Welles's associates said that if the deal is consummated, the actor-producer will sue RKO, the distributors, and attempt to force the picture's exhibition. In many cities National controls all theatres and in others the picture will be relegated to back-street houses where it will have no standing because it has not been shown in the first run theatres. According to RKO, in the three cities in which it has been shown at popular prices—San Francisco, Denver and Omaha—the film's revenue on opening day exceeded that of *Kitty Foyle* [one of RKO's biggest money-makers].

PB: Did you notice an influence on Hollywood films from *Kane*?

OW: You couldn't mistake it. Everybody started having big foreground objects and ceilings and all those kind of compositions. Very few people had ever even used a wide-angle lens except for crowd scenes.

PB: But the effect wasn't in terms of story construction?

OW: No, the things that I *valued* didn't seem to have much effect on anybody. But the most obvious kind of visual things, everybody did right away.

PB: A quote from Andrew Sarris: "*Citizen Kane* is still the work that influenced the cinema more profoundly than any American film since the *Birth of a Nation*."

OW: I don't think that's true. Because *Birth of a Nation* had genuine innovations—the close-up, the moving shot, everything—the whole language of film is in it. And people could take that in a simple, direct way. I think *Citizen Kane* has influenced more movies in the last years than it did before. In the early days, all it did was put some ceilings on sets and some deep focus; it changed *set-ups*, which don't mean a thing. But the use of time and all that has only begun now. And it isn't direct, that influence.

I'm not a pro-innovation man. But I am supposed to be an innovator, and I have quietly given myself a few bows for all of these things that it turns out I didn't invent. I *did* invent, but my big inventions were in radio and the theater. Much more than in movies. Nobody knows that. I invented the use of narration in radio.

PB: Yeah.

OW: Which made [Norman] Corwin possible and all that. He never wrote till I started. I'm the man who took the gelatins out of lights in the theater.

PB: And made it just a white light?

OW: Yes. White light. That's the basis of all lighting. That I know I did. But in the movies I'd thought I'd done all these things and I find they've already been done. So it's a good argument in favor of my point that directors shouldn't look at too many pictures.

PB: But the important similarity between the two films is that *Birth of a Nation* summed up all the techniques that had come before in silent films. It brought everything to a head, and *Kane* did that, too, for the sound film.

OW: Yes, it summed things up, to a point. But it's not the technical advances that I think are important about *Kane*, it's the use of time and the way people are handled—that kind of thing.

PB: From the technical point of view, the most important thing in *Kane* perhaps is the use of the sound track.

OW: Yeah, but nobody followed that. They can't. They don't know how. That's a particular trick, and it hasn't influenced anybody. They could learn to do it, but they don't. You can't just say, "Now let's do the overlapping thing." But it can be learned very easily. In movies, though, nobody asks anybody anything. In the great days of painters, they used to go and stay in the atelier and see how the man made that brush stroke. But now everybody sees a movie and says, "I can do it." Nobody really wants to learn—except in an academic way, on a theoretical basis.

PB: But in practice—

OW: In practice—just go and find out how Gregory La Cava got that joke across. You can go to him and he'll tell you. But nobody has the chutzpah to just do it.

PB: All right, how do you do it?

OW: It can be taught in about two hours. We need three very good actors and a little exercise in it. I can't explain it, we have to illustrate it.

PB: I made some stabs at it in *Targets*—

OW: And it worked.

PB: No, it was sloppy because you couldn't understand what was being said as well as—

OW: That's the thing—you have to drill them so that the right syllable comes at the right moment. It's exactly like conducting an orchestra. You have to say, " 'Can't' comes in now. Once again." Because the operative word is "can't" and you come in under there. It's very, very mechanical. It's cold as hell, ice cold—exactly like conducting.

PB: When you first went to Hollywood, you were quoted as saying, "If they let me do a second picture, I'm lucky."

OW: I was so right.

PB: You knew that even before you went out there.

OW: Yes.

PB: You've always been aware of what you were getting yourself into.

OW: Damn right.

PB: You had an awareness of your own character.

OW: And of Hollywood.

PB: Well, I mean *you* within your circumstances. Like you and Hearst, and you and the "War of the Worlds" broadcast. You always seemed to know what you were getting into. That's much more interesting than if you didn't know.

OW: Much more fun. The surprises have been in degree, that's all.

PB: What did you think when you got the Oscar for the best original screenplay?

OW: You're a rat. I always deny that. I always pretend I never got an Oscar.

PB: Well, the picture was nominated in nine categories that year, for director and—

OW: Never mind. You're spoiling my fun.

Orson is not without justification in denying the Oscar he shared with Man-kiewicz—it was almost an insult. The Academy Awards are notoriously influenced by sentiment. Welles was the outsider, and not a humble one, either, on whom sanction could be generously bestowed. Envy, jealousy, fear, whatever—the Hollywood majority just didn't like him. In every category, the award went to one of their own. (Even best screenplay was no doubt more a gesture to old-time pro Mankiewicz than an award to Welles.) Best picture was Darryl Zanuck's production of How Green Was My Valley, *which also won best direction (John Ford's third Oscar), best art direction, and cinematography (Toland was a Hollywood man, but, tinged by Welles, his trend-setting photography was officially ignored). Best actor went to an old favorite, Gary Cooper, for Howard Hawks's* Sergeant York. *I'd [PB] be the last to say these pictures were without merit,*

Ford and Hawks being two of my favorite directors; they were certainly at the forefront of the films of that year, but Kane *was the film of a decade. The most telling Oscar was for music: Bernard Herrmann was nominated twice that year— for* Kane *and for* All That Money Can Buy *(another RKO release), and the academy gave him the award—for* All That Money Can Buy.

When the Oscars were announced (February 26, 1942), Welles was in Rio shooting It's All True. *On April 5, 1942, he sent his co-winner a belated note:*

> *Dear Mankie:*
>
> Here's what I wanted to wire you after the Academy Dinner:
>
> "You can kiss my half."
>
> I dare to send it through the mails only now I find it possible to enclose a ready-made retort. I don't presume to write your jokes for you, but you ought to like this:
>
> "Dear Orson: You don't know your half from a whole in the ground."
>
> > *Affectionately,*
> > *Orson*

Even now, after thirty years, Citizen Kane *is like watching a consummate artist grappling for the first time with the intoxication of his found vocation. All his passions—theater, magic, circus, radio, painting, literature—suddenly fused into one. This may explain why to so many people—even those who've seen Welles's other pictures (not so many have, actually)—*Kane *remains the favorite. It is not his best film—either stylistically or in the depth of its vision—but its aura is the most romantic: not just because he was twenty-five when he made it and strikingly handsome in it, not the content or thrust of the narrative that gives it romance, but the initial courtship of an artist with his art.*

No other director discovering the medium was as ready or as mature. The signs were right. So were the circumstances, and they were never the same again: free choice of material, complete control before and during shooting, final word on the cutting, the full financial and technical resources of the best moviemaking facilities in the world. Orson never had all these elements combined on one movie again. (It's also the only film of his to receive, if not exactly decent distribution, at least national prominence and publicity.) Kane, *therefore, is the only time*

Orson Welles was able to put on the screen exactly *what he wanted from every standpoint.*

It was late in Guaymas. The sun was down, but there was still an orange glow on the bay. Welles was struck by the beauty of the scene, and we looked at it for some time without speaking. He seemed melancholy. Kane *was his first film, and the fact that, despite all the fine work in movies he has done since, people still remember him mainly for that one is not a small source of unhappiness. It is a similar situation in radio. So many of his programs were far better, more inventive and beautiful than the "War of the Worlds," but that's the only one people want to talk about. And here we'd spent the whole day on* Kane, *the one film he least likes to discuss. Still, I chanced a final comment.*

PB: It seemed to me that your memory of your mother is re-flected in the scenes with Kane's mother.

OW: Not at all. She was so different, you know.

PB: I don't mean the character, but the affection of Kane—

OW: Really no comparison. My mother was very beautiful, very generous, and very tough. She was rather austere with me.

PB: Well, the mother in *Kane* was not a sentimental mother—

OW: It isn't that. There's just not any connection.

PB: It's not so much the mother herself but the emotion of *remembering* a mother. As in the scene where you meet Dorothy Comingore and tell her you're on a trip in search of your youth, and she has that line, "You know what mothers are like." And you say, in a sad, reflective tone, full of memories, "Yes." It's one of my favorite moments in the picture.

OW: No, Peter, I have no Rosebuds.

PB: But do you have a sentiment for that part of your past?

OW: No. . . . I have no wish to be back there. . . . Just one part of it, maybe. One place. My father lived sometimes in China, and partly in a tiny country hotel he'd bought in a village called Grand Detour, Illinois. It had a population of 130. Formerly it was ten thousand, but then the railroad didn't go through. And there was this hotel which had been built to service the covered wagons on their way west through southern Illinois (which is real Mark Twain country, you know, and people like

Booth Tarkington). My father spent a few months of his year there, entertaining a few friends. They never got a bill. And any legitimate hotel guests who tried to check in had a tough time even getting anyone to answer that bell you banged on the desk. Our servants were all retired or "resting" from show business. A gentleman called Rattlesnake-Oil Emery was handyman. One of the waitresses had done bird calls in a tent show. My father was very fond of people like that.

Well, where I do see some kind of Rosebud, perhaps, is in that world of Grand Detour. A childhood there was like a childhood back in the 1870s. No electric light, horse-drawn buggies—a completely anachronistic, old-fashioned, early-Tarkington, rural kind of life, with a country store that had above it a ballroom with an old dance floor with springs in it, so that folks would feel light on their feet. When I was little, nobody had danced up there for many years, but I used to sneak up at night and dance by moonlight with the dust rising from the floor. . . . Grand Detour was one of those lost worlds, one of those Edens that you get thrown out of. It really was kind of invented by my father. He's the one who kept out the cars and the electric lights. It was one of the "Merrie Eng-lands." Imagine: he smoked his own sausages. You'd wake up in the morning to the sound of the folks in the bake house, and the smells. . . . I feel as though I've had a childhood in the last century from those short summers.

PB: It reminds me of *Ambersons*. You do have a fondness for things of the past, though—

OW: Oh yes. For that Eden people lose. . . . It's a theme that interests me. A nostalgia for the garden—it's a recurring theme in all our civilization.

PB: Kane lost his Eden when the bank took him from his home, and you lost yours—

OW: —in Grand Detour? It was called Grand Detour because the Rock River circles there—it's almost an island. I never even saw the ruins of my father's hotel. It really was a marvelous little corner in time, a kind of forgotten place. . . .

PB: How old were you in those years?

OW: I don't know exactly. It was just before and during my time at Todd. It burned down the year before he died, with all his jade collection in it. And he came out of the fire in his nightshirt after everybody thought that all was lost—came out of the flames with a bird cage and, under his arm, a framed picture of Trixi Friganza. She'd been one of his old girlfriends. . . . Can I go now?

PB: OK.

OW: Good night.

Editor's Notes to the Welles Interview

JONATHAN ROSENBAUM

◆ ◆ ◆

G IVEN THE VIRTUALLY mythological status of *Citizen Kane* in Welles's career, it isn't surprising that it has generated by far the most debate of all his films. Two publications in particular should be cited: "Raising Kane," by Pauline Kael, which appeared originally in two successive issues of the *New Yorker* (February 20 and 27, 1971) and then as a lengthy preface to the script, published later the same year (*The "Citizen Kane" Book*, Boston: Atlantic/Little, Brown, and Robert L. Carringer's *The Making of "Citizen Kane"* (Berkeley: University of California Press, 1985). Kael's essay was replied to at length by Bogdanovich and Welles in a point-by-point refutation published by Bogdanovich as "The *Kane* Mutiny" in *Esquire* (October 1972), which included certain portions of the previous interview. Other rebuttals included Ted Gilling's interviews with George Coulouris and Bernard Herrmann in *Sight and Sound* (Spring 1972), polemics by Joseph McBride (*Film Heritage*, Fall 1971) and myself (*Film Comment*, Spring 1972 and Summer 1972), and remarks in the Welles biographies by Barbara Leaming (*Orson*

Welles, New York: Viking, 1985) and Frank Brady, (*Citizen Welles,* New York: Scribner's, 1989).

The major focus of Kael's essay is its defense and celebration of screenwriter Herman J. Mankiewicz as the principal, neglected creative force behind *Kane.* According to Kael, the script was written almost entirely by Mankiewicz, and Welles had actively plotted to deprive him of any screen credit:

> Welles probably made suggestions in his early conversations with Mankiewicz, and since he received copies of the work weekly while it was in progress at Victorville, he may have given advice by phone or letter. Later, he almost certainly made suggestions for cuts that helped Mankiewicz hammer the script into tighter form, and he is known to have made a few changes on the set. But Mrs. Alexander, who took the dictation from Mankiewicz, from the first paragraph to the last, and then, when the first draft was completed and they all went back to Los Angeles, did the secretarial work at Mankiewicz's house on the rewriting and the cuts, and who then handled the script at the studio until after the film was shot, says that Welles didn't write (or dictate) one line of the shooting script of *Citizen Kane.*
>
> . . . Mankiewicz began to realize that he'd made a very bad financial deal, and that the credit might be more important than he'd anticipated. After talks with Mrs. Alexander and the Mercury people who visited on weekends, he decided he was going to get screen credit, no matter what his bargain with Welles had been. Meanwhile, Houseman . . . discovered once again, and as so many others had, that it wasn't easy to get your name on anything Orson Welles was involved with. Houseman was apparently fed up with arguments, and he says he waived his claim when he saw how determined Welles was; he left for New York and got started on preparations for *Native Son.* But Mankiewicz was an experienced Hollywood hand and veteran of credit brawls who kept all his drafts and materials, and a man who relished trouble. He had ample proof of his authorship,

and he took his evidence to the Screen Writers Guild and raised so much hell that Welles was forced to split the credit and take second place in the listing.

Later in the same essay, Kael recounts another story:

> Nunnally Johnson says that while *Citizen Kane* was being shot, Mankiewicz told him that he had received an offer of a ten-thousand-dollar bonus from Welles (through Welles' "chums") to hold to the original understanding and keep his name off the picture.... Mankiewicz said he was tempted by Welles' offer. As usual, he needed money, and, besides, he was fearful of what would happen when the picture came out—he might be blackballed forever. William Randolph Hearst, like Stalin, was known to be fairly Byzantine in his punishments. At the same time, Mankiewicz knew that *Citizen Kane* was his best work, and he was proud of it. He told Johnson that he went to Ben Hecht with his dilemma, and that Hecht, as prompt with advice as with scripts, said, "Take the ten grand and double-cross the son of a bitch."

I asked Nunnally Johnson if he thought Mankiewicz's story was true, and Mankiewicz had actually got the offer and had taken Hecht's advice. Johnson replied, "I like to believe he did." It's not unlikely.

Bogdanovich's "The *Kane* Mutiny" replies to all three of these charges. The first charge, which even Robert Carringer calls "a flagrant misrepresentation," has no factual basis beyond a willful confusion about how the script was written, apparently fostered by various statements from John Houseman—Welles's producer and partner in the Mercury stage and radio productions, who had gone through a violent break with Welles in Hollywood during the work on *Heart of Darkness*, and was later hired back to assist Mankiewicz on the *Kane* script.

Houseman repeated the notion that Mankiewicz was the script's sole author many times, in many contexts, up until his death, without ever explaining many anomalies about this—such as his own cable to Mankiewicz from New York, quoted by Frank Brady in *Citizen Welles*, which reads in part (passages in square brackets are my own): "Leaving tonight for Carolina to confer with Paul Green and Richard Wright [on *Native Son*]. . . . Received your cut version and several new scenes of Orson's. . . . After much careful reading I like all Orson's scenes with exception of Kane-Emily sequence [apparently the breakfast montage, which is found in none of Mankiewicz's drafts]." It should be added that even though Houseman is often a relatively reliable source on certain matters regarding Welles's work, his memoirs are highly misleading and inaccurate concerning aspects of the *Heart of Darkness* project (which he claims never developed beyond a first-draft script, despite many scripts and other documents to disprove this) as well as *Kane*.

Welles explained the screenwriting process of *Kane* in a letter to the London *Times* (November 17, 1971), in an account that no scholar has contested:

> The initial ideas for this film and its basic structure were the result of direct collaboration between us; after this we separated and there were two screenplays: one written by Mr. Mankiewicz, in Victorville, and the other, in Beverly Hills, by myself. . . . The final version of the screenplay . . . was drawn from both sources.

Although the printed shooting script of *Kane* credits both Mankiewicz and Welles, in that order, just as the film's final credits do (with the consequence that Welles, as legally established coauthor, received royalties on *The "Citizen Kane" Book*, along with Kael and with Mankiewicz's heirs), Kael's first charge, which has remained unmodified in all subsequent editions of the book, continues to be believed by a good many readers. Her second charge—that Welles tried to deprive Mankiewicz of any screen credit—has never been substantiated either, although Carringer curiously concludes that "it seems to be true." Carringer's evidence is Mankiewicz's contract with the Mercury Theater (he had no contract with RKO), which "contained the standard waiver of rights of authorship," and letters from Arnold Weissberger

(Welles's lawyer) to Welles and RKO's legal department. All this *does* point toward a possible denial of screen credit to Mankiewicz—following the precedent of the Mercury radio adaptations, which assigned no scriptwriter credits and fostered the false impression of Welles as sole adapter—but nothing in the evidence cited by Carringer indicates that Welles was an instigator of this plan, or even necessarily a supporter of it.

Kane can be seen in two diametrically opposed fashions. One can see it as the first feature of a maverick independent filmmaker, and the only one in which he was accorded both full use of a Hollywood studio *and* final cut. Alternatively, one can view *Kane* as the ultimate vindication of the Hollywood mainstream, showing that major creative talents (including Welles, Mankiewicz, and cinematographer Gregg Toland) could be brought together and used to their fullest advantage.

According to Kael, *Kane* is a culmination of 1930s newspaper comedies, a picture whose greatness stems from the collaboration of disparate talents rather than a single guiding intelligence (also Carringer's thesis), and a "*shallow* masterpiece" (her emphasis). The net result was to make Welles's best-known work also seem like one of his safest. (Years earlier, however, Kael had described *Kane* in a short review as "the most controversial one-man show in film history," making it clear that the "one man" in question was Welles, not Mankiewicz; and she was one of the most eloquent and passionate defenders of Welles's *Falstaff*; see her book *Kiss Kiss Bang Bang* [Boston: Atlantic/Little, Brown, 1968] for both reviews.)

Regarding Welles's troubled relationship with Houseman, which is alluded to only elliptically here, one should consult Barbara Leaming's Welles biography and Bogdanovich's "The *Kane* Mutiny" to get Welles's side of the story. (For Houseman's side, see the first volume of his memoirs, *Run-Through* [New York: Simon and Schuster, 1972].) During my meeting with Welles in 1973, the question of Houseman and his memoirs came up when I alluded to some of Houseman's skeptical remarks about the *Heart of Darkness* project. After Welles insisted that Houseman was in no position to have known much about the project because he wasn't even around for any of the story conferences, he went on to say

(I quote from memory), "He's the worst kind of enemy someone can possibly have, because he gives the impression to others"—meaning me in this case—"of being sympathetic." "That's really a pity," I replied, "because his discussion of the Mercury radio shows is probably the most detailed account of them that's appeared anywhere in print." There was a long, smoldering silence at this point—the only moment during our lunch when Welles betrayed any anger—after which he said quietly, with a touch of both sorrow and sarcasm, "So be it."

It's worth adding, however, that *Citizen Kane* was not the last Welles project that Houseman was involved with. Between the completion of *Kane* and its release, the two collaborated once again, on their last stage production together in New York, an adaptation of Richard Wright's powerful, bestselling novel about American racism, *Native Son*, starring Canada Lee as Bigger Thomas, which Wright himself helped to adapt, and which enjoyed a successful run. Like the Welles productions of *Julius Caesar* and *Shoemaker's Holiday*, the show ran without an intermission; its main action was set in a courtroom (where the audience was encouraged at certain points to regard itself as a jury), with eight flashbacks, and, like the novel, centered around Bigger Thomas's murder of a young white woman. (One of the flashback settings was the tenement flat of the Thomas family, where one of the Rosebud sleds used in *Citizen Kane* figured as a prop.)

When Welles recalls "playing himself" on the "March of Time" radio show, it is possible that he is misremembering the actual occasion and alluding to his performance of a scene from Archibald MacLeish's *Panic*, a week after he performed that play on the stage in March 1935, rather than his production of his black *Macbeth* two years later.

A few basic dates might be helpful in understanding Welles's discussion of his childhood. He was born May 6, 1915. His mother, Beatrice Ives Welles, died May 10, 1924; his father, Richard Head Welles, died December 28, 1930. His parents separated when he was six, and his relationship with Dr. Maurice Bernstein—who was close to his mother, and who became his official guardian after his father's death—virtually went back to his infancy. He attended the Todd School from 1926 through 1930. For the most detailed discussion of this period, see Barbara Leaming's *Orson Welles*.

Regarding Preston Sturges, his first play was *The Guinea Pig*, which ran for 64 performances; *Strictly Dishonorable*, which opened about eight months later in 1929, wound up running for 557 performances.

Thornton Wilder, whom Welles first met in 1933, was instrumental in getting Welles his touring job with Katharine Cornell by giving him an introduction to Alexander Woollcott; the tour lasted from 1933 to 1934.

Akira Kurosawa's *Rashomon* (1951), the first of his films to get worldwide attention, is set near Kyoto in the eighth century, and describes a rape and murder from the viewpoints of the four people present, each of whom contradicts the other three concerning the basic facts of what happened.

The term "pan focus" was used in *Life* magazine's May 26, 1941, article about Welles, shortly after *Kane*'s release. For the same illustrated story, Toland shot three still photographs to demonstrate the differences between "pan focus," "the old way," and "a conventional close-up."

Dorothy Comingore entered films as Linda Winters in Columbia comedy shorts of the mid-1930s after some stage experience in stock. She appeared in Three Stooges comedies and some low-budget Westerns and did some bits in a few other films in the late 1930s (e.g., *Scandal Sheet* and *Mr. Smith Goes to Washington* in 1939) before landing the lead female part in *Citizen Kane*.

For further comments from Welles on the nonfunctionality of producers and agents, see his feisty and controversial article for the February 1941 *Stage*, "Orson Welles Writing about Orson Welles," reprinted in *Hollywood Directors, 1941–1976*, edited by Richard Koszarski (New York: Oxford University Press, 1977).

Regarding Welles's fondness for birds and his parrot in Spain, the latter can be seen with him in *Treasure Island* (1972)—a film that he scripted as well as acted in—along with his pet monkey, Mimi.

Targets (1968), Bogdanovich's first feature, scripted by him, with uncredited assistance from Samuel Fuller, and based on a story by Bogdanovich and Polly Platt, alternates two narratives, both set in Los Angeles, which come together in the final sequence: a horror actor (Boris Karloff) decides to retire, claiming his films can't compete with the horrors of contemporary life, and a Vietnam veteran (Tim O'Kelly) goes mad, kills his family, climbs a tower, and shoots people passing on the freeway.

For more information about the cut brothel sequence in *Kane*, see Mankiewicz and Welles's shooting script in *The "Citizen Kane" Book* and (for illustrations) Carringer's *The Making of "Citizen Kane."*

The Scripts of *Citizen Kane*

ROBERT L. CARRINGER

◆　◆　◆

THE BEST-KNOWN controversy in film criticism of recent years has been over the authorship of the *Citizen Kane* script. Pauline Kael first raised the issue in a flamboyant piece in the *New Yorker* in 1971. Contrary to what Orson Welles would like us to believe, Kael charged, the script for the film was actually not his work but almost wholly the work of an all-but-forgotten figure, one of Hollywood's veteran screenwriters, Herman J. Mankiewicz:

> Welles probably made suggestions in his early conversations with Mankiewicz, and since he received copies of the work weekly while it was in progress ... may have given advice by phone or letter. Later, he almost certainly made suggestions for cuts that helped Mankiewicz hammer the script into tighter form, and he is known to have made a few changes on the set. But Mrs. Alexander, who took the dictation from Mankiewicz, from the first paragraph to the last,

and then, when the first draft was completed and they all went back to Los Angeles, did the secretarial work at Mankiewicz's house on the rewriting and the cuts, and who then handled the script at the studio until after the film was shot, says that Welles didn't write (or dictate) one line of the shooting script of *Citizen Kane*.

The principal evidence was an early draft of the script which Kael was able to show had been written mostly by Mankiewicz. She fleshed the case out with testimonies from various Mankiewicz relatives, professional associates, and friends, all purporting to show how much the script was really his. The evidence was all one-sided and the case was wholly circumstantial, but nevertheless "Raising Kane" presented an authentic critical problem that could neither be dismissed nor ignored. Welles has always worked by being involved in several things at once. Especially in the frantic early years of the Mercury Theater, it was often necessary for others to take over some of the time-consuming preparatory chores like scripting: Although the Mercury radio scripts were often written by others as a matter of course, their authorship was frequently attributed to Welles. Why would it be unusual for the same thing to happen on a Mercury Theater film? Without any hard and fast evidence to prove otherwise, even a circumstantial case for Mankiewicz's authorship of the *Citizen Kane* script was enough to raise lingering suspicions, if not outright doubts.[1]

Fortunately enough evidence to settle the matter has survived. A virtually complete set of script records for *Citizen Kane* has been preserved in the archives of RKO General Pictures in Hollywood, and these provide almost a day-to-day record of the history of the scripting. Once this record is reconstructed and all the available pieces of evidence are matched to it, a reasonably clear picture emerges of who was responsible for what in the final script. The full evidence reveals that Welles's contribution to the *Citizen Kane* script was not only substantial but definitive.

There are seven complete drafts of the *Citizen Kane* script in the RKO files.[2] The first is dated 16 April 1940; the latest set of revisions in the final draft is dated 19 July. The first three might be more accurately termed "gatherings" than drafts. Once the project was under way, the various production departments—budgeting, art, casting, research, and so on—had to have a temporary first draft in order to start preliminary preparations as soon as possible. Then a temporary second draft would have to be available so that the departments could make necessary reconsiderations and changes. Since, at these early stages, the script would be gathered for production purposes, the gatherings do not necessarily indicate that a new creative plateau had been reached in the evolution of the story. Meanwhile, as a script gathering was being typed, revisions were being made daily and sent on to the stenographic department. The revision pages were then individually assigned a new date (usually the date of typing) and inserted into a script carrying an earlier master date. (One early script gathering has almost 200 such pages.) As the start of shooting neared, a mimeographed script, called "Final," was prepared for wide distribution to members of the cast and production staff. In the case of *Citizen Kane*, "Final" was the fourth draft, and subsequent drafts (all newly mimeographed) were called "Revised Final," "Second Revised Final," and "Third Revised Final." The mimeographed scripts also have inserted individually dated revision pages, usually on blue paper.

The first two drafts of the *Citizen Kane* script were written by Herman Mankiewicz and John Houseman in seclusion in the desert at Victorville, California, during March, April, and May 1940. Officially, Houseman was there as editor. But part of his job was to ride herd on Mankiewicz, whose drinking habits were legendary and whose screenwriting credentials unfortunately did not include a reputation for seeing things through. Detailed accounts of the Victorville interlude have been given by Houseman in his autobiography and by Kael in "Raising Kane." There was constant interchange between Victorville and Hollywood, with Houseman going in to confer on the script and Welles sending up emissaries (and going up on occasion himself) and regularly receiving copies of the work in progress. Welles in turn was working over the draft pages with the assistance of his own secretary, Katherine Trosper, and handing the revised screenplay copy in its rough state over to Amalia Kent, a script supervisor at RKO noted for her skills at breaking this kind of material down into script continuity form, who was readying it for the stenographic and various production departments.[3]

First Draft

The first draft of the script with a complete beginning, middle, and end is dated 16 April 1940 and titled *American*.[4] It is over 250 pages (the final shooting script was only 156 pages), and even at that length there are still huge gaps in the continuity to be filled in. Though *American* is only a pale version of what is to come, it must nevertheless be examined in careful detail. The material at this state is almost wholly the work of the writer and his editor. When Welles himself becomes heavily involved in the writing, it will become apparent almost at once how greatly his ideas on how to deal with the material differ from theirs. One measure of the success of the film is the degree to which it is divested of the conceptions of the early drafts of the script.

American opens in the manner of the German expressionists, with directions for the camera to move through an iron gate and, after a series of dissolve-views of the dilapidated grounds of Kane's estate (called "The Alhambra" at this point), to enter the front door, proceed across the great hall, ascend the staircase, and pass down a long gallery filled with art objects, arriving at last at Kane's bedroom, where a nurse is just entering with a hospital table. From inside we are to hear a voice say, faintly, "Rosebud." We are to see the falling snowflakes, then the glass globe held by the figure on the bed. He is to say "Rosebud" three more times. The early segments of action—a newsreel biography, the discussion in the projection room, visits to Susan Alexander Kane at the nightclub and to the Thatcher Memorial Library, and a flashback to Kane's childhood in Colorado—appear in the order and with the overall logic they will eventually have.

The first major difference from the final script appears after the Colorado sequence. In *American* the Thatcher manuscript, instead of going immediately to the newspaper years, continues with an account of the financier's visit to Kane in Rome on his twenty-fifth birthday. Kane is installed in the oldest, most expensive Renaissance palace in Rome. A party is in progress when Thatcher arrives. The guests are a thoroughly disreputable lot— "pimps, Lesbians, dissipated Army officers, homosexuals, nymphomaniacs and international society tramps." That evening Thatcher and Kane meet alone to discuss the future management of Kane's interest. Thatcher presents Kane with a large bound book detailing his holdings. As Kane thumbs through it he seems to stumble accidentally on one item, the New York *Enquirer*, a faltering newspaper acquired some years before in a foreclosure proceeding. Kane says he thinks it "might be fun to run a newspaper" and forbids Thatcher to dispose of the *Enquirer*. Thatcher's story continues with his encounter with Kane in the *Enquirer* offices a few years later, written as it will appear in the film except that in the business of Cuba it is Leland (called Brad at this stage), not Wheeler, who, as the *Enquirer's* correspondent on the scene, is instructed to keep on providing tropical colors and leave it to his editor to provide the war. Thatcher's narration concludes with an encounter in the board room of Thatcher and Company many years later, when it is revealed to the old man and his son (and heir apparent in the business) that Kane's papers are about to expose certain questionable bond flotation practices by the nation's leading investment bankers.

Bernstein's story begins by returning to Rome and telling the sequel to Kane's meeting with Thatcher. Bernstein reveals that he gave up his wholesale jewelry business to go in with Kane and how the two of them plotted secretly to take over the *Enquirer* and made plans to do away with its "ladylike" and "sissified" content and to transform its deadly dull layout. (Duplicity was necessary, Kane thought, because Thatcher would have disposed of the *Enquirer* if he had got wind Kane was interested in it.) Kane's first day at the *Enquirer* is presented substantially as it is in the film. The circulation-building phase, however, is very different. There are scenes showing Benton, editor of the *Chronicle*, reacting to his new rival—dismissing him as a young upstart, then becoming more and more nervous at his success, and finally offering to buy him out. Benton's personal secretary, Reilly, appears in these scenes. Later he comes over to Kane with the rest of the *Chronicle* staff. Though he is eventually eliminated, he has a prominent role through several drafts of the script.

Bernstein also tells of a discussion at dinner one evening between himself, Kane, and Leland (now back from Cuba and installed as dramatic critic) about Thatcher's efforts to ruin the *Enquirer* by bringing pressure on its advertisers. Kane predicted such efforts would cease almost at once. Next day when a crony of Thatcher's on the traction trust pays a threatening call to Kane's office, Kane produces incriminating letters Reilly has stolen for him and forces the man and his associates into leaving the *Enquirer* alone. Next in Bernstein's story are two familiar incidents—a conversation in Kane's office when Kane and Leland discuss Kane's impending vacation in Europe on his doctor's advice and Kane's return from Europe with a surprise announcement for the society editor. Back in the present, Thompson shows Bernstein a letter from attorneys representing Emily—now Mrs. Whitehall Standing—saying she regards her marriage to Kane as a distasteful episode in her life which she would prefer to forget and declining to be interviewed.

Next in *American* is the story of Kane's life with Emily. It is organized as a discrete narrative segment, but there is no frame device or other explanation of its narrative status. Though the letter of disclaimer from her lawyers has eliminated Emily as one of the informants, at this stage she is clearly still being considered as a kind of undeclared narrative presence. First are shots of the White House wedding. Next is a scene in the Lincoln Room in which Emily's father tells Kane the Nortons dislike his politics and crusading but are convinced nonetheless Emily chose wisely. Then come scenes of a honeymoon in the remote Wisconsin woods. Kane has had his yacht taken down and shipped there and reassembled on a small lake. The happy couple is attended by an army of chefs and servants. Kane is finding it difficult to keep his promise of two weeks free of newspapers and other business. Suddenly, in an old piece of newspaper used for wrapping, an item catches his eye. He breaks the honeymoon short and rushes back to attempt to head off a lease of government oil reserves to an oil trust. Kane gains an audience with President Norton and they exchange heated remarks. When the president refuses to call off the lease, Kane begins a campaign against him in his papers. A son, Howard, is born to the Kanes, but Kane's preoccupation with his work and his increasingly savage attacks on the president open a breach in the marriage. The president is seriously wounded in an assassination attempt; reportedly the assassin had an inflammatory *Enquirer* editorial in his pocket; angry crowds gather in front of the *Enquirer* building. Though the president recovers and the public outrage eventually dies down, Emily cannot forget; she will remain married to Kane to keep up appearances and avoid hurting his political ambitions, but she no longer loves him. At about the same time Leland starts to protest to Kane about a new policy being instituted in the dramatic section by Reilly, but Kane puts him off. Shortly after, Leland is transferred to the Chicago paper at his own request.

Kane becomes a candidate for governor on the Independent Voters' League ticket; though his opponent is Judge Grey, his real antagonist in the campaign is Boss Rogers, who saw to it that Kane was denied the regular party's nomination. Kane is thought to be a certain loser, but his antipolitics, antiparty themes appeal to the voters, and his campaign catches fire. There is a gigantic rally at Madison Square Garden on the eve of the campaign. After Kane gives his speech, he is handed an urgent message to "come to my place tonight—Susan." Kane loses by a slim margin. The *Enquirer* headline charging "fraud at polls" is not merely a political stance, since it is generally believed the election was stolen from Kane. He demands a recount but relents when he senses it probably won't do any good. Emily, who has stuck by him to avoid damaging his chances in politics, leaves to file for a divorce and takes their son with her. Before she goes she tells Kane she has known about Susan Alexander for some time.

Leland's story comes next. In Leland's remarks to Thompson there is material later deleted—a long passage in which he describes his and Kane's days in school together and tells how he came to be associated with Kane on the *Enquirer*, and another passage in which, as he reflects over their long friendship, he wonders if Rosebud may somehow be connected with himself. His narration begins during the early days at the *Enquirer* and includes several scenes of him and Kane dining together at expensive restaurants and going to the theater, usually in the company of cheap women. It continues with the celebration party, which had been introduced in Bernstein's narration; as dancing goes on in the background, Leland questions Bernstein about the loyalties of the new staff, as he does in the film. Next Leland is sent off to Cuba as the *Enquirer*'s special correspondent at the front. He is shown in a quiet pastoral scene in Cuba while headlines and articles in the *Enquirer* carrying his by-line tell of native uprisings, massacres, and other eyewitnessed atrocities taking place there. Leland returns from Cuba in a rage and protests this gross distortion of his reports. Kane accepts his resignation as war correspondent but uses his charm and the prospect of wine and women and continued good times to get back into his good graces. One evening at the theater Kane and Leland and their inevitable girls run into Kane Sr., "a dandy as ever was," in the company of a "young tart"; later at Leland's apartment when Kane Sr. introduces her as his new wife, Kane flies into a murderous rage and attacks the old man.

The Leland narration continues by filling in or expanding things already introduced: Leland and Bernstein talk about why Leland didn't accompany Kane to Europe (because Leland's a "stuffed-shirt," a "New England schoolmarm," and Kane was going to have fun); Leland and Emily look on as a proud father admires his three-week-old son; Kane skips dinner at home (the second time that week) to pursue his campaign in the *Enquirer* against the president; and Kane, Bernstein, and Leland huddle together at the office on the evening of the assassination attempt as an angry mob mills outside. Now Reilly's new policy—actually an outright promotional scheme—is revealed: in effect, theatrical producers are to be guaranteed favorable notices in exchange for advertising considerations. If Leland's review of a particular show is too negative, a more favorable review by someone else will be substituted. The scheme apparently has Kane's blessing. Leland is outraged and insists on being transferred to Chicago; Kane lets him go. An added note explains that despite his independent campaign posture Kane made a political deal to ensure his election. When his opponents got wind of it, Kane scooped them and exposed himself in his own papers. The bad publicity cost him enough votes to make the race close and make it possible for his opponents to steal the election. Other inserts show Kane emerging with Susan from a justice of the peace and Leland trying unsuccessfully to compose a congratulatory telegram. The final portion of Leland's account covers Susan's debut. It includes background material that was to be eliminated: Leland meets the Kanes at the special train which transports them to Chicago; on this occasion telltale allusions are made to Susan's fondness for jigsaw puzzles and Kane's injunctions against further drinking. There is a celebration luncheon attended by the mayor and six governors. Leland passes out at his typewriter before he finishes his review. A box on the theatrical page of the Chicago *Enquirer* the next day states that the review will be run a day late. Leland receives a $25,000 severance check; he tears it up and returns it along with the Declaration of Principles. A messenger delivers the envelope to Kane in his stateroom on the train. Kane quietly disposes of it. Susan, absorbed in her jigsaw puzzles, never knows.

After Leland's narration there is a sixty-page numbering gap. The missing portion would include Kane's first years with Susan—their meeting, the development of their relationship, their marriage, and her singing career. In this draft Susan's story does not begin until she and Kane have already retired to the Florida estate, which, after the numbering gap, is renamed Xanadu. Her first scene features Bernstein as a reluctant visitor always fidgeting about the work he left behind in New York. He confesses to Kane he also feels out of place because the other guests, mostly Susan's friends, are so much younger than Kane and he. Kane insists he stay over and appear in costume at a Wild West party the following evening. Susan goes off to the stables with a handsome young man, Jerry Martin, to see a new colt, and despite her mild protestations to Jerry that he has got her all wrong, it is clear something is in the offing between them. Susan brings a pitcher of cocktails to Bernstein in his room; she tosses down three drinks as she describes how empty the lives of the moneyed can be. At the Wild West party an obviously bored Susan dances in a slow, old-fashioned style with Kane while all the rest do lively modern dances. Susan and Jerry dance, then wander off together in search of drinks. When Kane decides to go for a swim at 1:00 A.M., he and Raymond come upon Susan and Jerry embracing in the bathhouse. Kane makes a remark to Raymond about a "rat that ought to be killed," and the next afternoon Raymond reveals that Jerry Martin has been found dead on the Xanadu grounds, apparently as a result of being thrown from his horse. Kane brings the news to Susan, still in bed with a hangover. She reads the truth in his eyes.

Next we see them a year later on their yacht. They have been on an extended around-the-world cruise; Susan pleads to be taken home. Next is a montage of puzzles, inserted to suggest her increasing frustration and boredom at Xanadu. The rest of her story from this point is substantially as in the film—the Everglades picnic, the argument between Susan and Kane in their tent, Susan's decision to leave, and the separation scene in Susan's room. Back in the present, Susan says she's sorry she couldn't help about Rosebud, but tells Thompson he ought to see Raymond because "he knows where the bodies are buried." Raymond haggles with Thompson over how much whatever information he gives is worth and then continues the story from Susan's departure (it was 1929). Kane puts out a news item over the wire saying her leaving was "under the terms of a peaceful and friendly agreement," orders a picture run as usual after dinner, and goes to her room and takes away the little glass globe.

Next is an account of how Kane lost his papers in 1935. For years Kane has stripped his newspapers of cash to finance his extravagant personal ventures. Now a massive loan is needed to keep the papers going. Thatcher Jr. makes control of the business management of the papers a condition of the loan. Kane, Bernstein, and Reilly are seen dining alone in silence at Xanadu.

A few years later Kane's son, Howard, is killed when he and

some other members of a "half-baked, idiot fascist movement" try to seize an armory in Washington. Typically, Kane dictates a self-serving press release for his papers which begins, "Deprived of the father's guidance to which he was entitled . . ." He attends the funeral and is seated next to Emily and her new husband. Afterward Raymond finds Kane apparently unconscious on the floor of the bathroom in his hotel. In the last shot of him he is being attended by a nurse on the grounds of Xanadu. Finally the screen is filled with newspaper headlines announcing his death. Raymond and Thompson take leave of one another.

Near the end *American* degenerates into buffoonery and farce. The scenes at Xanadu are written substantially as they will eventually appear down to Thompson's all-important summation of Kane. As he begins, a photographer rudely interrupts him, and he breaks off. Later as he and the others wait for a train to New York he starts in again and is again rudely interrupted and told to save it for later. There the matter is dropped. *American* ends with Rosebud going into the furnace, a reversal of the opening shots, and a final glimpse of Kane's monogram on the immense iron gate.

Though Welles used to play down the connection, it is by now almost universal knowledge that William Randolph Hearst was the general model for Charles Foster Kane. Some of Hearst's memorable lines, his scandal mongering, his ideological inconsistencies, the awkwardness of his May-December romance with Marion Davies—all these things in the film based on Hearst were more or less commonly known at the time. What is not generally known is just how strong a presence Hearst was in the formative stages of the scripting. That presence in *American* is overwhelming; most of this installment of the script is quite literally a reworking of specific incidents and details from Hearst's life. Some of it was too scandalous to have appeared in respectable print, such as an alleged liaison of Marion Davies's which resulted in a death aboard Hearst's yacht under mysterious circumstances, almost certainly the inspiration for the Jerry Martin affair.[5] But most of it had been published previously in newspaper and magazine articles and in books. Mankiewicz had been a newspaper man himself and knew nearly every story about Hearst by heart. But he was also almost certainly drawing on published sources as well. Two works in particular, both published just a few years before the writing of *American*, seem to have been special sources for the information in *American* about Hearst: a florid and highly romanticized "authorized" biography by Mrs. Fremont Older, wife of a Hearst editor, and a biography in the muckraking tradition by Ferdinand Lundberg. Mrs. Older struggles valiantly to put all of Hearst's activities, even the seamiest, in the most favorable light; Lundberg does just the opposite. Read one after the other, these two books can leave an impression of Hearst that is very much like the position the film finally arrives at about Kane: that he is a figure of contradiction and paradox whose true motives and real self continually elude even his most persistent interpreters.[6]

The title *American* may have been inspired (as Pauline Kael suggests) by Hearst's general fondness for attaching that label to his enterprises. But it was also used in a similar way in the title of Mrs. Older's book. The newsreel narration sometimes sounds suspiciously like Mrs. Older's rhetorical flights, such as her description of the aging publisher in his years of decline at San Simeon:

> Camp Hill has become the Casa Grande on the Enchanted Hill of San Simeon. Here in remote grandeur, forty-three miles from a town of any size, and two hundred miles from a large city, William Randolph Hearst, this invisible Charlemagne of the mountains, seems to his twenty-million readers almost like a myth. Few have seen him, save in the news-reel.
>
> In 1919, Hearst gave to San Simeon a new meaning. The forty-five-thousand acres inherited from his father became the nucleus of what has grown to be an imperial domain. Here, with the clarity of isolation, the publisher on the crest of his mountain range surveys his fifty miles of coast line on the Pacific, and edits forty-one newspapers and magazines. (p. 528)

The events dealt with in the newsreel could be an outline for a public biography of Hearst. The first detail used to illustrate Kane's impact on his times is his involvement in mercy efforts after the San Francisco earthquake. *American* calls for shots of "special trains with large streamers: 'Kane Relief Organization.' " The model is Hearst's publicity-orchestrated sponsorship of relief efforts after the famous earthquake of April 1906. Oil scandals and women's suffrage, the first two issues enumerated to illustrate Kane's association with controversial public affairs, were both areas of long-standing and highly visible involvement by Hearst. Like Kane, Hearst was notorious for his flip-flopping of support on political issues and personages, from labor to fascism and from the Bolsheviks to FDR. Hearst, like Kane, also "hastened his country's entry into one war" and "bitterly . . . opposed our participation in another." The comic touch in the newsreel where Kane is termed, successively, from separate quarters, a communist, a fascist, and an American is undoubtedly inspired by a passage in one of Hearst's old campaign speeches reprinted by Mrs. Older:

> I am attacked on one side by the organs of socialism as an enemy of radicalism, and on the other side by the organs of Wall Street as an enemy of conservatism. I am opposed by both extremes . . . but my program is not extreme, simply Americanism. (pp. 310–11)

Another humorous touch in the newsreel directly inspired by Hearst is Kane's expulsion from "Nurenberg [sic] University" for placing a chamber pot on the school tower. Hearst had been expelled from Harvard after he sent a chamber pot to each faculty member with a photograph of the recipient inside (Lundberg, p. 20).

Numerous details in Kane's newspaper career have precise counterparts in Hearst's life. Like Kane, Hearst had a virtual financial empire at his disposal, out of which he selected one insignificant item, an anemic and unprosperous newspaper, the San Francisco *Examiner*. (Kane's paper at this stage is the *Enquirer*, which is closer to Hearst's paper than the spelling—*Inquirer*—eventually used.) Thatcher acquired the paper in a foreclosure proceeding and was offered $100,000 for it, precisely the amount of the bad debt through which Hearst's father acquired the *Examiner* in 1880 (Lundberg, p. 20). Kane tells Thatcher he thinks it "might be fun to run a newspaper"; Mrs. Older's husband, a Hearst editor, recalls that at the time Hearst took over the *Examiner* he was thought of as "the son of a millionaire who thought it might be good to 'take a fling' at journalism" (p. vii).

The original models for Kane's two closest associates on the paper, Bernstein and Leland, are Hearst men—S. S. Carvalho, his shrewd, single-minded, intensely loyal Jewish business manager, and Eugene Lent, his boyhood chum in San Francisco, traveling companion in Europe, Harvard classmate and associate on the Harvard *Lampoon*, and one of his first employees on the *Examiner*. Virtually all the steps Kane takes when he assumes control of the *Enquirer* are based directly on or inspired by Hearst's behavior in the early days at the San Francisco *Examiner* and later when he took over the New York *Journal*. Hearst threw himself into his work and practically lived in the editorial offices of his papers in those days; Mrs. Older reports that he seldom left the *Journal* offices in New York until three or four in the morning. One of his first tasks was to redesign completely the appearance of the paper. Hearst was legendary for issuing orders for the paper to be made over after the pages were locked up or even after it was on the presses. "The paper must be right, nothing else matters," a resisting editor is said to have been told on one such occasion (Older, p. 139; also see p. 151). Hearst actually dropped the price of the paper as a circulation ploy (as Kane is shown contemplating), throwing fear and panic into the ranks of enemy papers. Hearst pursued an aggressive and virtually intimidating policy of soliciting advertising, as Kane does in *American*. Hearst also hounded his news sources mercilessly, as Kane does in the episode on Mrs. Silverstone of Brooklyn.

The circulation-building sequences of *American* are based largely on Hearst's rivalries with other publishers in his early newspaper days. Lundberg points out that by 1889 the *Examiner* had reached a Sunday circulation of 62,000; in *American* when circulation reaches 62,000 Kane has a sign with that figure painted on a wall opposite his rival's window and on 300 other signs around the city. Kane's cocky offer to buy out his influential rival is based on a similar offer Hearst made to James Gordon Bennett of the New York *Herald* (Lundberg, p. 115). The episodes involving the publisher Benton in *American* are based on actual events involving Hearst's archrival, Joseph Pulitzer of the New York *World*, the most successful newspaper publisher in America before Hearst. Hearst succeeded with the *Journal* as Kane succeeds with the *Enquirer*, partly by imitating the format and typographical layout of his rival and partly by conducting high-priced raids on his talent. "In three months," Lundberg reports, "Hearst had taken Pulitzer's whole Sunday staff of editors, artists, and writers" (p. 53). When Hearst's *Journal* passed Pulitzer's *World* in circulation, Hearst, who had a reputation for entertaining his staff royally, "gave a large dinner at Delmonico's celebrating the fact" (Older, p. 143).

Like Kane, Hearst also built up circulation through his relentless attacks on moneyed interests on behalf of the common man. Within his first few months as owner of the *Examiner*, he had enlisted in a half dozen such crusades (Older, p. 79). Throughout his career he waged continuous war against the syndicates that conspired to get control of a commodity or service and manipulate it for financial gain—the various "trusts": traction, utilities, gas, ice, oil, coal, and so on. Very often the enemy was Hearst's perennial nemesis, J. P. Morgan, the model for Walter Parks Thatcher, with whose banking firm the big trusts were often in league. The scene in which Kane backs down Thatcher and the traction trust with incriminating evidence is also modeled on fact: Hearst arranged for sensitive documents to be stolen from an official of Standard Oil and used them for years to blackmail or discredit his enemies (Lundberg, pp. 122–35). When Thatcher (through Thatcher Jr.) has the last word by taking over the papers, it is a fictionalization inspired by an actual fact. The financial condition of Hearst's papers was so shaky during the depression that it was necessary to secure massive bank loans. Lundberg reported, "Although nominally controlled by Hearst, the Hearst publishing properties are actually controlled through the instrumentality of these bank loans by a Wall Street syndicate headed by the National City Bank of New York" (p. 310).

Kane's involvement with politicians and his own political campaign are told within the framework of his first marriage. Emily Norton, the president's niece, actually bears little resemblance to Hearst's first wife, showgirl Millicent Willson. Nevertheless, many of the personal details and most of the political material are reworkings of Hearst legends and facts. When the writers have Kane in the Lincoln Room at the White House admiring a painting of Lincoln, they have in mind Hearst's well-known idolatry of Lincoln. Emily's father remarks snidely that Lincoln can be a great inspiration even though he never advocated income taxes or municipal ownership of public utilities, two of Hearst's favorite causes. Kane's extravagant gesture of bringing the yacht on his honeymoon is probably inspired by the well-publicized incident of Phebe Hearst in New York sending her son in California a yacht so large it had to be disassembled for shipment across the isthmus of Panama on railroad cars (Older, p. 166). The interruption of the honeymoon is modeled on an actual incident reported by both Older and Lundberg: Hearst was vacationing in Egypt when an obscure item about a cherished political cause in a days-old newspaper caught his eye and sent him racing back to America to intervene. The Hearst cause was the defeat of a treaty that would leave the Panama Canal unfortified; in making Kane's cause the blockage of the lease of Teapot Dome and other oil reserves to the oil interests, *American* attaches typical Kane behavior to the most celebrated political scandal of the early twentieth century.

Kane begins a restless campaign against the oil leases. After the assassination attempt on President Norton, copies of Kane's savage personal attacks on him in the *Enquirer* are found in the would-be assassin's pocket. The newsreel directions in *American* say this footage is to be "modeled on Florida attempt upon President Roosevelt" (p. 18), but audiences of the time would have remembered the McKinley assassination and Hearst's widely reputed implication in it. Hearst had engaged in unusually virulent attacks on McKinley. After McKinley's second election the following admonition appeared in a Hearst paper editorial: "If bad men cannot be got rid of except by killing, then the killing must be done" (Lundberg, p. 89). The attacks continued right up to the assassination. Various New York newspapers reported that the assassin, Leon Czolgosz, had on his person a copy of a *Journal* attack upon McKinley and other inflammatory clippings (Lundberg, p. 94). There was public outrage, and Hearst was burned in effigy in a number of cities.

Kane's campaign for governor is based mainly on reported circumstances of Hearst's 1905 campaign for mayor, with other details added from Hearst's unsuccessful 1906 campaign for governor. It was said that Hearst decided to run as an independent candidate for mayor after Charles Murphy of Tammany (the model for Boss Rogers, who is later renamed Gettys) denied him the regular party's nomination. The principal theme of Hearst's mayoralty campaign, like Kane's, was Tammany and the political bosses (Lundberg, p. 102). In his various campaigns Hearst had gigantic rallies in Madison Square Garden. In his campaign for the governorship he made conspicuous use of his two-year-old son. A line in Hearst's capitulation speech in the governorship race may be the source for the theme of Kane's campaign speech at the Garden:

> I congratulate the bosses on their foresight in defeating me, for my first act as Governor would have been to lift the dishonest officials by the hair of their unworthy heads. (Older, p. 315)

In *American* Kane actually wins the gubernatorial race, but it is stolen from him by the Murphy forces; a montage in the newsreel shows assorted views of the fraud—an election watcher being dragged out of his polling place, fake ballots being made up in a back room, and a ballot box being thrown from a rowboat into the East River. This material is based directly on Lundberg's description:

> *Hearst won the election.* He was the victor by several thousand votes, it has since been established, but the Tammany bruis-

ers, heeding their instructions from Murphy, went berserk. Hearst's campaign people were assaulted and ballot boxes were stolen from the Hearst wards and dumped into the East River. (p. 103)

Some of the most significant personal complications of Kane's life in *American* are also traceable to Hearst material. Of Hearst's early newspaper days in New York Lundberg writes:

At this period Hearst was seen at all the theatrical first nights, he frequented Delmonico's and the other fashionable restaurants, rode in one of the newfangled expensive French automobiles. He was usually accompanied by two of the prettiest girls that could currently be found along Broadway. Hearst's hobbies, since the Harvard days, have been the theater and the girls. (p. 58)

Several scenes in *American* are included to demonstrate these same traits in Charles Foster Kane. Not only was Hearst a womanizer, but he was also notoriously undiscriminating in his choice of female companions. His well-known fondness for shopgirl and showgirl types is undoubtedly the inspiration for Kane's attraction to Susan Alexander. The promotional scheme that causes the rift with Leland is probably based—as is the incident of the opera review which will appear in the second draft—on Hearst lore:

Hearst has been a silent partner in other Broadway productions, and his newspapers brought the public in by one means or another, usually by extravagant praise. It has meant peremptory dismissal for a Hearst reviewer or critic to denounce a show or a film in which Hearst has an interest. (Lundberg, p. 302)

Hearst's great love for his mother and her strong influence on his development were well known. Characterizations of her in Mrs. Older's biography such as that she "determined that what was achieved by her with such effort should come easily to her son ... that he should have every advantage, every incentive and aid to go forward" (p. 5) may have influenced the characterization

of Kane's mother. Kane's strong attachment to his mother's possessions is probably also inspired by Hearst. Mrs. Older speaks of
Phebe Hearst's " 'real' lace . . . bought by her husband . . . [which]
to-day . . . is carefully stored at San Simeon" (p. 7), and Lundberg
records that Hearst maintained a large warehouse full of antiques
in New York (p. 327). These two facts are telescoped for the scene
between Susan and Kane which appears in the second draft and
has Kane on his way to a warehouse to see some of his mother's
things. Finally, the strongest of all of Kane's attachments to
mother and youth may also have been inspired by Hearst. One
of Hearst's childhood friends was a neighbor, Katherine Soulé,
called "Pussy" by her playmates. She and Hearst often played
together in the Hearst walled garden as Phebe Hearst tended her
flowers. Miss Soulé recalled to Mrs. Older:

> Willie Hearst was conscious of all beauty. When his mother
> bought new French dishes he pointed out the rose buds to
> Pussy. One day his head appeared at the top of the fence
> and excitedly he called, "Pussy, come and see the 'La
> France'!"
> Pussy had never heard of a La France, and so she hastily
> climbed the ladder to see this new exciting object.
> "Why," she exclaimed, "It's just a rose!"
> "It's a La France," corrected the boy.
> A large pale pink rose was in bloom, and it must have
> been one of the first of that variety in California, for the La
> France rose was introduced in France by Guillot in 1867.
> Round and round the La France walked the two children.
> "Isn't it lovely?" exclaimed Pussy. "I can't believe it's real."
> "Pussy, if I wasn't afraid my mother would be mad, I'd
> cut the La France and give it to you." (p. 19)

American is no more rough than any other first draft, but it
has special problems ordinary first drafts don't have. Mainly these
stem from the use of Hearst biographical material. Essentially
American is a dramatization of Hearst anecdotes, legends, and ru-
mors of all kinds borrowed indiscriminately from a variety of
sources. To play the material in anything close to its state in

American would open the way to ghastly legal difficulties involving libel, invasion of privacy, plagiarism, and copyright infringement. Strictly from a legal standpoint, *American* would be unusable without a massive overhaul. There is also a dramatic side to the problem. Hearst was too free and easy a source of information for an unsteady writer like Mankiewicz. Most of *American* is quite simply *à clef* plotting with only the barest effort at characterization. Kane himself at this stage is more an unfocused composite than a character portrait, a stand-in mouthing dialogue manufactured for some imaginary Hearst. In this sense Hearst is one of the principal obstacles to the script's further development. Before any real progress with the characterization can be made, the ties to his life will have to be cut drastically. This de-Hearstification of the material begins immediately after *American* and continues right down to the very end of the scripting. A lot of Hearst material survives in the film, but far less than was there at the beginning. One reason Welles could maintain so confidently that Kane wasn't Hearst may be that he had eliminated so much Hearst material from the scripts that he thought he had actually somehow eliminated Hearst in the process.

The first set of changes after *American* known to survive are contained in a forty-four-page studio typescript carbon, dated 28 April and marked "Mankiewicz" in an unknown hand. The revisions begin with two outright curiosities. The first revision calls for the Colorado sequence to end with the camera coming to rest on the sled and revealing the Rosebud trademark and label; an added note describes the way the scene originally ended and suggests shooting it both ways. The second revision calls for Thompson to let out a loud "Bronx cheer" as he closes the Thatcher manuscript and gives it back to the guard. Some very significant changes are also introduced in these pages. A decision has been made about what to do with Emily's material (most of it is to be reassigned to Leland), and the framing segments with Bernstein and Leland have been rewritten to reflect this change. The stolen-election motif borrowed from Hearst's 1905 campaign has been abandoned; now Kane actually loses. The cause is presented in two important new scenes—one in which Emily insists

Kane make a call with her after the rally in Madison Square Garden and its sequel, the encounter in Kane and Susan's "love nest." A follow-up scene is added on election night in which an enraged Emily confesses to Leland how she really feels about Kane and what all these years with him have been for her:

> *Emily*: Why should anyone vote for him? He's made it quite clear to the people what he thinks of them. Children—to be told one thing one day, something else the next, as the whim seizes him. And they're supposed to be grateful and love and adore him—because he sees that they are well-fed and well-clothed. And only pay a nickel in the street cars. . . . Personal lives? There are no personal lives for people like us. . . . If I'd thought of my life with Charles as a personal life, I'd have left him . . . five years ago [after the assassination attempt]. Maybe that's what I should have done, the first time he showed me what a mad dog he really was. . . . I didn't ask him for anything—any love or affection—not a thing except to keep up appearances—for *his* sake and Howard's and—to behave decently like an ordinary, civilized human being. But he couldn't do that. And so he and a cheap little— . . . If you're asking me to sympathize with him, Brad, you're wasting your time. (pause) There's only one person I'm sorry for. . . . That—that shabby little girl.

Herman Mankiewicz testified in the Lundberg case, in response to a question about the mechanics of plotting, that the alternate ending with the sled was written at Welles's specific insistence.[7] Is it not reasonable to suppose that other of these changes also originated with him?

Second Draft

The next full draft carries the handwritten identifying date 9 May 1940. It is stenographically edited to 325 pages (to indicate that everything in *American* had been accounted for, by whatever means) but actually has text on only about 300 pages. Approximately half these pages carry no individual date; the other half are inserted revision pages dated 30 April and 14 May, all within the Victorville period.

At the beginning of this draft the camera-moving instruction is dropped and the opening is written as it will be in the shooting script. Now Kane calls "Rosebud" only once. The news digest opens with two quotations from Coleridge's "Kubla Khan." Among the Hearst materials eliminated from the newsreel are the details of Kane's school history, his expulsion from college in Germany, and the information about the election fraud. An all-important set of directions about Thompson appears at the end of the projection room sequence, again perhaps as a result of consultations with Welles. Though these directions do not actually appear in the shooting script, nevertheless they are followed precisely in the film:

> It is important to remember always that only at the very end of the story is Thompson himself a personality. Until then, throughout the picture, we only photograph Thompson's back, shoulders, or his shadow—sometimes we only record his voice. He is not until the final scene a "character." He is the personification of the search for the truth about *Charles Foster Kane*. He is the investigator.

The scenes in Rome are written very differently. The business conference with Thatcher has been restructured. Bernstein comes in and abruptly informs Thatcher he is Kane's business manager. Thatcher dislikes him at once, obviously for ethnic as well as professional reasons, and insists that Kane send him from the room when they discuss business. (Kane refuses.) Kane inspects the book and casually selects the *Enquirer*. (When the follow-up scene is played later, Bernstein provides a new shading to Kane's scheme to fool Thatcher—he had actually been receiving copies of the *Enquirer* daily for two years prior to their meeting.) The later encounter between Thatcher and Kane, the yellow journalist, is moved from Thatcher's manuscript in this draft and placed in chronological order in Kane's career, so that it appears as the last of the running-a-newspaper sequences in Bernstein's story.

Another curious restructuring of this sort takes place in the Bernstein material. Bernstein's story begins with the sequel to the meeting with Thatcher in Rome. It continues, however, not with the early days of publishing but with new material not in *American*—Kane coming to the Chicago offices after Susan's debut to find Leland passed out at his typewriter. (This incident in turn is broken into two segments, with the sequel of Kane finishing the review presented later, in Leland's story.) Now come the publishing sequences—the early days at the *Enquirer*, the circulation buildup, the encounter with Thatcher—and then the departure for Europe and Kane's return with an engagement announcement. There is considerable pruning and shaping in this area. Various scenes of the first *Enquirer* days are telescoped. Others are pared or eliminated outright. Hearst material goes—conferences with the rival publisher, among other things, and a few of those tiresome scenes of restaurant- and theater-going. Kane's departure for Europe is now played on the deck of a Cunard liner about to sail, a change doubtless made to accommodate a bit of Welles-sounding horseplay. As the liner is about to cast off, directions read: "From offstage can be heard the steward's cry, indispensable in any Mercury Production, the old familiar cry of 'All Ashore That's Going Ashore!' "

At this point in *American* the material assigned to Bernstein ended. In the new draft, material which appeared later in *American* is now placed here. First are the Xanadu scenes with Bernstein as an uncomfortable social guest. The Jerry Martin business has been eliminated and a new character, Charles Foster Kane, Jr., age twenty-five, written in. The following line of Bernstein's is probably intended to explain why there is no heir apparent to the publishing empire: "I'm sorry young Mr. Kane didn't work out at the office, Mr. Kane—I guess he ain't cut out for newspaper work." Back in the frame Bernstein tells Thompson what hurt Kane most was not Susan's leaving him but having to give up the papers to Thatcher and Company. Then comes the sequence in which Thatcher Jr. informs Kane that Thatcher and Company is taking over the papers.

In *American* Bernstein's testimony ended with his reading of the

letter from Emily's lawyers. After that came the material that
could have been Emily's. In the first changes the letter was taken
away from Bernstein and replaced with the suggestion that
Thompson look up Leland. In the new draft most of the Emily
material is inserted in Leland's story in the chronological order
in which it would have occurred *in Leland's life*. As a consequence,
Leland's narration separates into three distinct segments. The first
extends from his early days with Kane at the paper when the two
were inseparable associates and companions to the first signs of
disagreement between them over Kane's handling of the Cuban
war. This segment closes with Kane's sailing for Europe. Back in
the frame Leland now reads the letter from Emily's lawyers, and
his story resumes with Leland telling about Kane and Emily, from
their early serene days together, through the attacks on the president, the assassination attempt, the political campaign, and finally Emily's departure. The third segment of Leland's narrative
covers Leland's departure for Chicago, the opera review incident,
and his final break with Kane. Two new scenes are added here.
In one, after Leland's transfer to Chicago, Reilly appears in Kane's
office with Leland's returned severance check; the Declaration of
Principles is also in the envelope. (Later on, when Reilly and his
scheme are eliminated, this incident will be rewritten as the coda
to the opera review.) The other added scene is the sequel of the
opera review incident: Leland waking up to find Kane finishing
his review. There is also considerable shifting from the previous
order of the material in Leland's revised story, as well as considerable paring. Again, much of the eliminated material is Hearstian, such as Kane's admiration for Lincoln and his constant shopgirl or showgirl companions.

Scenes of Kane's early years with Susan appear for the first
time in the second draft. The details of their first meeting are
somewhat different from those in the shooting script. Susan and
Kane bump into one another on the street and as he moves aside
he steps on a plank covering a bad place on the sidewalk and is
splashed with mud. Susan laughs; Kane reacts as a crusading editor would: "If these sidewalks were kept in condition—instead
of the money going to some cheap grafter—" In the description

of Susan's room we are told of a few personal belongings on her chiffonnier: "These include a photograph of a gent and lady, obviously Susan's parents, and a few objets d'art. One, 'At the Japanese Rolling Ball Game at Coney Island,' and—perhaps this is part of the Japanese loot—the glass globe with the snow scene Kane was holding in his hand in the first sequence." Kane tries all sorts of diversions to help Susan forget her toothache; he sings a popular tune, does a soft-shoe, and makes shadowgraph figures on the wall. Susan's stern landlady appears to protest the door being closed, but once she sees who Susan's visitor is she backs off and closes it herself. Susan's singing lessons, her opera career, and her attempted suicide now appear, written substantially as they will appear in the final script. Next in *American* was the Xanadu material with Jerry Martin. With that eliminated, next in the second draft are scenes aboard Kane's yacht (the Kanes have been on a long cruise) and the picnic in the Everglades. Next is the scene in Susan's room when she has packed to leave, and afterward the instructions appear for the first time for Kane to smash up her room.

The incident of Thatcher and Company taking over the papers, which would be Kane's next major crisis chronologically and which actually came next in *American*, has been moved to Bernstein's story in the second draft. After that came the death of Kane Jr., and in the second draft the aftermath of it has been expanded. Now we move to the chapel at Xanadu after the funeral for the burial. Kane is overcome with grief. As he stares at the row of crypts he begins to prattle about his mother, who is buried here. He recalls how she loved poetry and begins to read from the verse inscription on the wall of the crypt. (It begins with the first line on the inscription at the City of Brass in *1001 Nights*, "The drunkenness of youth has passed like a fever.")

In the wrap-up sequence at Xanadu the scene with the wise-cracking reporters waiting for the train has been eliminated. In the epilogue a working new direction is added, that the final shot will come to rest on a No Trespassing sign.

Important progress is made in the second draft of the script. Several redundant scenes have disappeared as well as a good deal of Hearst material and that lengthy, ludicrous business involving Susan's lover, Jerry Martin (though some equally ludicrous scenes, such as those involving Kane's father, are still in). Good, durable scenes between Kane and Susan have been added. Perhaps the most inspired touch in the new script (and seemingly the most characteristically Wellesian) is the part where Kane finds Leland passed out at his typewriter and finishes his review in the same lacerating vein in which Leland had started it. Sections of dialogue have been more finely sculpted, and roughly a third to a half of the lines are written substantially as they will be played in the film.

On the other hand, there are still fundamental structural and dramatic problems at this stage. Among the most glaring is the handling of Kane's decision to enter newspaper publishing. The scenes in Rome set up too complicated an explanation which blunts the impact of so momentous an event—Kane's staging a dissolute party to make Thatcher think he's a worthless playboy; Kane's pretending the *Enquirer* is a casual decision when in fact he has carefully prepared to take over the paper. The Rome business will continue to present problems of this sort until it is finally eliminated altogether. Serious structural imbalances are also created by the ordering in the second draft. So much crucial material in Kane's life has been partly or wholly assigned to Bernstein— the encounter with Thatcher, the break with Leland, the deterioration of his marriage to Susan, the loss of the papers—that Bernstein almost attains the status of what would be devastating for the story, a privileged narrator. It may be that for part of it Mankiewicz was simply indulging himself;[8] or, since Bernstein is allowed to confide certain special things about Kane in this draft, it may be that some serious consideration was being given to making him a kind of focal point for Kane's story. In any case, a reverse trend soon becomes evident in the next drafts, as some of the material assigned to Bernstein here is shifted back to its original position. Other narratives suffer accordingly with the shift of material to Bernstein. Thatcher, for instance, is now left without any scenes between him and the adult Kane. Emily's material also continues to pose a major problem. Assigning it to Leland loads his narration down with dramatic crises—not only the two that are his, Reilly's scheme and the opera debut, but three more of Emily's—the assassination attempt, Susan, and the election loss. Eventually these will have to be telescoped into a dramatically manageable number of crisis moments. On balance, the second draft might be best characterized as a much-improved rough draft. It is not until the all-important third draft that the *Citizen Kane* script undergoes its most significant dramatic distillation.

Third Draft

There are clues in the second draft that Welles may have been guiding the script at this stage to a much greater degree than has been conceded. In any case, in the new draft his direct involvement can be documented and precisely identified. According to Houseman, he and Mankiewicz returned from Victorville and delivered their script to RKO on Monday, 27 May. Mankiewicz then left for five weeks to pursue an assignment at MGM. After waiting around a few days for the script to be typed, Houseman took a train to New York. At the same time Houseman was on his way East, Welles, who had been in New York to appear at an RKO sales convention, was on his way back to Hollywood.[9] Revisions began again on 1 June, the day after Welles's return. Over the next two weeks around 140 new revision pages are inserted into this draft. The circumstances themselves suggest that most of these changes can probably be attributed to Welles. Corroborating evidence makes that almost certain.

There is considerable minor tampering in the first third of the new draft. The Colorado sequence has been reworked, apparently to bring the characters into sharper focus. Several lines assigned to Mrs. Kane in earlier drafts are reassigned to Kane Sr. and to Thatcher. The changes seem intended to soften her. For instance, when the adults go outside to tell the boy he is being taken away, Mrs. Kane no longer introduces Thatcher (apparently she is too upset) and he must introduce himself. At the same time Kane Sr. is made to come off in a worse light. For instance, Thatcher's

line "fifty thousand dollars a year . . . to be paid" is moved so that
it now precedes Kane Sr.'s line of capitulation, "let's hope it's all
for the best." The problematic Rome sequence also has a new
look. When Kane and Thatcher meet, Kane has a new conception
of their relationship. He thinks he's been deliberately kept abroad
by Thatcher these seventeen years and asks sarcastically whether
he'll have to go through the immigration process when he returns to America. (He tells Bernstein later he thinks Thatcher
did it so he could have his own way with Kane's fortune.) Bernstein also has a somewhat different manner. He is deliberately
oafish and offensive with Thatcher. Two structural changes are
made in Thatcher's narration. The financier's encounter with
Kane over the traction trust has been removed from Bernstein's
story and returned to Thatcher's, where it was in the first draft.
The follow-up scene, however, showing the Thatcher interests
taking over control of the papers, has now been eliminated.
(Eventually it will be redrafted by Welles himself during the
shooting.)[10]

The principal changes in the third draft are concentrated in
the segments of narration belonging to Bernstein and Leland.
Several expository sequences, some of them quite lengthy, have
been eliminated outright. Among these are a dinner at Rector's
with Kane and Leland and their girls; the appearance of Kane Sr.
and his new wife; the honeymoon sequences with Emily; a sequence early in his marriage with her showing Kane doting over
his young son but already imperiling his family life because of
his preoccupation with his work; a sequence when Kane and his
family and a group of politicians are gathered to announce his
entry into politics; and all the material pertaining to Susan's and
Kane's arrival in Chicago for her opera debut. All of Bernstein's
Xanadu scenes have been dropped, and so have the encounters
between Kane and a rival publisher. Several key episodes of Kane's
career have been compressed. The circulation buildup is now
shown in a montage: the composing room, the Declaration of
Principles on a front page, a wagon with a sign "*Enquirer:* Circulation 26,000," various shots of the paper being delivered, a new
number (62,000) painted on a window, and Kane, Bernstein, and

Leland looking in this window and discussing the rival paper. The scenes showing how Kane checkmated Thatcher and his cronies in the Hearst style with pilfered documents have been eliminated, and there appears instead a three-and-a-half-page montage of the *Enquirer's* growing impact on the American scene in the 1890s. This montage ends with a close-up of Kane's passport (it reads "Occupation—Journalist"), which provides a bridge to the scene of Kane's departure for Europe on the Cunard liner. Another montage is added to depict the passage of time during Kane's absence: through the *E* of the *Enquirer* letters on the building we see Bernstein slaving away at his desk through the various seasons. The assassination material has been condensed in much the same fashion. The scenes showing how Kane's home life suffers as he becomes more deeply involved in the oil scandal story are eliminated. After Kane's encounter with the president there is a rapid montage containing cartoon and editorial attacks on the president, ending with a close-up of the word TREASON, then the assassination itself—a hand firing a gun, hands extending from uniforms and struggling with the first hand, the White House in the background, a ticker tape spelling out the news.

Some new material has been added in these portions of the third draft. Georgie, the madame, makes her first appearance in the story. When Leland is protesting Kane's handling of the Cuba business on the day of the newspaper party, Kane mollifies him with talk of a special "girl" Georgie has lined up for him, and the party eventually adjourns to Georgie's. On the day of the assassination attempt, years later, Kane is at Georgie's when Reilly calls to break the news. (Georgie's part stayed in despite Hays Office objections and her scenes were actually shot, but she was eventually edited out.) An important new speech is added for Leland just as he is about to tell Thompson what he knows about Kane's life with Emily:

LELAND: He married for love—(a little laugh). That's why he did everything. That's why he went into politics. It seems we weren't enough. He wanted all the voters to love him too. All he really wanted out of life was love.—That's Charlie's story—

it's the story of how he lost it. You see, he just didn't have any to give. He loved Charlie Kane, of course, very dearly—and his mother, I guess he always loved her. As for Emily—well, all I can tell you is Emily's story as she told it to me, which probably isn't very fair—there's supposed to be two sides to every story—and I guess there are—I guess there're more than two sides—

Also newly added are two sequences of Kane and Emily on a ship bound for Europe, added to replace the deleted honeymoon material. This exchange occurs at their first meeting:

KANE: Would you do me a favor?
EMILY: I think so.
KANE: Slap me, Emily. Slap me hard.
EMILY: Why?
KANE: I'd rather not tell you till I've kissed you, but believe me, Emily, I deserve it. (Pause)
EMILY: You've been following me around the deck, haven't you?
KANE: All night.
EMILY: How long are you willing to follow me?
KANE: Forever.

In the second new sequence they are making wedding plans. Kane is impetuous and eager to get back and marry at once; Emily wonders if she'll ever know Kane and whether they'll be happy together.

The assassination attempt and its aftermath are still presenting serious problems in the third draft. When Kane hears the news, his first reaction is an order not to play the assassination down but to give it full coverage in the Kane papers. Then, without waiting for further word on the president's condition, Kane writes an editorial praising the fallen leader. Leland points out that this new posture doesn't make sense, since only the day before Kane had called the president a traitor. Kane says he has been right all along but now he must think of Emily. This incident is probably intended to show how Kane will go to any length to sell papers but will always insist on the high-mindedness and selflessness of his motives. On the heels of this comes the first Leland crisis. Leland brings up the matter of the promotional scheme and puts it bluntly: "I will not write a good review of a play because somebody paid a thousand dollars for an advertisement in the *Enquirer*." Then Leland, acting as peacemaker, comes to what he says is the real purpose of the discussion: Emily and the fact that she's going to leave Kane and her various reasons for it. From this the discussion moves to the motives behind Kane's behavior, and their exchange concludes with what will eventually become the "want the voters' love" and "love on my own terms" exchange. Kane and Leland leave the building under police protection (an angry mob holds Kane responsible for the assassination attempt), and as Kane drives off, Leland's last words are that he wants to be transferred to Chicago. Next are scenes of Kane at home pleading with a distraught Emily not to leave him now. After this is the scene with Reilly informing Kane that Leland returned his check with the torn-up Declaration of Principles. The problem of a surplus of crises in this area of the story persists. The eventual solution will be to merge four crises into two—to drop the assassination attempt and the promotional scheme and build everything around the love nest and the opera debut—but such a solution is not yet in sight.

While the script was undergoing this set of revisions, Houseman was back in New York making preparations for an upcoming stage adaption of Richard Wright's *Native Son*. Sometime around the middle of the month he received a revised script from Mankiewicz. He wired back on 16 June:[11]

Dear Mank: Leaving tonight for Carolina to confer with Paul Green and Richard Wright. Will report in detail. Received your cut version also several new scenes of Orson's. Approve all cuts. Still don't like Rome scene and will try to work on it my humble self. After much careful reading I like all Orson's scenes including new montages and Chicago opera scenes with exception of Kane Emily sequence. Don't like scene on boat. Query any first meeting scene

between them. However, do feel there must be some inti-
macy between them before oil scandal comes to shatter it
stop Simply don't understand sequence or sense of Orson's
telescoped Kane Leland Emily assassination scenes. There
again will try and make up my own version. Please keep
me posted. Love to Sarah.

In scarcely two weeks after the script was in Welles's hands,
major changes had been made. First, about seventy-five pages of
the Mankiewicz-Houseman material—most of it in the form of
expository and character-dialogue sequences—had been eliminated. Typically, many of the deleted sequences have been replaced with snappy or arresting montages. It is the first unmis-
takable appearance of the witty bravado style that is the film's
most characteristic trait. Creative ellipses of this type will continue to be one of the most apparent signs of Welles's hand in
the scripting. Several brand-new scenes have also appeared—
Houseman's wire identifies their origin—among them, the shipboard meeting with Emily and Kane's composing an editorial
praising the fallen president. Other characteristic changes have
also appeared. The opera material Houseman refers to is a lengthy
direction indicating we are to see the second playing of Susan's
debut from her point of view, unquestionably one of the most
inspired touches in the film. Welles has also begun to set his hand
to three of the most problematic areas of Kane's private life: taking over the paper, Emily, and the break with Leland. Not much
of the material introduced by Welles at this point will survive in
the form in which it first appears. Nevertheless, the revisions are
both characteristic and significant. In a very short time Welles has
already worked some fundamental changes on the nature of the
script.

Fourth Draft

The fourth draft,[12] called "Final," is the first on which the name
Citizen Kane appears. It is dated 18 June, three days after the re-

visions of the latest date in the third draft. It contains forty-three new (blue) revisions pages, dated 18 June and 19 June. There are numerous minor revisions, things like an adjustment of the facts in the newsreel and the frame story and the polishing of dialogue. Leland, for instance, is now given one of his best lines; Kane, he says, was "disappointed in the world. So he built one of his own." But the principal changes are deletions. The entire Rome business is finally eliminated; all that remains of it now is a brief allusion Bernstein makes to Thompson. It had been torturous from the first, with too much sidetracking into secondary motives such as how Kane came to know Bernstein and how and why they hatched their plot to fool Thatcher. With it all out of the way, Kane's action is now all the more striking and interesting for its impulsiveness—just a single sharp line in a letter, "I think it would be fun to run a newspaper." Welles's two shipboard scenes with Kane and Emily are out again, though the lengthy, talky scenes depicting the widening problems in their marriage are still in; the solution to how best to deal with their relationship is still not in sight. Also out, possibly for Hays Office reasons, is Susan's landlady and her capitulation about the door; now it remains open, and Susan herself asks who Kane is. The script had begun to firm up in its third draft. After these revisions and excisions in the fourth, only a few glaring problems remained to be solved, and the essential dramatic foundation of the film was now set.

Fifth Draft

Herman Mankiewicz went back on the RKO payroll on 18 June, approximately the date the fourth draft was completed, and stayed on through 27 July, five days after the full shooting schedule had begun. (During his five-week absence he had written the first draft of the script of *Comrade X* for MGM. He received no screen credit for this.) There were still several major decisions to be made about the script after 18 June, and undoubtedly Mankiewicz was involved in some of these, but his principal responsibilities during this period likely consisted of helping to sculpt the scenes more finely in rehearsal and shepherding the record of the changes.

The new draft, dated 24 June and called "Revised Final," incorporates revisions since 19 June and additional blue-page changes dated 27 and 28 June and 2 July. The most significant changes in this draft involve Kane's first wife and their son. From the first draft, Emily Norton has been alive in 1940. Now the letter from her lawyers is out, and the newsreel informs us she died in 1914. Appearances of a grown-up son of Kane were removed earlier, and now the remaining allusion to him—his presence offscreen at Xanadu and his burial in the Xanadu chapel—are also removed. The scene after the election disaster in which Emily talks at length to Leland about the various problems in her marriage has also been eliminated. The early romance of Emily and Kane is now reduced to a single shot—an insert of a diamond ring on a hand, after which the camera pulls back to reveal the lovers kissing. The deterioration of the marriage is dealt with in a single scene. Emily is in the bedroom with the morning *Enquirer*. The headline reads, "President Mum on Oil Theft." A doting Kane enters to kiss her good-bye; she remonstrates gently with him about his unreasonableness toward the president. This way of playing it, of course, is the original basis for the breakfast table montage. Several lesser revisions are worth noticing, most of them in the running-a-newspaper sequences. A few of the Welles montages are out—the circulation buildup as he wrote it, the growth of the *Enquirer* in the 1890s, and the change of seasons. Kane's departure for Europe is introduced in the party sequence, making the Cunard dock scenes redundant. The dialogue of Kane's dramatically troublesome confrontation with Leland over Cuba is rewritten once again.

Another set of changes in this draft is of special interest. Revised pages for the projection room sequence carrying the date 2 July are inserted. Shooting on *Citizen Kane* began on 29 June with the projection room sequence. These pages have been rewritten to conform to the way the scene was actually shot. By comparing the revision pages with the previous draft one has precise examples of how the script was undergoing changes in the shooting.

In the script, there was a lengthy digression in this sequence almost at once (right after the remark "Seventy years of a man's life"): a long quotation from a derogatory obituary of Kane by Arthur Ellis in *"American Review"*.[13] It has now been eliminated completely, and on the screen Rawlston comes at once to the heart of the matter—the need for an "angle." (It had been "motivation" in the script, a word with considerably less resonance for the meaning of the film.) A Hearstian allusion to Kane's labor record is removed. Rawlston's reply when Thompson begins to raise an objection—"Nothing is ever better than finding out what makes people tick"—is replaced with a direct order: "Find out about Rosebud." Several fragments of lines are reassigned from Rawlston to the background voices. All these changes help to step up the pace and contribute to the frenetic energy of the projection room sequence as it is played on the screen. Clearly the script was constantly being altered, as would be customary, say, in the rehearsals of a play, to fit the necessities of the performance.

Sixth Draft

This draft, dated 9 July, is 155 mimeographed pages, and is called "Second Revised Final."[14] One fundamental change has been made in it. The assassination attempt on the president and Kane's alleged complicity in it, along with the lengthy aftermath involving, first, Kane and Leland, and then Kane and Emily, eighteen pages altogether, has been eliminated entirely (all that remains about the assassination is a brief mention in the newsreel), and corresponding adjustments have been made. The account of Kane's first meeting with Susan, originally a part of her narration, has been moved into Leland's story to replace the assassination material. In this position their meeting is followed by the political campaign; now there is only one political crisis to be dealt with. Raymond has been given several new lines, including his best: "Rosebud? I'll tell you about Rosebud. How much is it worth to you?" The paper is now spelled *Inquirer*. Two extremely important new conceptions also appear. The first is the solution of how to deal with Kane's first marriage, in the celebrated breakfast table montage: "NOTE: The following scenes cover a period of nine years—and played in the same set with only changes in lighting, special effects outside the window, and wardrobe." The second provides what may be the film's most striking, and certainly one of its most resonant, images. The previous draft called for an unidentified scene "still being written" after Kane leaves Susan's smashed-up room; it appears in the new draft—the instruction to walk down the corridor between facing mirrors. In terms of actual progress toward the final version of the script and the completed state of the film, the sixth draft is second in importance only to the third.

Seventh Draft

The final script is dated 16 July 1940, less than a week before the start of the regular shooting schedule on 22 July. It does not reflect changes suggested in a 15 July letter from the Hays Office.[15] As in previous drafts, numerous small revisions have been made; for instance, the scene in the newsreel of Kane being interviewed dockside after a trip to Europe has been added, and adjustments have been made in such problematic sequences as Kane's encounters with Thatcher over the traction trusts, with Leland over Cuba, and with Emily at the breakfast table. Two important structural changes have been made, both involving Kane's relationship with Leland. In the previous script the newspaper party was broken into two segments, with the first half in Bernstein's story and the second half (the long discussion of Cuba and the adjournment to Georgie's) in Leland's, with Kane's European trip and engagement in between. In the new script the party is played continuously. The opera review incident had also been broken into two segments through several drafts, half in Bernstein's story and the continuation in Leland's; now the sequence is played continuously at the later point. As the story was originally conceived, we were to see the growth of the disharmony between the two friends in a series of encounters over various issues—Cuba, the attacks on the president, the promotional scheme, inattention to Emily, the election loss, Susan, and the opera review. These new revisions are a continuation of the process through which the number of issues and encounters is cut down. Eventually their argument over Cuba will be eliminated too.

One later set of changes is also inserted into this script—a revised version of the tent scene in the Everglades dated 19 July (shot 105 in the published script). This material was to be shot on 22 and 23 July, and the dialogue was being firmed up in rehearsal. Several of Susan's more sententious lines are eliminated, and one passage which seems too uncomfortably close to something Leland said earlier—"Only love me! Don't expect me to love *you*"—is significantly revised. As in previous examples, this material will be changed further during the shooting.

Herman Mankiewicz's principal contribution to the *Citizen Kane* script was made in the early stages at Victorville. The Victorville scripts elaborated the plot logic and laid down the overall story contours, established the main characters, and provided numerous scenes and lines that would eventually appear in one form or another in the film. The Mankiewicz partisans would have us believe that this is the heart of the matter and that by the end of Victorville the essential part of the scripting was complete.[16] Quite the contrary. It is true that certain *sections* of the script were close to their final form at Victorville. Principally these are the beginning and end, the newsreel, the projection room sequence, the first visit to Susan, and Colorado; that is, the Rosebud gimmickry and the elaborate plot machinery used to get Charles Foster Kane on and off stage—but none of the parts involving the adult Kane people actually knew. At this stage in the scripting Charles Foster Kane is little more than a succession of poses fictionalized from Hearst. Work has scarcely begun on the most glaring problem in the material, making Kane into an authentic dramatic portrait, defining what the Kane phenomenon represents, and indicating how we are supposed to feel about these things. The Victorville scripts contain dozens of pages of dull, plodding material that will eventually be discarded or replaced altogether. And, most tellingly, there is virtually nothing in them of that stylistic wit and fluidity that is the most engaging trait of the film itself.

Major revisions began as soon as the script passed into Welles's hands, and several important lines of development can be discerned in subsequent phases of the scripting. One of these is the elimination of dramatically questionable material, especially of a large amount of material drawn from Hearst. Another is a fundamental alteration of the nature of many of the scenes; this may be described generally as a shift from scenes played continuously to scenes fragmented according to montage conceptions. Yet another is the evolution of Charles Foster Kane as a character. The principal strategy is the replaying of certain key situations and moments in his life over and over again as a means of testing and discovering the character.

Houseman's wire makes clear who was responsible for the first major set of revisions. That the subsequent installments are also attributable chiefly to Welles is indicated both by the circumstances and by the nature of the revisions. All the familiar signs of Welles's presence are evident in the scripting after Victorville: the stylistic flair that was so lacking in the Victorville scripts, certainly, but also the specific ways he works. Unlike most writers, Welles's customary approach to revision is not to ponder and polish but to discard and replace. He works rapidly and in broad sweeps, eliminating whole chunks and segments at a stroke and, if necessary, replacing them with material of his own devising. If the new material lacks the boldness or sense of dramatic hyperbole he is after—the "Welles touch"—he starts over again, discarding and replacing, and sometimes repeats the whole process several times until he gets what he wants. The evolution of the breakfast table montage is a perfect example. First some of Mankiewicz's rather humdrum scenes involving Kane and Emily are discarded. New scenes are substituted. The overall conception in the early Welles stages is still very conservative and conventional and theatrical: a series of expository scenes between Kane and Emily showing the gradual deterioration of the marriage, leading to an emotionally charged resolution after Kane loses the election. More scenes are discarded, including Welles's own; new ones appear. At last out of trial and error comes the master stroke—a way of playing it using tiny bits and pieces from all the previous scenes but forging them into a brilliantly original combination, the montage at the breakfast table. Other forms of revision in the later scripts are also familiar. On his major productions Welles begins rehearsing with his actors as soon as possible, rehearses extensively, and freely changes the material in rehearsal. He is also adept at handling last-minute scripting emergencies and does the rewrites himself on the spot, often at speeds that astonish even his oldest associates.

Besides being Welles's first film, *Citizen Kane* also marks one of the few times in his career when he was working from an original story idea rather than adapting an existing work. Mankiewicz was hired to furnish him with what any good first writer ought to be able to provide in such a case: a solid, durable story structure on which to build. What Mankiewicz gave him Welles approached as he always approaches "story material," not as a blueprint to be approximated or realized but as a source work at the service of an original, independent creation, and he adapted it with the same freedom and disregard for authority with which he adapts a Shakespeare play or a thriller by Nicholas Blake. His somewhat frenetic scripting habits are unusual by Hollywood standards. They are, in fact, habits one associates with "live" mediums like radio and theater, where one learns quickly to perform with grace and aplomb under the pressures of deadlines, fate, and all the vagaries of the moment. Nearly a decade of such experience in the Mercury Theater had endowed Welles with special talents for expeditious solutions and the necessary skills to be, of all major film directors, perhaps the one least dependent on the ordinary services of a screenwriter. In the eight weeks between the time the Victorville material passed into Welles's hands and the final draft was completed, the *Citizen Kane* script was transformed, principally by him, form a solid basis for a story into an authentic plan for a masterpiece. Not even the staunchest defenders of Mankiewicz would deny that Welles was principally responsible for the realization of the film. But in light of the evidence, it may be they will also have to grant him principal responsibility for the realization of the script.

Notes

1. Pauline Kael, "Raising Kane," *New Yorker*, 20 and 27 February 1971, rpt. in *The "Citizen Kane" Book* (Boston, 1971), p. 38. John Houseman gives a detailed account of the way the Mercury Theater radio shows were prepared in "The Men from Mars," *Harper's Magazine*, December 1948, pp. 74–82. Concerning the "War of the Worlds" broadcast, he claims that Welles "had virtually nothing to do with the writing of the script." "Raising Kane" set off a storm of protest. Most of the replies were either invocations of then-fashionable "auteur" doctrines or testimonies to Welles's prodigious skills by those who knew or had worked with him. Welles himself wrote a brief letter of reply to the editor of the London *Times* ("The Creation of *Citizen Kane*," 17 November 1971, p. 17). The more or less official reply was made in his behalf by critic-director Peter Bogdanovich. Bogdanovich's case was based mainly on testimony by Welles partisans and Welles himself; judged strictly on the nature of Bogdanovich's evidence his argument was not much stronger than Kael's ("The Kane Mutiny," *Esquire*, October 1972, pp. 99–105, 180–90). Richard Meryman's *Mank: The Wit, World, and Life of Herman Mankiewicz* (New York, 1978) deals at length with the authorship controversy but sheds no new light on it.

2. There are also several sets of revision pages for individual sequences done between drafts, plus copies of special scripts with scene and set designation but no dialogue, prepared from the main drafts for budgeting, art work, and other purposes. I thank Al Korn, vice president of RKO General Pictures, for making access to these files possible, and John Munro-Hall, West Coast manager of RKO, for his active support and assistance. I also thank Vernon Harbin, an administrative employee of RKO for forty-five years, for elaborate behind-the-scenes explanations of the studio's operations and practices during the *Citizen Kane* period, and Amalia Kent, veteran Hollywood script supervisor, not only for her recollections of her work supervising the *Citizen Kane* and other Welles scripts, but also for much valuable technical information on scripting procedures at RKO in the 1940s. *Citizen Kane* © 1941 RKO Radio Pictures.

There are several *Citizen Kane* script items in the archives of the Mercury Theater which are not in the RKO files; I have identified these in footnotes at the appropriate places. I have been able to see these materials only briefly in a general inspection of the Mercury archives, but their former custodian, Richard Wilson, a long-standing Welles associate, a production assistant on *Citizen Kane*, and himself a specialist on the history of the script, has kindly read this essay, told me he thinks it an accurate account of the script's history, and assures me there is nothing in the Mercury files to controvert its main argument and its essential points. (The Mercury Theater archives have been sold to the Lilly Library at Indiana University, Bloomington.) I thank Wilson for this assistance and also for valuable information he provided me about Welles, the Mercury Theater, and *Citizen Kane*. I have also examined miscellaneous *Citizen Kane* script materials in the Film Study Center, Museum of Modern Art; Theatre Arts Library, UCLA; and Wisconsin Center for Film and Theater Research. I am also grateful to John Houseman and Pauline Kael, who have both responded immediately and forthrightly to my various inquiries, and to Sara Mankiewicz for the opportunity to examine her husband's copies of the *Citizen Kane* script.

3. John Houseman, *Run-Through: A Memoir* (New York, 1972), pp. 445–61. "Raising Kane," pp. 29–39. Amalia Kent had impressed Welles with her work on the problematic first-person script for his unproduced *Heart of Darkness* film, and she worked directly with him in various script supervision capacities on other of his RKO projects, including *The Magnificent Ambersons* and the unproduced *Smiler with a Knife*. She also continued as the script supervisor throughout the shooting of *Citizen Kane* and prepared the cutting reports for the film's editor, Robert Wise. Kael gives the impression that Rita Alexander, Herman Mankiewicz's private secretary, was performing all these specialized studio functions herself.

4. I have seen two script fragments which predate *American*. One, in the Mercury Theater files, is a ninety-two-page typescript original, undated, containing early versions of the opening, the newsreel, the projection room sequence, and the Thatcher narration and story. It has handwritten corrections, probably by John Houseman; one of these crosses out the original surname, Charles Foster *Rogers*, and writes in *Craig*. The other, in the RKO files, is a seven-page typescript carbon of the newsreel sequence, with the date 18 April entered separately in typescript original. It contains various material that did not survive in *American*, for instance, a direction for an inserted shot of a tattered deed

left by the defaulting boarder. In it the Kanes are the *Craigs* and Bernstein is *Annenberg*.

5. See Kenneth Anger, *Hollywood Babylon* (1965; reprint, San Francisco, 1975), pp. 96–104. Anger also reports an instance of a Hearst trait shown in *American*: his releasing phony news items to cover up personal scandals.

6. Mrs. Fremont Older, *William Randolph Hearst, American* (New York, 1936); Ferdinand Lundberg, *Imperial Hearst* (New York, 1937); all further citations to these two books will appear in the text. In 1947 Lundberg brought suit against the makers of *Citizen Kane* for copyright infringement. Mankiewicz freely admitted on the stand he had read both books and said he regarded them both as biased: "Mrs. Older's book falls into the class of what I would call, if Mr. Hearst were running for office, a campaign life; and Mr. Lundberg's book is the counterpart to it, the book designed to show that the opposition candidate never helped an old woman across the street or gave a horse a piece of sugar" (testimony, 30 November 1950, p. 66). As to the charge of infringement, he insisted he had known *firsthand* things about Hearst that had appeared in print *only* in *Imperial Hearst*. The trial ended in a hung jury and RKO settled out of court. The records of *Lundberg v. Welles et al.* (hereafter cited as Lundberg case) are at the Federal Records Center in Baronne, New Jersey.

7. Lundberg case, Mankiewicz testimony, pp. 103–4.

8. John Houseman testified in the Lundberg case that Bernstein was Mankiewicz's favorite character in the script (Houseman testimony, p. 112).

9. Houseman, *Run-Through*, p. 457; Lundberg case, Mankiewicz testimony, p. 161; RKO Employment Records for Herman Mankiewicz; MGM Employment Records for Herman Mankiewicz; *Film Daily*, 31 May 1940, p. 2.

10. Richard Wilson recalls that shooting was halted while Welles went off and rewrote this scene.

11. Houseman to Mankiewicz, night letter, 16 June 1940; carbon in the John Houseman Collection, Special Collections Library, UCLA. Printed by permission of John Houseman.

12. There is a 137-page script fragment in the Mercury Theater archive dated 5 June. It is a typescript original which contains a full text up to Leland's departure for Chicago, followed by a two-page sketch covering Susan's opera debut. It contains new material not in the third

draft (for instance, Leland reciting Walt Whitman during the Rome party) but also earlier material that is eliminated from the third draft (for instance, the honeymoon in the North Woods). There is a handwritten *M* on the front cover, and the letter *M* is typed in after the page number of each page. On the cover page of a carbon copy of this same item is a handwritten notation, "Mank version." Apparently it is a partial revision of the second draft proffered by Mankiewicz but largely ignored by Welles. This item is not in the RKO files.

13. Mankiewicz had cribbed it from William Allen White's obituary of Frank A. Munsey and inserted it in *American*. See George Britt, *Forty Years—Forty Millions* (New York, 1935), p. 17.

14. This was the script submitted to the Hays Office. The copy in the Mercury Theater files is a typescript carbon with some scenes penciled through, possibly by Welles.

15. The Hays Office letter is reprinted in *The "Citizen Kane" Book*, p. 90.

16. Sara Mankiewicz said this to me in a discussion we had of her husband's work on the scripts. It is one of Pauline Kael's main lines of argument.

Style and Meaning in *Citizen Kane*

JAMES NAREMORE

❖ ❖ ❖

The Magician

ACCORDING TO ORSON WELLES'S one-time producer John Houseman, Welles was "at heart a magician, whose particular talent [lay] not so much in his creative imagination (which is considerable) as in his proven ability to stretch the familiar elements of theatrical effect far beyond their normal point of tension."[1] Left-handed as the compliment may seem, Welles was, among other things, a professional magician ("You know an awful lot of tricks," Susan Alexander says to Charles Foster Kane during their first meeting, as he casts shadows on the wall to amuse her. "You're not a professional magician, are you?"), and his movies delight in visible trickery. In *Citizen Kane*, for example, the camera moves in to a close-up of a group photograph of the *Chronicle* staff while Kane talks about what good men they are; suddenly Kane walks right into the photo, and as the camera pulls back from the assembled journalists we find ourselves at an *Inquirer* party six years later. Such moments draw upon a cinema of pleasurable illusion as old as Méliès, and many people are attracted to Welles's work precisely because of them. Before analyzing *Kane* as a narrative, therefore, let us consider its surface—not so much the elaborate special effects as the typical dramatic scenes, in which the "magical" style takes on meaning.

An obvious place to begin is with the wide-angle, deep-focus photography that became one of the most distinctive features of Welles's style. His methods were to change somewhat, growing more fluid, various, and in some ways more daring in his later films as he gained experience and encountered other photographers after Gregg Toland. He seldom returned to a truly elaborate depth of field, as in those deliberately grotesque shots in *Kane* (probably designed by Toland) in which a giant head only a few inches from the camera is in equally sharp focus with a figure that seems to be standing a mile away. Nevertheless, the principle of exaggerated perspective was suited to his temperament and remained an essential quality of his work. Like many other features of his style, it creates a slightly hallucinatory effect, marking him from the beginning of his career as anything but a purely representational or conventional artist.

This last point will become clearer if we examine one of the best known and most written about moments in *Citizen Kane*: the boardinghouse segment, where we meet Kane in his youth. The camera pans slowly across a handwritten line of Thatcher's memoirs—"I first met Charles Foster Kane in 1871"—and then, accompanied by Bernard Herrmann's lilting, crystalline "Rosebud" theme, the image dissolves from the white margin of the page into an unreal land of snow where Charlie (Buddy Swan) frolics with his sled. At first the black dot against pure white echoes the manuscript we have been reading, but it swoops across the screen counter to the direction the camera was moving, in conflict with the stiff, prissy banker's handwriting, suggesting the conflict between Kane and Thatcher that runs through the early parts of the movie. The camera moves in closer and an insert establishes the setting when one of the boy's snowballs strikes the sign over Mrs. Kane's boardinghouse. (Herrmann's music suddenly stops.) Following this shot is a single, characteristically

Wellesian, long take. The camera retreats from the boy and moves through the window where his mother (Agnes Moorehead) stands admonishing him not to catch cold; she turns, accompanied first by Thatcher (George Colouris) and then by her husband (Harry Shannon), and walks the full length of the parlor, the camera tracking with her until it frames the whole room. She and Thatcher sit at a table in the foreground, and the camera holds relatively stationary for the rest of the scene. By this means Welles deliberately avoids conventional editing and lets each element—the actors and the decor of the home—reveal itself successively, until everything is placed in a rather symbolic composition. (See figure 1.)

Toland's photography is much sharper than any reproduction of a frame from the sequence can indicate. The depth of focus enables us to see everything at once, and the wide-angle lens slightly enlarges the foreground, giving it dramatic impact. As is typical in *Kane*, the action is staged in terms of three planes of interest: in the foreground at the lower right, Mrs. Kane and the banker sit negotiating the child's future; in the middle distance, Mr. Kane makes agitated pacing movements back and forth,

FIGURE I.

whining and complaining to his wife; and far away, framed in the square of the window as if in the light at the end of a tunnel, Charlie plays in the snow. While the parents and banker converse inside, the sound of the boy's play can be heard through the window, which Mrs. Kane has insisted must be left open. According to the RKO cutting continuity, the boy's shouts are "indistinct," but if you listen closely you will hear some of his lines. As his mother prepares to sign him over to a guardian and thus dissolve her family, the boy shouts, "The Union forever! The Union forever!"

Undoubtedly Welles's theatrical experience led him to conceive movie images in this way; indeed the stage sets for his famous modern-dress *Julius Caesar* in 1937 had been designed to allow for a similar in-depth composition. Actually, however, the long takes in *Kane* are in one sense less conventionally theatrical than the typical dialogue scene in a Hollywood feature, which does nothing more than establish a setting and cut back and forth between close-ups of the actors. Hollywood movies, in Welles's day as in our own, tend to emphasize the faces of stars; *Kane*, by contrast, puts a good deal of information into its individual shots, introducing a sense of visual conflict in the absence of cutting and close-ups. The spectator has an immediate impression of the whole, of several conflicting elements presented not in sequential fashion, but simultaneously, as if the camera were slicing through a cross section of the moment, looking down a corridor of images and overlapping events. Thus Welles designs the boardinghouse scene in such a way that we can't help gazing toward the window that neatly frames and encloses the boy's play, seeming to trap him at the very moment when he feels most free. At virtually the same time, we are aware of Mrs. Kane seated with the banker in the foreground, her face the image of stern puritanical sacrifice. Thatcher hovers officiously, while in the middle distance, caught between son and mother, the weak, irresponsible Mr. Kane keeps saying he doesn't like turning the boy over to a "gardeen." The faces, clothing, and postures of the actors contrast with one another, just as the slightly blurred, limitless world of snow outside the window contrasts with the sharply focused, gray interior.

The shot was meticulously organized in order to stress these conflicts; in fact it took Welles and Toland four days to complete the boardinghouse sequence as a whole because everything had to be timed with such clockwork precision. As a result, *Kane* has a somewhat authoritarian effect on the visual level. Welles may not be so Pavlovian a director as Sergei Eisenstein, but he keeps the actors and the audience under fairly rigid control, using the extreme depth of Toland's photography in highly expressive ways. As in the shot described above, the actors often assume unnatural positions, their figures arrayed in a slanting line that runs out in front of the camera, so that characters in the extreme foreground or in the distance become subjects for the director's visual commentary. Actors seldom confront one another face to face, as they seem to do in the shot/reverse shot editing of the ordinary film. The communication scientists would say that the positions of figures on the screen are "sociofugal," or not conducive to direct human interaction; and this slight physical suggestion of an inability to communicate is fully appropriate to the theme of social alienation which is implicit in the film.

Space in conventional Hollywood films of the late 1930s and early 1940s was certainly less symbolic than this. Oddly, however, Welles's uses of deep focus and long takes have frequently been praised for their heightened "realism." The notion derives chiefly from French theorist André Bazin, whose famous essay "The Evolution of the Language of Cinema" has been a major influence on Welles's critics. In the essay, Bazin argued that between 1920 and 1940 there had been two kinds of filmmakers—"those directors who put their faith in the image and those who put their faith in reality."[2] By "image" he meant "very broadly speaking, everything that the representation on the screen adds to the object there represented" (24), and by "reality" he meant an unmanipulated phenomenal world that could leave its essential imprint on the film emulsion. According to Bazin, a director had two ways to "add" to real-world objects: by means of "plastics" (lighting, sets, makeup, framing, and so on), and by means of editing or montage, which creates a meaning "not proper to the images themselves but derived exclusively from their juxtaposition" (25). In Bazin's view, such practice was challenged by Welles; thanks to the depth of field in *Kane*, Bazin wrote, "Dramatic effects for which we had formerly relied on montage were created out of the movements of the actors within a fixed framework" (33).

In Welles, as in his predecessor Jean Renoir and his contemporary William Wyler, Bazin saw "a respect for the continuity of dramatic space and, of course, its duration" (34). Indeed, he said, the alternation of montage sequences and long takes in *Kane* was like a shifting back and forth between two tenses, or between two modes of telling a story. The latter technique, however, was more important for Bazin. Because the many deep-focus shots in *Kane* eliminated the need for excessive cutting within a scene, because they theoretically acted as a window upon the plenitude of the phenomenal world, and because they gave the spectator a "choice" of what to look at in any shot, he praised the film as a step forward in movie realism. Furthermore, he argued, the deep-focus style was appropriate to ideas expressed in the script. "Montage by its very nature rules out ambiguity of expression," he wrote, and therefore "*Citizen Kane* is unthinkable shot in any other way but in depth. The uncertainty in which we find ourselves as to the spiritual key or the interpretation we should put on the film is built into the very design of the image" (36).

Bazin was certainly correct in describing *Kane* as an ambiguous film and as a departure from classical Hollywood convention; nevertheless, in his arguments about realism he underemphasized several important facts. For example, if in some scenes Welles avoided using montage to "add to the object represented," this left him all the more free to add in another way—through what Bazin called "plastics." Interestingly, some of the deep-focus shots in the film were made not by simple photography but by a kind of invisible montage, a combining of two or more images in a complicated optical printing process that creates the illusion of a single shot. (See, for example, the scene in which Kane, seated at a typewriter, completes Leland's opera review while Leland stands in the distance; the two figures in this shot were photographed separately and their images joined to look as if they occupied the same space and time.) *Kane* is in fact one of the most obviously stylized movies ever made; the RKO art department's contribution is so great, Welles's design of every image so constricting, that at times the picture looks like an animated cartoon. This very artificiality is part of the film's meaning, especially in sequences like the election rally and the surreal picnic in the Xanadu swamplands. Technically (but not stylistically), *Kane* is the ultimate studio production; there is hardly a sequence that does not make us aware of the cleverness of various workers—makeup artists, set designers, lighting crews, and perhaps most of all Orson Welles.

Yet the public statements of both Welles and Toland seem to foreshadow or confirm Bazin's notions about realism. Toland claimed that Welles's idea was to shoot the picture in such a way that "the technique of filming should never be evident to the audience," and in his well-known *American Cinematographer* article about the photography of the film we repeatedly encounter comments such as the following: "The attainment of approximate human-eye focus was one of our fundamental aims"; "The *Citizen Kane* sets have ceilings because we wanted reality, and we felt it would be easier to believe a room was a room if its ceiling could be seen"; "In my opinion, the day of highly stylized cinematography is passing, and being superseded by a candid, realistic technique."[3] The last statement finds an echo in Bazin's notion that *Kane* was part of a general movement, a "vast stirring in the geological bed of cinema," which would restore to the screen the "continuum of reality" and the "ambiguity of reality" (37). The same general argument can be heard in Welles's own remarks to Peter Bogdanovich in the interview published in this volume: "in the early days of my life as a filmmaker . . . I talked a lot about that 'giving the audience a choice' business. It strikes me as pretty obvious now."

One should remember that the term "realism" (often used in opposition to "tradition") nearly always contains a hidden ideological appeal, and has been appropriated to justify nearly every variety of revolution in the arts. But if realism is intended simply to mean "verisimilitude," then Welles, Toland, and Bazin are at best half right. True, deep focus can preserve what Bazin called the "continuum" of reality, and three-dimensional effects on the screen (which owe considerably to Welles's blocking and Toland's lighting) can give the spectator the impression of looking into a "real" space. Nevertheless Toland is inaccurate when he implies that the human eye sees everything in focus, and Bazin is wrong to suggest that ether reality or human perception is somehow "ambiguous." On the contrary, human vision is exactly the opposite of depth photography, because humans are incapable of keeping both the extreme foreground and the extreme distance in focus at the same time. The crucial difference between a camera and the human eye is that the camera is nonselective. Even when we look at the deep-focus compositions in *Kane*, we do not see everything in the frame at once; we are aware of an overall composition which exists simultaneously, but, as Bazin has noted, we need to make certain choices, scanning the various objects in the picture selectively. Welles seems instinctively aware of this fact, because he designs his images quite rigidly, sometimes blacking out whole sections of the composition or guiding our attention with movement and frames within the frame. He gives us more to look at than in the average movie, but the information crowded on the screen has been as carefully manipulated as any montage.

Still another and perhaps more important factor should be taken into account in any discussion of the phenomenal "realism" of Welles's technique. Toland claimed that he was approximating the human eye when he stopped down his camera to increase the depth of field, but what he and most other commentators on the technique do not emphasize is that he also used a wide-angle lens to distort perspective. *Kane* was photographed chiefly with 25-millimeter or even shorter lenses, which means that figures in the extreme foreground are elongated or slightly ballooned out, while in the distance the lines formed by the edge of a room converge sharply toward the horizon. Thus if Toland gave the spectator more to see, he also gave the world an unnatural appearance. Furthermore, Welles's use of the wide angle, as in the shot of Mrs. Kane walking from the window to the opposite end of the parlor, fundamentally alters the relationship between time and space, calling into question some aspects of Bazin's argument about duration. Here, for example, is an extract from an interview with the British cinematographer-director C. M. Pennington-Richards, who is describing properties of the wide-angle lens:

> Of course using wide angle lenses the time-space factor is different. If you've got a wide angle lens, for instance a 1" lens or an 18mm, you can walk from three-quarter length to a close-up in say four paces. If you put a 6" lens [i.e., a telephoto] on, to walk from three-quarter length to close-up would take you twenty paces. This is the difference: During a scene if someone walks away and then comes back for drama, they come back fast, they become big fast. There is no substitute for this—you only can do it with the perspective of a wide-angle lens. It's the same with painting; if you want to dramatize anything, you force the perspective, and using wide angle lenses is in fact forcing it.[4]

These comments signal the direction that any discussion of photography in *Kane* should take. Most directors operate on the principle that the motion picture image should approximate ordinary human perception, but Welles used the wide angle to create what the Russian formalist critic Victor Shklovsky would call a "defamiliarization." In retrospect, what was truly innovative about *Kane* was not its sharp focus but its in-the-camera treatment of perspective. Depth of field was less unusual than Toland and later historians have made it seem; like the photographing of ceilings, it was at least as old as D. W. Griffith and Billy Bitzer— indeed there are beautiful examples of it in Chaplin's *The Gold Rush* (1925). A certain "normality" of spatial relationships, however, was practiced throughout the studio years, when filmmakers used a variety of lenses but usually sought to conceal optical distortions by means of set design, camera placement, or compensatory blocking of actors. Welles's favorite director, John Ford, had used wide-angle lenses extensively in *Young Mr. Lincoln* (1939) and *Stagecoach* (1939), and Gregg Toland had made some interesting experiments with them in *The Long Voyage Home* (1940), sharing a title card with Ford; but in all these films the slight visual distortion seems at odds with their directors' tendency toward invisible, self-effacing uses of the camera. In 1941, the same year as *Kane*, Arthur Edeson photographed John Huston's *The Maltese Falcon* at Warner Brothers using a 21-millimeter lens, which, at least theoretically, created as much distortion as in Welles's film. The space in *Falcon*, however, seems cramped; nearly the whole action is played out in a series of little rooms with the actors gathered in tight, three-figured compositions. The difference lies in the fact that Huston stayed within limits of studio conventions, underplaying Edeson's offbeat photography, whereas Welles used the lens distortion openly, as an adjunct to the meaning of the story. In *Kane*, as in German expressionist cinema, space becomes demonic, oppressive; ceilings are unnaturally low, as if they were about to squash the characters; or, conversely, at Xanadu rooms become so large that people shrink, comically yet terrifyingly dwarfed by their possessions. (This effect is enhanced by the set design. At one point Kane walks over to a huge fireplace and seems to become a doll, warming himself before logs as big as whole trees: "Our home is here, Susan," he says, absurdly playing the role of paterfamilias.)

Again and again Welles uses Toland's photography not as a realistic mode of perception, but as a way of suggesting a conflict between the characters' instinctual needs and the social or material world that determines their fate. The short focal length of the lens enables him to express the psychology of his characters, to comment upon the relation between character and environment, and also to create a sense of barely contained, almost manic energy, as if the camera, like Kane himself, were overreaching. Fairly often he stages important conversations between characters against some counterpointed piece of business, as if he were trying to energize the plot by throwing as much material as possible onto the screen. One of the most obvious examples is the party sequence in the *Inquirer* offices, where Leland (Joseph Cotton) and Bernstein (Everett Sloane) debate about Kane's character (see figure 2). Here again, the shot establishes three planes which are set

FIGURE 2.

in conflict with one another. To the left is Leland, a young, hand-some, fastidious WASP, frowning with disapproval. To the right and slightly nearer is Bernstein—slight, ugly, Jewish, and as loyal as a puppy. Leland is bareheaded, but Bernstein wears a Rough Rider's hat as a sign of his allegiance to Kane's war in Cuba. The contrast is further emphasized by the dialogue: throughout the scene Leland refers to Kane as "Charlie," implicitly recognizing that he belongs to the same social class, whereas Bernstein always refers to his boss as "Mr. Kane." (We have just heard a song about Kane: Charles Bennett, the entertainer at the head of the chorus line, asks, "What is his name?" The chorus girls sing, "It's Mr. Kane!" Then the whole crowd joins in, singing, "He doesn't like that Mister / He likes good old Charlie Kane!") The brief conversation between the two men is important to the plot because it underlines Leland's growing disillusionment and Kane's increasing ambitions. In the original Mankiewicz-Welles script, it was played at an interlude in the party. By the time of the actual filming, however, Welles decided to stage the conversation simultaneously with Kane's dance. Leland and Bernstein have to shout to be heard over the raucous sounds of the orchestra and chorus, and our eyes are continually pulled away from them toward the antics in the background. Even when Welles cuts to a reverse angle, we can still see Kane and one of the girls reflected in the glass of a window (see figure 3). Notice that this shot contains an echo of the composition in the boardinghouse; once again Kane is supposed to be at play, and once again a window frame seems to mock his apparent freedom.

The violent overlappings and baroque contrasts occur not only on the visual level, but also on the soundtrack. Welles didn't invent overlapping dialogue any more than he and Toland invented deep focus, but the complex, hurried speech in *Kane* and the various levels of sound within a scene are especially effective corollaries of the complex photographic style. Here again, the technique is more expressive than purely realistic. The listening ear doesn't make sense of overlapping speech or the chaos of sounds in the real-world environment; like the eye, it needs to select some things and screen out others. The microphone, on the other hand, is as nonselective as the camera. Hence the sounds in *Kane*, like the images, have been carefully orchestrated and mixed to blot out unwanted distractions and to serve sym-

FIGURE 3.

bolic functions, even while they overheat the spectacle and make the viewer work to decipher it.

Because Welles was a celebrated practitioner of radio drama, critics have often pointed to the "radio-like" attention to sound in *Citizen Kane*. (The first words Welles speaks in the film, after the whispered "Rosebud," are a reference to his Mars broadcast. "Don't believe everything you hear on the radio," he chuckles.) The most interesting aspect of the sound design is the degree to which music, dialogue, and sound effects become adjuncts to the layered principles of deep focus, so that the various types of sound counterpoint with or comment upon one another. There are also moments when dialogue and incidental sound have been made somewhat "realistically" chaotic, because the director is willing to sacrifice clarity for pure speed. By the early 1930s, a fast-talking, breezy manner had become virtually the norm for American movies, and Welles was especially fond of the technique. His use of overlapping speech is an important key to the overall style in *Kane*, where so much depends on superimposition and simultaneity, with one scene dissolving into the next, one account of Kane's life slightly overlapping the succeeding account, one actor biting the other's cue. In its first half, the film is as rapidly paced as a Howard Hawks comedy, not so much for the sake of realism as for the sheer thrill of the zesty atmosphere.

The sense of pace and energy depends more on editing than is usually noted. Even Bazin, who was interested chiefly in the long take, recognized that superimpositions were characteristic of Welles's work. What Bazin did not emphasize, as Brian Henderson has pointed out, is that "the long take rarely appears in its pure state." In fact, Henderson notes, "the cut which ends a long take—how it ends and where—determines or affects the nature of the shot itself."[5] For example, toward the end of the scene in Mrs. Kane's boardinghouse, Agnes Moorehead rises and walks back toward the window, the camera following her. She pauses, and Welles cuts to a reverse angle, looking past her face toward the opposite side of the room as she opens the window and calls out to Charles. The sequence as a whole is composed of a shot/reverse shot, but there are some interesting differences between this particular editing style and standard Hollywood practice. For one thing, the cutting is not keyed to the statement-and-reply rhythm of the dialogue. Instead it imposes a structure on the narrative, holding off the change of camera viewpoint and the crucial close-up until the most effective moment. Equally important, the editing of shots such as this one, photographed with a wide-angle lens, creates a slightly more violent effect than the editing of normal perspectives and makes the audience more aware of the cutting process. The exaggeration of space gives the reverse angle an unusual force, as if we had been jerked into a radically different viewpoint. Thus Mrs. Kane's face looms up in the foreground, and the impact of the image is reinforced when she calls loudly out the window to Charles. The cut emphasizes the mother's pain and her pivotal role; behind her, we can see the figures of the father and the banker standing awkwardly in the distance, dwarfed by the size of her head. (See figure 4.)

Because of the many wide-angle views in Kane, shot/reverse shot editing takes on new dramatic possibilities. Consider, for example, the scenes of Kane and Susan separated by the vast halls

FIGURE 4.

of Xanadu, where a simple over-the-shoulder editing style becomes a powerful and witty statement about alienation and loneliness. Elsewhere in the film, Welles avoids reverse views altogether, playing out whole scenes in one take and "editing" by revealing successive playing areas. Sometimes he will throw a brief wide-angle shot on the screen with stunning effect, as in the *Inquirer* party, where a distorted close-up of a smiling black man coincides with a blast of music. In a few other scenes, however, he uses an ordinary shot/reverse shot style and even an ordinary lens, as in the meeting between Kane and Susan in her apartment. Ultimately, the chief difference between *Kane* and the standard film has less to do with a total avoidance of classical continuity editing than with the perspective of the shots Welles puts on the screen, plus his tendency to animate the space around the actors. Generally he keeps the camera at a distance, using the wide-angle lens to increase the playing area so that he can draw out the individual shots and fill them with detail. Welles wanted the audience to "read" a complex imagery, and wanted to choreograph dramatic movements of the camera and actors within a single shot. His work ran somewhat against the grain of classic studio movies, which used a paint-by-numbers editing style and encouraged the audience to forget technique and identify with the players.

The acting in Welles's early films is determined by similar principles, being slightly overwrought and at times self-consciously inflated. During the argument between Kane and Thatcher in the newspaper office, Welles and George Coulouris project their lines to a greater degree than in an ordinary movie, as if they were oblivious to the idea that acting for a camera ought to be low-key and naturalistic. The entire Thatcher section of the film is a subtle, deliberate echo of Victorian melodramatics, but even the later episodes are particularly high-pitched, creating a sort of repressed hysteria. Agnes Moorehead, Ray Collins, and Dorothy Comingore are a bit more wide-eyed and loud than they need to be; Collins, for example, underplays the villainy of Jim Gettys, but he stays in one's mind as a vivid portrait largely because he handles the quieter lines of dialogue almost like a stage actor, preserving the illusion of calm while he speaks at a high volume. Later, in the scene where Susan (Dorothy Comingore) attacks Kane for allowing Leland to write a negative review of her singing, the sound technicians seem to have added an extra decibel to her already piercing voice: "*What's that?*" she shouts as Kane opens a letter from Leland. "A declaration of principles," he says, almost to himself. "*What?*" she screams, the sound cutting at the audience's ears and making Kane flinch as if from a whiplash.

Welles's own remarkable performance in the central role is in keeping with this stylized quality. His resonant, declamatory voice speaks the lines rapidly, almost throwing away whole phrases but then pausing to linger over a word, like a pastiche of ordinary excited speech. A masterful stealer of scenes, Welles also knows that if he glances away from the person to whom he is speaking, he will capture the audience's attention. His slightly distracted look, plus the gauzy photography he prefers for his own close-ups, gives his acting what François Truffaut calls a "softly hallucinated" tone, something of a counterpoint to the more nightmarish mood of the rest of the movie. (Welles's screen persona and some of his directorial mannerisms may have developed less out of taste or theory than out of necessity. A massive, fascinating presence, he was nevertheless somewhat flatfooted and graceless in movement, and his best performances were in the roles of very old men. As the young Kane, he is usually photographed sitting down; when he does move—as in the dance at the *Inquirer* party or in the scene where he destroys Susan Alexander's room—his stilted, robotlike behavior is acceptable because it is in keeping with the highly deterministic quality of the script and the visuals.)

Keenly aware of his acting range, Welles designs most of his own scenes in *Kane* to accommodate his physical limitations; partly as a result of this habit, he is also very fussy about the movements of the other actors, who, as we have seen, are locked into rigidly structured patterns. Unlike Hawks, Ford, or any of the action directors of the time, he gives us very few moments when the camera sits passively and allows an actor's body its own natural freedom. And yet there are individual scenes, such as the one when Kane destroys Susan's bedroom, in which the emotions are so intense that the actors seem no longer to be pretending. These moments are as unconventional as the slightly exaggerated, artful playacting. By the early 1940s, American movies had developed a slick, understated acting style that avoided behavioral extremes. *Kane* was slightly different. It made the audience conscious of psychological pain in a way that was more common to the theater; it may have been a dream world, a wonder show, but it was also capable of touching upon important emotional truths.

Welles was of course assisted by the RKO technical staff and learned a good deal from watching the films of his Hollywood predecessors, including Ford, Ernst Lubitsch, and F. W. Murnau. In turn, his own work was to influence American cinema throughout the 1940s. Nevertheless, if the classic studio style ever existed (and by "classic" I mean movies that used chronological narrative, invisible editing, minimalist acting, and a muted photographic expressionism—everything designed to immerse the audience in content and make them forget the manipulations of style), then Welles was a challenge to the system. His movies contain a fine frenzy of performance and information, and the progress of his American career was to be a fairly steady movement away from the conventions of cinematic reality toward the bizarre and surreal. Most of his later pictures in Hollywood, made under severe contractual restraints and without the full participation of the Mercury Theater company, are characterized by a dazzling aesthetic unrestraint. (See *The Lady from Shanghai* [1947] and *Touch of Evil* [1958].) The density and bravado of his style in *Kane* may even have helped RKO executives fuel the myth of extravagance that still surrounds his life and work. Welles never went drastically over budget and was never responsible for a true financial disaster; nonetheless the idea persisted that he was a waster of studio money. This, together with his satiric vision of America, severely limited his ability to work in Hollywood.

Welles's artistic flamboyance also had a somewhat paradoxical effect on the films themselves, because his leading themes were the dangers of radical individualism and unlimited power. He was preoccupied with tyrannical egotists or Faustian types who try to live above the law and who ultimately become prisoners of guilt, self-delusion, and old age; meanwhile, his public philosophy was consistently humanistic and liberal. The question naturally arises, then, whether there was a tension or contradiction between Welles's politics and the personality implicit in his style. In my view there was such a tension—a productive one, however, as can be seen if we now examine more closely the maze of conflicts and oppositions that structures *Citizen Kane*'s overall narrative.

The Labyrinth

There are two snow sleds in *Citizen Kane*. The first, as everyone knows, is named Rosebud and is given to Kane by his mother; the second is a Christmas present from Kane's guardian, Thatcher, and is seen so briefly that audiences are unaware that it, too, has a name. If you press the pause button on the DVD edition of *Kane*, you will discover that for a few frames sled number two, which is called Crusader, is presented fully to the camera. Where the original has a flower, this one is embossed with the helmet of a knight. The symbolism is fairly obvious: Kane repays Thatcher's gift by growing up to be a crusading, trust-busting newspaperman, out to slay the dragon Wall Street. Deprived of maternal care, he turns himself into a phony champion of the people, an overreacher who dies like a medieval knight amid the empty gothic splendor of Xanadu.

Crusader was a tiny joke that Welles could throw away in a film that bristles with clever asides. I mention it chiefly because I'm foolishly proud of knowing such trivia, but also because it's a convenient way to point up the duality in Kane's character and in the very conception of the film. The contrast between Crusader and Rosebud is only the most superficial instance of the way images, characters, and ideas are set off against one another. Kane has not only two sleds but two wives and two friends. The camera makes two visits to Susan Alexander and two journeys to Xanadu; it even shows two close-ups of Rosebud, once as it is being obliterated by the snows of Colorado at Mrs. Kane's boardinghouse, and again as it is incinerated in the basement of Kane's Florida estate. Finally, in the most vivid clash of all, we are given two endings. First, the reporter Thompson quietly tells his colleagues that a single word can't sum up a man's life, and the camera moves away from him, lingering over the jigsaw pieces of Xanadu's art collection. After Thompson's exit, however, the camera begins tracking toward a furnace, where it reveals the meaning of Rosebud after all. In its last moment the film shifts from intellectual irony to dramatic irony, from apparent skepticism to apparent revelation.

At every level the movie is a paradox: Kane himself is in some ways as much like Welles as he is like Hearst. The style of the film is both derivative of earlier Hollywood models and critical of them. The leftist implications of the project adversely affected Welles's entire career, and yet in many ways the attack on Hearst is somewhat oblique. Actually, *Kane* is almost as deeply concerned with the movies themselves, and with the potentially deceptive, myth-making qualities of the media, which are epitomized by the Hearst press. In other words, it has a complex attitude not only toward its subject, but toward its own cinematic bravura.

These tensions and contradictions can be seen in the two contrasting movements at the beginning of the film—a dreamy, expressionistic portrayal of Kane's death, followed by a newsreel depiction of his life. As David Bordwell has pointed out, Welles seems to be paying homage to the dual fountainheads of cinematic perception—the fantasy of George Méliès and the realism of Louis Lumière.[6] But even though the two modes are placed in dialectical relation, they achieve only a negative synthesis; each suggests the voyeurism inherent in the medium, and each leaves Kane an enigma.

In the first shot, we see a No Trespassing sign that the camera promptly ignores. To the strains of what Bernard Herrmann called a funereal "power" music, we rise up a chainlink fence toward a misty, bleak, studio-manufactured sky, a series of dissolves providing glimpses of Kane's private world. As we pass beyond the gigantic *K* atop the fence and progressively nearer to a lighted window in a castle, we encounter a surreal montage:

monkeys in a cage, gondolas in a stream, a golf course. In the background, Kane's castle looks a bit like the home of a sorcerer, its strangeness enhanced by the stereoptic quality of the art work, which was created by the Walt Disney animators. (The Disney unit worked at RKO in this period, and was ideally suited to design the spooky, compellingly kitschy Xanadu, which seems both a wonder of the world and a monument to bad taste—a fairytale castle of the sort that Disney himself would later use to symbolize his theme park.) Our approach to this bizarre domain is as voyeuristic as anything in a Hitchcock movie; the camera is drawn like a moth to the lighted window, but at the moment when it arrives the light clicks out.

Similar forward movements; usually accompanied by dissolves, are used throughout the film; for example, when the camera twice crawls up the walls of the El Rancho nightclub and moves toward a broken skylight, enabling us to peer at Susan Alexander. Often the movement is blocked or slightly inhibited, as in the climactic moments, when we glide forward over the flotsam of Kane's life and approach a sled, only to have it carried away by a workman; a dissolve then takes us to a furnace, where the camera continues moving forward directly into the flames, at last coming to rest on the burning Rosebud. Here, as elsewhere, the camera becomes a sort of character—a restless, ghostly observer, more silent and discreet than the journalists who poke about among Kane's belongings, but linked to them in certain ways. Like Kane's own newspapers, the camera is an "inquirer," and the periodic frustrations it encounters—a door closing, a light clicking out, a sled being pulled away—are like subtle affronts to the audience's curiosity.

Inside Xanadu, Kane's death is shot in the style of the early European avant-garde. A gigantic close-up of the dying man's lips is the largest single image, but when the lips move and whisper the crucial word, they create a slightly ludicrous impression: Kane's mustachioed mouth resembles the mountains of a strange planet, and his whisper is as loud as a shout. An inexplicable close-up of a snow-covered cottage (a still photo superimposed with moving snow) turns out to be a paperweight, and when the

camera pulls back to reveal this fact some confusion lingers, because everything—Kane's hand, the paperweight, and the background—is covered with snowflakes. When the paperweight rolls
down the steps and crashes (another piece of trickery created by
several images spliced together), we cut to the most confusing
shot of all: a reflection in a convex piece of broken glass, creating
an elaborate fish-eye effect which is virtually a parody of the lens
Gregg Toland used to photograph the movie. We can barely make
out a nurse opening a strange ornamental doorway and entering;
another cut, to a low angle near the head of Kane's bed, shows
the nurse placing a sheet over a shadowed body.

These fragmentary glimpses tantalize the audience, capping the
effect suddenly by introducing a blare of music and the "News
on the March" title card. Once the newsreel gets under way, we
settle momentarily into a more logical mode, grounded in presumably objective, documentary facts that explain the origins of
the strange castle and provide an overview of Kane's life. But if
the private Kane was seen too subjectively and too close up, the
public Kane is seen too objectively and usually from too far away.
Welles and about a fourth of the Mercury players had previously
worked in the radio version of Henry Luce's famous newsreel,
the "March of Time," and they create a wonderfully accurate
parody of its hyped-up journalism, borrowing freely some of its
famous catchphrases, such as "this week, as it must to all men,
death came to. . . ." (As many critics have noted, the parody of
the Luce press serves to expand the film's critique of mass media
beyond the Hearst organization.) For all its self-important tone,
however, "News on the March" offers mainly a compilation of
Kane's public appearances, usually filled with scratches and photographed from awkward vantage points. Repeatedly Kane is
shown alongside politicians, aligning himself first with the pro-
gressives and then with the fascists. In his early career he waves
and smiles at the public in awkward gaiety, but later he becomes
somber and camera-shy. We are told that "few private lives were
more public," but are given only a few images of the Great Man's
domestic habits: a doctored photo of one of his Xanadu parties;
a shot of him sitting beside an empty swimming pool, swathed

in towels and going over a manuscript; a peep through a latticed gate, as a hand-held camera with a telephoto lens shows the old man in a wheelchair. Even "1941's biggest, strangest funeral" is shown only as a brief shot from an awkward angle; the image is grainy (Toland's imitation of newsreel stock is always perfectly accurate), and we see only a few rich mourners in the distance, over the massed heads of reporters.

Throughout the "documentary," there is a comic disparity between the awesomeness of Kane's possessions and the stilted old codger we actually view, as if the newsreel were trying to establish him both as a mythical character like Noah or Kubla Khan and as something of a joke. He supports the wrong politicians; he marries a president's daughter and then gets caught in a sex scandal; he drops wet concrete over his Edwardian coat at a public ceremony; he vouches for the peaceful intentions of Hitler. He is so bumbling and foolish that little remains of him but his wealth, and even that is treated as a believe-it-or-not curiosity. But the film also invites us to dislike the reporters who poke microphones and cameras in Kane's face. This feeling is reinforced when Welles suddenly breaks the illusion by cutting to a side view of the screen and the projector lights, and then making an aural joke: the projector clicks off and the pompous musical fanfare groans to a stop, as if somebody were giving "News on the March" a raspberry.

The ensuing conversation among reporters is one of the most self-reflexive moments in the film, shot in an actual RKO screening room which has been made to look like a region of the underworld. The air is smoky and the reporters are sinister shadows, as they largely remain throughout. Rawlston, the newsreel editor (Philip Van Zandt), is shown from a radically low angle, gesturing against what Welles called a "Nuremberg" light beaming down from the projection booth. He and his yes-men correctly perceive the shallowness of the newsreel, but their solution is to find an "angle." "It isn't enough to tell us what a man did," Rawlston says, "you've got to tell us who he *was*." The solution is Kane's dying word, a gimmick typical of Hearst's yellow journalism. Rawlston gives Thompson (William Alland) a tap on the shoulder and a shark's smile, ordering him to go out and get Rosebud, "dead or alive." And yet the audience isn't allowed to feel superior. We've already been made curious about Rosebud, which has exactly the same function for Welles and Mankiewicz as it does for Rawlston. Just as the newsreel lacks impact until some oversimplified "key" has been concocted to explain Kane's life, so the movie lacks impact without an enigma and a nicely punctuated ending. Perhaps significantly, Herman Mankiewicz, Joseph Cotten, and Erskine Sanford (the last two of whom appear later as characters in Kane's life) are barely visible in the shadows of the room, playing the roles of reporters who scoff at Kane's dying words. Everybody is involved in a dubious pursuit. The opening sections of the film have initiated a search, but they are filled with so many ironies and opacities that they threaten to undermine the project before it starts.

The story now becomes a series of reminiscences by witnesses to Kane's life. Here it's important to note that Welles's film is fundamentally different from Akira Kurosawa's *Rashomon* (1951): it doesn't present separate versions of an unknowable reality, but instead gives us different facets of a single personality. Kane's life is depicted more or less chronologically, through the memories and judgments of five characters who knew him at progressively later stages. We never have the feeling that these characters are distorting the truth, even though Leland recounts domestic events he could not possibly have seen. For all its interest in subjectivity and psychology, *Kane* has a rational structure; it's about contradiction and complexity, not about relativity.

Thompson's quest is initiated with a thunderclap and a gothic rainstorm, in comically scary contrast to Rawlston's last words ("It'll probably turn out to be a very simple thing"). We see a garish, dripping poster of a blond woman, and the camera moves upward, sliding over the roof of the El Rancho and down toward the skylight. Once again the search for Rosebud seems tawdry, notably so in a deep-focus shot that concludes Thompson's abortive interview with Susan. As Thompson steps into a phone booth and closes the door, the headwaiter (Gus Schilling) moves just a fraction to the left so that he is framed by one of the door's

FIGURE 5.

rectangular glass panels. In the distance, her head bowed drunk-
enly over a table, is Susan (Marion Davies was known to Hollywood insiders as a secret alcoholic), and we see a chain of male
predators arrayed in front of her: the waiter is trying to spy on
Thompson, who has been trying to learn about Kane; Thompson,
in turn, is conveying information to his boss at the other end of
the line (see figure 5). When Thompson exits the booth, he bribes
the waiter, who comments innocently, "Thank you, thanks. As
a matter of fact, just the other day, when the papers were full
of it, I asked her. She never heard of Rosebud." Fade out with
an ironic, playful chord of Herrmann's music.

Nearly all of the fragments of the narrative are structured this
way, with a mild shock or a witty image at the beginning and a
joke or an ironic twist at the end. The cynical, wisecracking tone,
however, has been put to the service of something more complex,
inflected by Welles's Germanic staging and by the indirect influence of impressionist novelists like Joseph Conrad and Scott Fitzgerald, who provided a model for the film's narrative technique.
The complexity is evident in the next sequence, which begins

with another joke. Herrmann plays his power motif with a flat, stale brass; the camera tilts down from the model of a huge, ugly statue of Thatcher; and we see Thompson speaking with a stereotypical lady librarian who tells him of the rules pertaining to manuscripts. The library reflects Thatcher's vanity and coldness: the inner vault seems as long as a football field, and at the far end is a small safe from which an armed guard extracts a volume of a diary. The mannish librarian stands at military attention while the guard, caught in the beam of another "Nuremberg" light, brings forth a glowing book. Meanwhile the shadowy Thompson looks a bit like Kafka's Joseph K., come before the Courts of Law. (See figure 6.) In other words, the aura of sacredness and sinister mystery is mixed with elements of hokum and profanity, so that we are aware of banal material goods being mystified into a spiritual netherworld. The lighting style resists being described either as satire, as seriousness, or as magic; instead it seems designed to underscore one of the film's leading themes—the transformation of money into myth.

The Thatcher portion of the film, which grows out of Thomp-

FIGURE 6.

son's reading of the diary, is at first somewhat Dickensian in mood, telling how a poor child rises suddenly to great expectations. Within a few moments, Charles Foster Kane is lifted from a snowy playground in front of his mother's boardinghouse and set down at a richly Victorian Christmas celebration, although in both places the atmosphere is chilly, the boy surrounded by menacing adult figures. George Coulouris (made up to look a bit like John D. Rockefeller) plays Thatcher in broad caricature, delivering his lines at top speed. In a charmingly exuberant and altogether anti-realistic montage, he constantly turns to face the camera, muttering in disgust as the young Kane grows up, founds a newspaper, and then attacks Wall Street. But Kane rises only to have an ignominious fall; the narrative as a whole covers the period between the winter of 1871 and the winter of 1929, when Kane, forced to turn part of the control of his newspapers over to his former guardian, broods on his failure and tells Thatcher that he would like to have been "everything you hate." In the final analysis, capital is in charge of Kane's life, and the market crash of the late 1920s does little more than solidify the power of America's major bankers. At the same time, a nostalgic evocation of the nineteenth century gives way to a somber present.

The portrait of Kane that emerges from these memoirs contains many ironies and ambiguities. In the boardinghouse scene, where we might expect to see him as the innocent victim of social determinism, he looks like something of a brat. By contrast, he is at his most charming during an early scene in the newspaper office, where his potential danger is underlined. Thatcher, who has been reading a succession of *Inquirer* headlines, lowers a paper ("Galleons of Spain off Jersey Coast") to reveal Kane sitting at his editorial desk, clad in shirtsleeves, sipping coffee with an amused, Machiavellian glint in his eye. In the same shot, Leland and Bernstein enter the frame, Leland taking a cigar from the desk (he is an addict, as we see later), and Bernstein scurrying past on official business. Kane seems a calm figure at the center of a storm, blithely dictating a telegram that echoes one of Hearst's most famous comments to a reporter ("Dear Wheeler, you provide the prose poems and I'll provide the war") and, in a large, climactic close-up, thumbing his nose at Thatcher's warnings ("You know, Mr. Thatcher, at the rate of a million dollars a year I'll have to close this place—in sixty years"). Generous with money and disrespectful toward stuffy Victorian authority, Kane declares that he is committed to the "people" as opposed to the "trusts." Thatcher and the elderly editor, Carter—a cold-hearted moneybags and a genteel incompetent—are perfect foils to his youthful rebelliousness, making his yellow journalism and attempt to start a war in Cuba seem like creative energy. But beneath the surface Kane is a different sort of character. "The trouble is," he tells Thatcher, "you don't realize you're talking to two people." On the one hand is the Kane we see, the pretty young man who claims to represent the public; on the other hand is the Kane who has investments in Wall Street and knows down to the penny the amount of his holdings ("eighty-two thousand, three hundred and sixty-four shares of Public Transit Preferred"). "If I don't look after the interests of the underprivileged," he remarks, in one of the places where contradictions are reconciled and class loyalty revealed, "maybe somebody will—maybe somebody without money or property."

When Thompson closes the diary and exits the library ("Thanks for the use of the hall"), he goes to interview Bernstein, who maintains the spell of Kane's charm. Bernstein talks mainly about the period between the founding of the newspaper and Kane's marriage to Emily Norton (Ruth Warrick), who was "no Rosebud." An apologist for Kane, he is also kindly and unpretentious—the only person who has remembered Susan after Kane's death ("I called her myself the day he died. I thought maybe somebody ought to"). Even his reactionary comment on the Panama Canal arises more from a defense of his dead friend than from any self-serving motive. Realistic about old age ("the only disease you don't look forward to being cured of"), as well as about his position in life ("Me? I'm chairman of the board. I got nothing but time"), he looks spry and at peace with himself, and the setting for his interview is conducive to a melancholy serenity: shadows fill the room, rain falls outside the high windows, and a fire burns in the hearth. Bernstein sits in a big leather chair, his face reflected in the polished surface of his desk as if in a quiet pool. Here, photographed in a long take which contains some of the most discreet camera movements in the film, he tells a story about seeing a girl in a white dress on the Jersey ferry (Welles's favorite moment, beautifully acted by Everett Sloane) and reminds us that he is the only character who has been with Kane until "after the end."

Yet the kindness and the cozy atmosphere don't conceal the fact that Bernstein is an overfaithful associate from a different social class than Kane, and that he functions as a kind of stooge. Kane will later tell his anti-Semitic wife, Emily, in no uncertain terms that the Jewish Bernstein may pay a visit to the family nursery, but there remains a significant distance between the two men. Kane and the patrician Leland arrive together at the *Inquirer* offices in a hansom cab, dressed in the height of New York fashion, while Bernstein tags along atop a delivery wagon, guarding Kane's property. Later, at the political rally and at Susan's concert, Bernstein can be seen in the company of Kane's goons. As Kane's financial agent and unquestioning companion, he is responsible for whatever dirty work needs doing, and he always places personal loyalty above principle. His prosperity at the end of his life, as Leland will later suggest, comes to him like a tip from his employer.

Bernstein's reminiscences are chiefly about adventure and male camaraderie. We see Kane sweeping into the *Inquirer* and turning it into a twentieth-century paper, meanwhile promising to be a knight-errant for the people, "a fighting and tireless champion of their rights as citizens." Only a few moments earlier, he had cynically concocted a lurid news item about sex and murder, during which he told Carter, "If the headline is big enough, it makes the news big enough." Bernstein acknowledges some of these warts on Kane's character, but he defends Kane anyway, describing him as a man connected with the manifest destiny of the country. And in fact, during Bernstein's flashback the film manages to show all the contradictions in liberal democracy through a single editorial desk. The newsroom becomes a focal point of social history, where we see the country moving through

various stages of democratization, each attempt at progress gen-
erating new conflicts and new evils. America moves from the age
of the tycoon, through the period of populist muckraking, and
into the era of mass communications, with turn-of-the-century
types like Kane being destroyed by the very process they have set
in motion.

Leland, whom Thompson now visits in a geriatric ward, is
often regarded as the spokesman for the "moral" of the film, but
while it is true that he serves as a sort of conscience for Kane,
he is as flawed and human as the doggedly loyal Bernstein. The
ultimate product of a fading and effete New England aristocracy
("One of those old families where the father is worth ten million
bucks and then one day he shoots himself and it turns out there's
nothing but debts"), Leland is an aesthete who despises the cap-
italists but can never join the workers. He lacks Kane's vitality
and is fascinated with Kane for that very reason. A dandy and a
puritan, he is very much the "New England schoolmarm" Kane
has named him, and the film may be hinting that his involvement
with Kane has sexual implications. Mankiewicz and Welles were
prohibited from showing a scene in a bordello where Kane unsuccessfully tries to interest Leland in a woman, but even without
that scene he seems to have no active sex life. As a young man
he barely conceals his admiration for Kane, and when he grows
disillusioned there is inevitably a "loose" woman involved. At the
big *Inquirer* party, his frowns of disapproval and complaints about
the war with Spain are played off against images of Kane making
time with one of the chorus girls. When the "love nest" with
Susan Alexander brings an end to Kane's political career, it is
Leland, not Emily Kane, who behaves like a jilted lover.

"A lot of us check out with no special conviction about death,"
Leland tells the reporter, "but we do know what we're leaving.
. . . we believe in *something*." This may be a valid criticism of Kane,
but Leland himself seems utterly lacerated with age, disillusionment, and cynicism, and the setting of his interview emphasizes
sterility and death—a purgatorial hospital sunroof where a few
ghostly figures in wheelchairs are attended by annoying nurses
and where even the sunlight seems cold. This atmosphere is par-

ticularly ironic in view of the story Leland tells, which deals with Kane's love life. A more intimate friend than Bernstein, he recounts the period between Kane's first marriage and his attempt to turn Susan Alexander into an opera star. The two wives are as much physical and social opposites as Leland and Bernstein have been, yet in their own way both are connected to Kane's desire to assert mastery. The celebrated breakfast table montage showing the disintegration of the marriage to Emily (whom Leland describes aptly as "like all the girls I knew in dancing school") is followed by the comic toothache scene in Susan Alexander's apartment, the allegro pace modulating into a sweet, intimate rendezvous. Aided by the least ostentatious, most persuasive makeup job in the film, Welles as Kane turns rapidly from an ardent husband wooing a president's niece into a tired businessman courting a salesgirl. He sentimentally imagines that Susan has a mother like his own, and the scene where he presides quietly over her recital is followed immediately by the opening of his campaign for governor—the sexual conquest linked to a hubristic attempt to dominate the populace. In fact, the closing line of Susan's song concerns the theme of power: it comes from *The Barber of Seville* and roughly translates as "I have sworn it, I will conquer."

The ensuing political rally is a good example of how the film creates large-scale effects with a modest budget. Its atmosphere is both American and Germanic, Kane's stem-winding campaign speech subtly evoking Hitler's harangues to his political hacks. In place of a crowd of extras, we see a painted, expressionistic image suggesting both Kane's delusions of grandeur and the crowd's lack of individuality. Everything is dominated by Kane's ego: the initial *K* he wears as a stickpin, the huge blowup of his jowly face on a poster, and the incessant "I" in his public speech. Now and then we cut away to the back of the hall, the oratory becoming slightly distant, Kane suddenly looking like a fanatical puppet gesticulating on a toy stage. He talks about "the workingman and the slum child," and meanwhile the frock-coated men behind him are arranged to resemble the bloated rich of a Thomas Nast cartoon.

During the rally, Kane's supporters—Leland, Bernstein, Emily, and Kane's young son—are isolated in close-ups, but his political rival, "Boss" Jim Gettys (Ray Collins), stands high above the action, the stage viewed over his shoulder, so that he dominates the frame like a sinister power. The showdown he subsequently arranges between himself, Kane, Emily, and Susan—a private conversation in perfect contrast to the rally—is one of the most emotionally tense and skillfully directed scenes in the film. There are more than a dozen shots in the sequence, one of them a rather long take, but no close-ups; the characters are dynamically blocked, with Kane, Susan, and Gettys alternately stepping into shadow as the tide of the conversation changes. Throughout, the voices of the women provide a counterpoint to the central male contest. Emily is quiet, determined, and formal: "There seems to be only one choice for you to make, Charles. I'd say that it's been made for you." Susan, completely ignored by everyone, pipes shrilly, "What about me? Charlie, he said my name would be dragged through the mud!"

Gettys, who is as much a monster as Kane, behaves courteously to Emily, even though he tells Kane that he is "not a gentleman." "You see, my idea of a gentleman. . . . Well, Mr. Kane, if I owned a newspaper and didn't like the way somebody was doing things . . . I wouldn't show him in a convict suit with stripes, so his children could see him in the paper, or his mother." One mamma's boy has taken revenge on the other, and as a result Kane explodes. "I can fight this all alone," he shouts, and then screams, "Don't worry about me. I'm Charles Foster Kane! I'm no cheap, crooked politician trying to save himself from the consequences of his crimes. Gettys! I'm going to send you to Sing Sing!" The last words fade weakly into traffic sounds as Gettys exits the apartment building and closes the front door.

Just at the moment when Kane's political ambitions are wrecked, the film shifts almost completely into its examination of his sexual life. In this respect *Kane* contrasts vividly with the usual muckraking accounts of William Randolph Hearst's career. Mankiewicz and Welles allude to many of Hearst's reactionary undertakings, but they understate the violence that was associated with his empire, suggesting it only through occasional asides and the imagery of the political rally. According to biographer Ferdinand Lundberg's *Imperial Hearst* (one of the sources of the film's script), during the newspaper wars of early twentieth-century Chicago, Hearst had employed gangsters to rout his competitors; gunmen like Dion O'Bannion had beaten up rival newsboys and even shot innocent civilians, while Hearst's editors blamed the trouble on "labor agitators." Through most of the century, Hearst was a vigorous opponent of unions and child labor legislation, and his mining interests in Peru were more or less forced-labor camps where workers were held at the point of guns. *Citizen Kane's* only apparent reference to such things is to briefly show Bernstein in the company of what look like hired toughs, and to have Leland berate Kane for his paternalistic attitude toward workers. Just when Leland meets the politically broken Kane in the abandoned newsroom and accuses him of swindling the public, the film veers off into the most intimate details of Kane's love affair with Susan.

In effect, however, Mankiewicz and Welles were not so much abandoning the social issues as condensing them and displacing them onto the story of Susan. If Susan Alexander is only roughly similar to Marion Davies, that is partly because Welles and Mankiewicz converted her into a symbol for Kane's treatment of the society at large. As Leland tells us, she represents for Kane a "cross section of the American public." When Kane meets her, she is a working girl, undereducated and relatively innocent, and his relationship with her is comparable to his relationship with the masses who read his papers. He showers her with wealth, but this merely confirms Leland's remark in the desolated, postelection newspaper office: "You talk about the people as though you owned them." Kane's treatment of Susan is a confirmation of this charge, and it also reminds us of the violence he is willing to use to have his way; thus in the last reels, which show Kane retreating more and more from public life, Susan is reduced from a pleasant, attractive girl to a harpy, and then to a near-suicide. The film emphasizes the fact that Susan sings unwillingly, at the command of her master. When Kane establishes their love nest, the relationship is summarized in a single shot: in the foreground Susan is poised awkwardly at a grand piano; farther back in the room, Kane is enthroned in a wicker chair, applauding slowly and grinning in satisfaction; still farther back, visible through the archway to another room, is a sumptuous double bed. After the marriage, Kane tells reporters, "We're going to become an opera star," and he hires Matiste (Fortunio Bonanova) to begin the arduous, comically inappropriate series of music lessons. The settings grow more opulent, while Susan becomes increasingly driven and humiliated. She begins to resemble those Peruvians toiling in Hearst's copper mines, though she is certainly getting better pay.

The choice of opera rather than movies for Susan's career is significant. It enables the film to make one of many references to Welles's own life (as a baby, he had appeared briefly in the Chicago Opera), while also referring to American tycoons like Samuel Insull and Robert McCormick, who sponsored operas; more important, it highlights the difference in social class between Susan and the patrons for whom she works. We see her kneeling on satin pillows, pitifully frightened and garishly made up, singing "Ah! Cruel" in a register beyond her voice to a dozing, tuxedoed audience, while up in the rafters a laborer holds his nose and shakes his head sadly. "I'm not high-class like you," Susan tells Kane in an even shriller voice when she kneels again on the floor of a hotel room and reads the Leland-Kane review. She attempts to quit the opera, reminding Kane that "I never wanted to do it in the first place," but Kane orders her to continue because "I don't propose to have myself made ridiculous." In a scene remarkable for the way it shows the pain of both people, his shadow falls over her face—just as he later towers over her in the party scene, when a woman's ambiguous scream is heard distantly on the soundtrack. Ultimately, however, Susan asserts her power. Leland has warned that the workingman will not always tolerate Kane's patronage: "you're not going to like that one little bit when you find out it means your workingman expects something as his right and not your gift." This is more or less why Susan leaves Kane. In some ways, the Susan Alexander plot replaces political with personal concerns, but in other ways it shows how public and sexual concerns are interrelated.

If the film makes a strong political and personal criticism of Kane, it nevertheless treats him ambiguously, with a mixture of satire, awe, and sympathy. In the newsreel, he is attacked for different reasons by both capital and labor. At his death, the *Inquirer* shows a distinguished-looking photo with the banner headline "Charles Foster Kane Dies after a Lifetime of Service" while the rival *Chronicle* shows him glowering under a dark hat brim, with a headline reading, "C. F. Kane Dies at Xanadu Estate." To Thatcher, Kane is a spoiled do-gooder who is a menace to business; to Bernstein, he is a hero who helped build the country; to Leland, he is an egomaniac who wants everybody to love him but who leaves only "a tip in return." No single response is adequate, and near the end the disparate judgments take the form of contradictory emotions. Thompson, functioning as the audience's surrogate, remarks to Susan Alexander, "You know, all the same I feel sorry for Mr. Kane." Susan, the only character we've actually seen Kane victimize and the only person in the film who could condemn him outright, gives Thompson a harsh look and a terse reply: "Don't you think I do?"

Susan's comment crystallizes the film's divided attitude. In the later sequences, where Kane nearly destroys Susan, the images of his massive form towering over the submissive woman are more than simple evocations of tyranny: the audience is invited to fear along with Susan, but also to feel sympathy for Kane, who is so pained by age and thwarted desire. This feeling is especially strong toward the end, where the most powerful and intense moments—the enraged breaking up of Susan's room and the discovery of the paperweight—are played off against the predatory Raymond (Paul Stewart) and the vast, chilly labyrinth of Xanadu. As the inquiry has deepened, the tone of the film has shifted subtly; the comic blackout sketches that characterize the Thatcher and Bernstein sections are replaced by a darker, more grotesque mingling of black comedy and tragedy that belongs to Leland and Susan—the scenes near the big Xanadu fireplace, for example, with Susan's voice echoing, "A person could go crazy in this dump," or the surreal picnic, with a funereal stream of black cars driving down a beach toward a swampy encampment, where a jazz band plays "This Can't Be Love" against a matted background of RKO bats borrowed from *Son of Kong* (1933). Each phase of the movie becomes more painful than the one before, until we arrive at the most cynical of the witnesses, Raymond, who is ironically responsible for the most intimate details: Susan leaves Kane, her image receding down a long corridor and then exiting Xanadu to the sound of an enraged cockatoo. (Both shots are good examples of the film's brilliant use of optical printing.) In response, Kane blindly destroys her room, the crisis bringing back his memories of childhood.

Thompson never emerges from the shadows, but at the end he becomes a slightly troubled and philosophic onlooker. Finally he gives up his search, knowing too much to expect a simple answer. We, of course, are in a more privileged position, and are given, if not a rational explanation, a vision of Rosebud. Here it might be noted that Welles was uneasy about the whole sled idea. He dismissed Rosebud in a famous remark, calling it "dollarbook Freud" and emphasizing that Herman Mankiewicz thought it up. Even so, some of the psychoanalytic ideas in *Kane* might have come straight from a textbook. According to Freudian terminology, Kane can be typed as a regressive, anal-sadistic personality. His petit-bourgeois family is composed of a weak, untrustworthy father and a loving, albeit puritanical mother; he is taken away from his mother during a period of sexual latency and reared by a bank; and as an adult he manifests what Freud describes as a pregenital form of sexuality in which "not the genital component-instincts, but the sadistic and anal are most prominent" (*General Introduction to Psychoanalysis* [1917]). Thus Kane is partly a sadist who wants to obtain power over others and partly an anal type who obsessively collects zoo animals and museum pieces. His childhood seems, in reality, far from idyllic; nevertheless, it is a childhood toward which he is compulsively drawn. All his energy is spent in trying to create his own world, similar to the imaginary one he enjoys in the snow near the beginning of the film, and in rebelling against anyone who asserts authority over his will. When he can no longer "look after" the little people, he begins to hate them. He tries to maintain a dangerous but awe-inspiring daydream, of which Xanadu is only the most obvious manifestation, and whenever the dream world is threatened, he responds with a child's rage. Thus when Thatcher interrupts Kane's play in the snow, the boy defends himself by striking out with his sled; when Jim Gettys interrupts the political game, Kane breaks into a terrifying but pathetic fury; and when Susan asserts her independence, he throws a literal tantrum, regressing to the state of a child destroying a nursery.

Whatever his influence in other spheres, Kane cannot control his own fate. (In 1941, with the New Deal in ascendance and the United States entering a war against fascism, it must have seemed to Welles that Hearst was in a similar position.) Forever imprisoned by his childhood ego, he treats everything as a toy: first the sled, then the newspaper, then the Spanish-American War. (Notice how the war is depicted as a child's game, with the *Inquirer* reporters sporting little wooden rifles and funny hats.) Toward the end there is Susan, with her marionette-style opera makeup and her dollhouse room in a fantasy castle. The final toy, the paperweight Kane discovers after his tantrum, is probably the most telling object of them all—a self-enclosed realm, immune from change, evoking a kind of fantasy about Kane's childhood in Colorado.[7] The sled burning at the heart of the furnace, its legend blistering in the heat and dissolving at the moment when it is discovered, tends to recall that same realm, and is both a quasi-Freudian explanation of Kane's psyche and a logical expression of his tortured romantic idealism—one of those images that the poet William Butler Yeats called "self-born mockers of Man's enterprise."

This is not to say that we have discovered the key to the film, for, as Thompson has tried to remind us, the meaning of any inquiry has less to do with a goal we arrive at than with a process we go through. Hence, after we discover the sled, *Citizen Kane* concludes with another reminder of the camera's inquisitiveness and a nearly complete reversal of the voyeuristic movement with which the story began. The camera retreats from the castle, staring at the awesome smoke of corruption in the sky and settling at last on the No Trespassing sign outside the gate. Our search is ended, but the narrative has been ambiguous and the style both magical and self-critical. Even the title of the film is a contradiction in terms.

Notes

1. John Houseman, *Run-Through: A Memoir* (New York: Simon and Schuster, 1972), p. 459.

2. André Bazin, "The Evolution of the Language of Cinema," in *What Is Cinema?* vol. 1 (Berkeley: University of California Press, 1964), p. 24; subsequent citations will appear in the text.

3. Gregg Toland, "How I Broke the Rules in *Citizen Kane*," in *Perspectives on* Citizen Kane, ed. Ronald Gottesman (New York: Hall, 1996), pp. 569–73.

4. Quoted in *Practical Motion Picture Photography*, ed. Russell Campbell (New York: Barnes, 1970), p. 176.

5. Brian Henderson, "The Long Take," in *A Critique of Film Theory* (New York: Dutton, 1980), p. 50.

6. David Bordwell, "The Dual Cinematic Tradition in *Citizen Kane*," in *The Cinema*, ed. Stanley Solomon (New York: Harcourt Brace Jovanovich, 1973), pp. 181–97.

7. If you look closely at *Citizen Kane*, you will discover that the snowy paperweight can be seen at two earlier moments, when it is almost hidden from view—first in Mrs. Kane's parlor, and then again in the young Susan Alexander's apartment. Apparently the two women, who are linked in Kane's mind, have identical paperweights.

Citizen Kane

The Sound Track

FRANÇOIS THOMAS

◆　◆　◆

A PART FROM A DIALOGUE TRACK that had mainly been recorded live on the set, the sound of *Citizen Kane* was pieced together in a studio. It cannot be attributed to any single contributor because its function was progressively determined during various stages of the film's creation and production. The role played by sound in the transitions from one scene to another was defined during the development of the screenplay (although several of the most striking transitions do not appear in the final shooting script) and took specific form during editing. Most of the dialogue was recorded on the set, whereas sound effects that give atmosphere and dramatic impact to each sequence were added at various points during editing and mixing. Co-screenwriter Herman J. Mankiewicz, production mixer Bailey Fesler, editor Robert Wise, and the sound-effects engineers each contributed suggestions at one time or another, as did composer Bernard Herrmann, whose music occasionally acts as a substitute for sound effects.[1] Chief among these collaborators was dubbing mixer James G. Stewart, who had been with RKO since 1931 and had headed postproduction sound operations since 1937. Stewart supervised each of the final steps that refined the sound track of *Citizen Kane*, and, with the still limited technical means at his disposal (magnetic recording did not replace optical sound until the beginning of the 1950s, when it greatly increased the potential to duplicate recorded sounds and mix them with others), he helped to shape a film whose every sequence is endowed with a unique sonic texture. It is, however, in no way to deny the considerable contribution of this unequaled technician to point out that the most crucial elements of what we hear in the film derive from the overall sound design: Orson Welles, sound architect as he already was in the theater and on the radio, composed a sound track of exemplary richness and precision.

The major principle of Welles's sound aesthetic, firmly established in his earliest theater productions, was to leave as little room as possible for silence. In *Kane*, the audience's attention is always demanded as much by the sound as by the picture, and a dense sound fabric is never loosened. Hence the abundance, unusual for a 1941 film, of dialogue, music, and other sounds but also, and most important, of their constant intertwining. The *Kane* sound track is characterized by the close interdependence of different components, which Welles blended into an intricate web; it contains no musical cues free from association with other sounds (the only brief exception being the obsessive "perpetual motion" music that accompanies the montage of Susan's jigsaw puzzles), nor any sequences based exclusively on dialogue or on sound effects. Far from remaining separate entities, the different sounds constantly alternate and overlap, both within sequences and during the numerous transitions required by the dramatic structure of the film.

This interweaving can first be observed in the organization of the dialogue, whose energy and density depends upon the elimination, or at least the restriction, of pauses between lines. Welles readily links lines together without permitting the slightest pause between them, and he frequently uses overlapping dialogue, which was already somewhat of a trademark for him, a heritage he later passed down to several generations of actors in theater and film. While theatrical convention calls for an actor to wait for his partner to stop speaking before taking the floor, Welles was one of the first directors of American theater to make abundant use of entangling lines. This technique was particularly evident in his 1937 and 1938 productions of Shakespeare's *Julius Caesar*, Thomas Dekker's *Shoemakers' Holiday*, and William Gillette's *Too Much Johnson*. (He did not confine himself to the sphere of contemporary comedy, where the fashion for overlapping had been set ten years earlier by Ben Hecht and Charles MacArthur's *The Front Page*.) Welles only rarely employed overlapping speech in his radio dramas, since sound and dialogue, which alone define the dramatic setting for each scene, needed to be immediately intelligible to the radio listener. Even so, a quick succession of lines, never permitting the slightest lull, often allowed "The Mercury Theater on the Air" to move at lightning speed. Where film is concerned, Welles had explicitly indicated numerous overlapping lines in the shooting script of his adaptation of Joseph Conrad's *Heart of Darkness* (his first project upon arrival at RKO). His most important predecessor in the use of this technique was Howard Hawks, who had briefly used overlapping dialogue as early as 1930 in a scene of *The Criminal Code* and who periodically resorted to it in his subsequent films, bringing it to a height in *His Girl Friday* (adapted by screenwriter Charles Lederer from *The Front Page*). The latter film was released in January 1940 and may have influenced *Citizen Kane*'s newspaper scenes. However, two major differences enable us to distinguish between the practices of Hawks and Welles. The rapid delivery and interweaving of lines in *His Girl Friday* are heard in the total absence of music until the film's final minutes, when the rhythm of the dialogue, confined from that moment on to two characters, is slowed down. By contrast, the intertwining of the lines in *Citizen Kane* does not preclude a rich musical score. Notice also that Hawks, whose chief aim is speed and exhilaration rather than density of meaning, generally resorts to a subterfuge in order to avoid hindering our comprehension of the dialogue; he regularly includes unnecessary sentence endings or minor interjections such as "Listen to me!" so that no important utterance escapes notice. Welles does not merely allow one line to cut slightly into the next, which is little more than an extension of theatrical convention; instead, he overlaps and deeply embeds one line into another.

This embedding is first established by two "on the spot" scenes in the *Kane* newsreel (Thatcher's testimony at the congressional investigation and Kane's radio interview), and it becomes especially evident in the film's first true talking scene, which takes place in the newsreel projection room. The journalists' conversation is conducted in shadows, from which only Rawlston and Thompson stand out, and the darkness tends to intensify the apparently chaotic intermingling of the dialogue. (In his theater productions, the scenes in which Welles most freely overlapped lines of dialogue were often played in darkness.) This sequence demands straight away an intense concentration as much on the voices as on the pictures. Here, the most important consideration in directing actors is the vocal aspect, and this is only the first instance of such a requirement, for overlapping is the rule in one out of every three lines in *Citizen Kane*.

This is not to say that a measured pace, or even a prolonged pause between lines, is unheard of in the film. Welles simply restricts pauses to scenes containing few or no overlapping lines, whereas he excludes them altogether from scenes in which overlapping predominates. Analogous to the rhythmic alternation in some films between day and night or indoor and outdoor scenes, *Citizen Kane* contains three alternating rhythms of dialogue—three types of scenes, which are characterized either by a delayed succession of lines, a linking of lines, or an overlapping of lines.[2] The distribution of these categories is above all a function of the dramatic chronology, which begins with the speed and verbal density of Kane's years in journalism and moves toward the spare, heavy language of the years passed in isolation in Xanadu. Among the brief scenes in which significant pauses are allowed are those that mark Kane's failed venture into politics and his futile efforts to launch Susan's singing career—for example, the scene when Bernstein chooses the *Inquirer*'s headline for the day after the election, and the dialogue between Kane and Susan after the latter's attempted suicide. Overlapping lines are the rule in the scenes resembling Hollywood comedy that take place during Kane's early years at the *Inquirer*, whereas overlapping disappears from nearly all of the scenes that compose Susan's story.

Citizen Kane goes by much too quickly for all of its lines to be grasped in a single viewing, but very few lines are actually inaudible or thwart the listener's efforts to understand them. Far from flattening out dialogue or rendering it incomprehensible, overlapping constantly accentuates meanings through the very fact of their collision. The technique is characterized by a clarity and precision of organization: never left to chance, it is practiced, through an amount of rehearsal that can only be imagined, down to the individual syllable. Welles virtually never allows one line to cut off another in the middle of a syllable; the interruption usually occurs either between two words or between two syllables of the same word. Between two syllables: in the offices of the *Inquirer*, when Bernstein asks Kane if he has "any answer" to a telegram from a correspondent in Cuba, Kane's reply of "Yes" anticipates the end of the question and coincides with the "-swer" in "answer." Between two words: during the first of a series of breakfasts with her husband, Emily Norton Kane says, "I've never been to six parties in one night in my whole life," and Kane, who has already assured her that she is very beautiful, repeats himself more softly, his "Extremely beautiful" coinciding with her "one night in my whole." One could provide many other examples such as these. With the same precision, Welles links together two sentences that overlap a third. As Kane exits his campaign rally, a politician in the crowd declares, "Jim Gettys isn't even pretending. He isn't scared anymore, he's sick." Kane's son exclaims, "Hello, Pop," at the same time as the words "even pretending," and Kane's reply ("Hello, son, how are you?") extends over the remainder of the line with the exception of the last word.

Welles even goes so far as to overlap three lines one on top of the other, as in the boardinghouse scene in which, in a very dense dialogue, Kane's parents argue in front of Thatcher about their son's future. In the middle of a string of eight consecutive lines, each one of which cuts into the preceding utterance, the father continues to protest while Thatcher, whom he has just interrupted, resumes his reading of the document he intends to have the mother sign:

KANE'S FATHER: *I don't hold with signing my boy away to any bank as guardeen just because . . . we're a little uneducated.*
KANE'S MOTHER: *I want you to stop all this nonsense, Jim.*
THATCHER: *The bank's decision in all matters concerning his education, his place of residence and similar subjects, is to be final.*

The mother's retort momentarily coincides with the father's word "guardeen," but then Thatcher's first two words ("The bank's") seem to drown both the end of the mother's line, which is cut off after the first syllable of "nonsense," and the words ("we're a") with which the father resumes the sentence he had left suspended. Three people are speaking at once, but each of the three voices remains clear and intelligible. As if this density were not sufficient, the muffled shouts of young Charles, who can be seen through the window as he plays war games in the snow, can be heard in the background.

The scene at the boardinghouse relies heavily on depth of focus, making us aware of the overlapping lines of dialogue and, more than in any other scene, the layering of sound sources that attest to the distance and the conflict between the characters. Thatcher confronts Kane's parents in their home while, outside, Charles sporadically shrieks and shouts out military rallying cries that metaphorically express what is at stake in the family altercation.[3] Charles's shouts are often drowned, but become audible now and again and consequently overlap the adults' dialogue. When Charles, who has just yelled out a series of battle cries, shouts, "Old Hickory, that's me!"[4] his sentence begins at exactly the same time as his father, back to the camera, makes his way toward the window and grumbles, "Why I can't raise my own boy is more than I can understand." Jim Kane momentarily obstructs our view of the child, but young Charles, who stresses the last syllable of his shout, speaks so firmly that his words are more perceptible than those of his father: in this case the faraway utterance is more easily heard than the statement made in close proximity.

Emphasis is a determining factor in our perception of overlapping syllables, words, and phrases: it permits the interweaving of lines that are not necessarily of equal rhythm and intensity. When Leland, following Bernstein's example, interrupts Kane and Thatcher's conversation at the *Inquirer*, he accentuates the second syllable of "borrow" in his first line ("I'll just borrow a cigar") so strongly that his "-row" exactly coincides with Bernstein's "how do you do," as the latter begins to reply to the banker. The repetitions of "er" that delay certain responses and consequently draw out sentences have a similar function. When Herbert Carter introduces the new boss to the journalists of the *Inquirer* ("The— er—new—er—new publisher") and Kane asks him to have the journalists sit back down ("Ask them to sit down, will you, please?"), Kane's entire sentence coincides with Carter's "new— er—new." A character entirely recreated during the shooting of the film, Herbert Carter is the favored victim of such overlapping and interruptions. When Bernstein, Leland, and a furniture-moving man successively jostle the old gentleman, asking him to let them by as they move Kane's things into his office, they punctuate the scene with nine repetitions of the words "Excuse me," while Carter does his best to continue a constantly interrupted sentence: "Bu—but a morning newspaper, Mr. Kane—after all, we're . . ."/"Excuse me"/". . . we—we're practically closed for twelve hours . . ."/"Excuse me"/"a day."

Overlapping is the ideal weapon in the balance of power between characters, who assert dominance either by cutting into a speech (sometimes cutting it off entirely) or by stifling another character's attempt to do the same—as "Boss" Jim W. Gettys expertly manages to do in conversation with Susan, and as the curator of the Thatcher Memorial Library does when speaking to Thompson. The best way for one character to assert influence over another is to complete a sentence the other has begun, a method of which Welles, the actor and director, is particularly fond. The most striking example of the technique occurs during the next-to-last breakfast episode, when Emily says, "Really, Charles, people will think . . ." and Kane puts an end to the conversation by finishing the sentence for her: "What I tell them to think."

The quick succession or overlapping of lines results in a rapid pace diminished only by techniques that are themselves rapid: a pause need not be prolonged in order to be felt as such, and, in a scene governed by overlapping lines, the occasional recourse to simple quick succession serves as a turning point leading to the reacceleration of the dialogue. The pause is therefore more likely to be found within a line than between two lines. Throughout, Welles and his actors show great flexibility in their use of hesitations, slowed rhythms, and momentary interruptions. The dignified Thatcher is the only character whose speech escapes almost entirely from these mannerisms. At the opposite extreme, Carter's speech is heavily affected by hesitation, as when he begins his lines by stammering ("I—I—I can't see that the function of a respectable newspaper . . .") or interrupts them by groping for words ("My—er—my—er—little—er—private sanctum is at your disposal, but I—I—I—I don't understand"). Among all the characters in Welles's films, only Joseph K. in *The Trial* and Silence in *Chimes at Midnight* occasionally go further in their stammering.

The few truly sustained pauses between lines in *Citizen Kane* occur at the very end of the dialogue between Kane and Susan at the time of their first meeting, when the young woman recalls her dead mother. This scene is also the only instance in which Welles permits himself a succession of reverse-angle close-ups. His rejection of regularly alternating lines of dialogue is therefore homologous with his reluctance to alternate reverse-angles and his scarce use of close-ups. The few intense close-ups in the film tend to emphasize a pause that sometimes precedes a verbal twist at the end of a sequence, as when Kane explains that, at the pace of one million dollars in annual losses, he will go out of business in sixty years, or when Leland predicts that his friend's Declaration of Principles will reveal itself to be as important as the Constitution, the Declaration of Independence, or his own first report card at school. In other words, the overlapping of lines, even more than the layering of different types of sound or sound levels, functions as a sonic counterpart to the visual depth of field.

The occasional absence of overlapping lines, however, in no way leads to a lack of visual depth. As mentioned above, overlapping is notably absent in the scenes at Xanadu, where a sense of spatial depth and dimension is provided by echoes. These echoes reign supreme in Kane's castle, as well as in the Thatcher Memorial Library and on the staircase of the love nest from which Kane bellows his threats to Gettys; but they are only one, relatively unspectacular aspect of a more general technique employed by the film: the frequent distortion of voices. Here again the stylistic device is established early on, by the first spoken word (Charles Foster Kane's last word), which is ostensibly whispered, but whose reverberation endows "Rosebud" with a paradoxical sonority and resonance.[5] Elsewhere, the speeches of the labor leader at Union Square and of Kane at Madison Square Garden are affected by the reverberations of loudspeakers. Voice quality is also altered by Leland's intoxication after the electoral defeat, which causes him to say "dramatic crimitism" instead of "dramatic criticism,"[6] and by Susan's raging toothache, which causes her to pronounce it as a "soothache." Everything, whether the noise of the rotary press in the composing room at the *Inquirer*, the hubbub of a stag party, or a glass partition or piece of furniture between two speakers, conspires to distort voices, making them strain or shout in order to be intelligible. The dialogue in *Citizen Kane* is thus made consistently eccentric, and the overlapping lines and atypical voices contribute to the film's unique style.

Beyond these considerations, the idea of overlapping can be extended to *Citizen Kane*'s entire sound design, which involves a thorough blending of various sound phenomena. The interaction of music with voices and sound effects, or of music within itself as certain melodies intermingle, facilitates transitions between one sequence and the next, whereas an overlapping and layering of speech and sound effects tends to dominate within dialogue scenes. Because dialogue and music alone are sufficient to fill the entire texture of the film's sound, ambient sounds and sound effects in *Kane* are not intended to form a simple background, nor do they merely alleviate the silence of passages devoid of dialogue or music. Rather, their role is to intensify the film's density of sound.[7] Certain scenes, such as the stag party at the *Inquirer* and Kane's election speech at Madison Square Garden, make use of a hubbub of voices or indistinct murmuring; but Welles, whose goal is to produce readable sound that is in no way a prisoner to realism, most often resorts to clearly defined, expressive sound effects which he chooses and inserts at will. By the same token, many sounds that would necessarily be produced by the actions on screen are not heard at all. The moving of Kane's possessions into Carter's office, accompanied by nondi-egetic polka music,[8] is accomplished without the slightest noise after the initial crashing of the furniture that collapses around Bernstein. As in his radio shows, Welles sometimes uses a single sound to color an entire scene: the clatter of horses' hooves as Kane and Emily leave in a barouche after their brief visit to the *Inquirer*, or the breaking waves that punctuate the dirge-like blues music playing behind a silent procession of black cars on their way to a picnic. Young Kane's departure from his home in Colorado to a new life in New York is suggested by two faraway train whistles and a rumbling locomotive mingled with background music and a moaning wind, while on the screen we see two shots of an abandoned, snow-covered sled.

Such examples indicate that sounds in *Citizen Kane* are not always realistically motivated by the images on the screen, or even by specific settings that can be imagined offscreen. True, many sounds merely accompany the visible gestures and movements of characters; seldom attracting the viewer's full attention, they serve a secondary value behind pictures. To a certain degree, the same rule applies to atmospheric sounds of wind or rain, which tend to serve the visual mise-en-scène. By contrast, many other sounds are symbolic and closely interdependent, each called for in turn by the sounds with which they come into contact. Every isolated or intermittent sound is rigorously timed to the dialogue—or, more rarely, to the music—and fitted into an intricate sound pattern.

During the course of a scene, sound effects are sometimes inserted in the middle of the actors' lines, enriching the already dense web formed by the dialogue. Like the occasional distortion of voices, this technique complements the overlapping of the dialogue; indeed it tends to be reserved for scenes in which the characters speak one after the other in quick succession. In order to be more audible, many of the briefest sounds (although this can also be said of a sustained clap of thunder) take advantage either of short respites that separate two lines or of pauses within sentences. As we shall see further on, they particularly enhance the deliberately morose scenes in which Thompson interviews Bernstein and Leland. They become especially noticeable when they are produced by the characters, as when Kane, during the second episode of the breakfast montage, throws a match into an ashtray as he pauses in the middle of a sentence ("Emily, my dear—your only co-respondent is the *Inquirer*"). Some of these inserted sound effects are used as ironic punctuation: the boat siren heard in the background during a newsreel interview with Kane serves to undercut his pomposity by filling in the pause between his motto, "I'm an American, always been an American," and his question to the reporter (played by Gregg Toland): "Anything else?"

Sustained intermittent sound effects often accompany or accentuate a particular sentence, and they strictly conform to its structure. This sonic accentuation, used to reinforce and intensify language, is inherited from Welles's years in theater, where he achieved similar effects through the use of percussion. When intermittent sounds break off, they tend to call attention to the dialogue immediately following their cessation. Thus, during Thompson's interview with Bernstein, the sound of thunder coincides sometimes with several lines and sometimes with an exchange of short sentences, but it never cuts a sentence or a word in half. Similarly, during the aforementioned newsreel/radio interview with Kane in "News on the March," a blaring siren drowns one of the interviewer's questions as well as the first sentence of Kane's reply; it then breaks off, giving emphasis to Kane's second sentence, in which he prophesies—from the vantage point of 1935—that Europe will not go to war.

Added during sound mixing and editing, the sound effects interspersed throughout many of the sequences give expressive touches to individual phrases and lines. They perform this function with considerable flexibility, the more so since, in most instances, their effect is almost subliminal. Thus, in the first scene between Thompson and Bernstein, the sound of a teletype machine replaces the sound of thunder as background noise and is meticulously placed with respect to the characters' words, which it never interrupts. Nevertheless, it occasionally stands out more clearly: five very rapid, regular beats punctuate Bernstein's words ("Mr. Leland never had a nickel"). Another beat, immediately following Bernstein's rhetorical question ("You know who you ought to see?"), gives the appearance of an anticipated reply before Bernstein himself responds, "Mr. Leland." The attack of Bernstein's words seems to coincide with the teletype machine, thus creating a very marked long-short-short-long rhythm.

On the hospital terrace where Thompson meets Leland, three recurrent offscreen sounds indicating ambient noise serve complementary purposes, providing a more clear punctuation: creaking or grating vibrations underlining individual sentences; metallic clangs heard in pauses between sentences; and the occasional distant noise of boat sirens. The sirens have realistic justification: the address of the hospital on 180th Street and the brief low-angle shot showing Thompson in front of the building indicate that we are near the Hudson River, on whose waters, before the upward tilt of the camera, two boats can indeed be seen. The other sounds, however, have no clearly identifiable onscreen source. At one point, a siren lightens the solemnity of the word "Xanadu" when Leland speaks it after pretending to be unable to remember the name of Kane's castle. Two very slight metallic sounds, faint as they are, establish a double punctuation on either side of the word "singer" when Leland explains to Thompson, "That whole thing about Susie being an opera singer, that was trying to prove

something." In effect, they serve as an aural equivalent to the
derisive quotation marks that the *Chronicle* had placed around Susan's supposed profession, which Kane had undertaken to remove
by launching her opera career. When Leland quotes the front
page of the *Chronicle* (of which the viewer has already caught a
fleeting glimpse in "News on the March"), a creaking sound
breaks off after the words CANDIDATE KANE CAUGHT IN LOVE NEST
WITH . . . and helps to stress the next words: "quote, 'SINGER,' un-
quote."

One of the film's most obvious uses of expressive sound involves the typewriter on which Kane completes Leland's opera
review for the *Chicago Inquirer*. The clacking typewriter lends itself
to frequent sound variations, to the point where it alone provides
a sonic armature or framework for the scene. In the office of the
drunk and sleeping Leland, Kane asks Bernstein for a typewriter.
Welles cuts immediately to the hammering of the keys, which,
with an exaggeratedly slow rhythm and an angry force, type out
the letters of the word "weak" in an enormous, emphatic close-
up. Cut to Leland's office, where Leland wakes and begins to speak
with Bernstein while Kane continues to type in the room beyond.
The formerly isolated foreground noise now becomes distant, and
from this moment on the sound of typing is accompanied by the
regularly spaced returns of the typewriter carriage. Without exception, the more prolonged sound of the carriage is placed after
the end of a rejoinder in the dialogue. The final confrontation
between Kane and Leland, who will never see each other again,
begins with a fresh and quite loud return of the carriage, which
exactly coincides with a cut to the outer office and which seems
all the more violent because Kane and the typewriter are now
seen as large elements in the foreground. The typing noises resume; then another carriage return immediately precedes Kane's
greeting to Leland, which he utters with his back turned: "Hello,
Jedediah." Kane demonstrates his control over Leland by ceasing
to type while speaking and by resuming immediately afterward,
thus partly drowning Leland's reply: "Hello, Charlie, I didn't
know we were speaking." Kane allows a brief lull to set in before
his last rejoinder: "Sure we're speaking, Jedediah. You're fired."

His line is followed by a final, exaggeratedly drawn-out carriage return, which puts an end to the conversation and to the two men's friendship. The skillfully calculated rebuke fits almost musically into the rhythm set by Kane's occasional realignments of the carriage and the sheet of typing paper as he speaks the last line. After five staccato sounds in a distinct rhythm—quarter note, quarter note, triplet (dotted eighth note, sixteenth note, quarter note)—the sixth note, which is called for by this rhythm, is withheld. The beat falls into a tense, electric silence, until Kane finally adds, "You're fired," and begins to work the carriage. The typing sounds resume and carry over *diminuendo* throughout the slow lap-dissolve into the next sequence, in which Leland finishes telling his story to Thompson; but during this dissolve, the sound of the carriage, having fulfilled its purpose, is no longer useful and is purely and simply eliminated. The image of Kane continuing to type disappears from the upper right-hand corner of the screen as he stretches his hand toward the carriage lever.

Beyond the role they play in any given scene, the interactions of sounds are crucial to the editing process because they are systematically used to establish transitions between scenes. Besides the tendency to overlap lines and avoid pauses, a basic principle in this film is the virtually uninterrupted movement between sequences, with few pronounced breaks. Two memorable jarring sounds provide exceptions to the rule. First, the title "News on the March," accompanied by loud theme music, leaps out after the slow, silent fade to black that follows Kane's death. Next, a deafening clap of thunder follows Rawlston's final instructions to Thompson: "Good. Rosebud, dead or alive. It'll probably turn out to be a very simple thing." These shocks, marking unusual transitions that employ direct cuts rather than dissolves, serve to punctuate and mark off the film's successive prologues (Kane's death and the newsreel, which are followed by the investigation itself).

As if in immediate compensation, however, the first foray into the El Rancho cabaret involves several sound sources that are intricately woven together. Two musical cues, the second of which momentarily drowns the first, are successively added to the sounds of the thunder and the rain: first, we hear a few discordant measures of nondiegetic music composed by Bernard Herrmann for high-pitched violins; then we hear a diegetic, instrumental arrangement of "It Can't Be Love" (the song later played by a small jazz ensemble during the picnic in the Everglades). As the camera seems to pass through the glass roof, the rain breaks off and the sound of Susan's coughing mingles with the rumbling thunder. Finally, the headwaiter's voice takes over as he introduces Thompson to Susan, and the ensuing conversation proceeds over the jazz music. In effect, the sound track conveys the same No Trespassing message as the sign at the beginning of the film; through a fog of sonic confusion, paralleled on the visual level by the glass roof blurred by lightning and rain, Thompson vainly attempts to pursue his investigation.

A large number of the sound transitions in *Citizen Kane* conform to two models, neither of which, however brilliantly achieved, is unique to the film: sometimes Welles begins a new sequence with a musical cue prompted by a line of dialogue at the end of the previous sequence, and sometimes he begins it with a line of dialogue that overlaps with music from the preceding sequence. In both cases, the music stops precisely between two sentences or phrases. A variation on the first approach can be heard during Bernstein's testimony, when the flood of his memories into the present is anticipated by nondiegetic ragtime music heard alongside his last sentence to Thompson: "He was with Mis-" [enter the ragtime] "-ter Kane and me the first day Mister Kane took over the *Inquirer*." The brief, high-pitched clarinet that overlaps his declaration is a *piano* prelude to the actual theme, which swells *forte* on the trombones immediately at the end of his sentence.

Throughout the film, Welles devises many other particularly inventive transitions, often designed to allow sequences to begin or to end in an imperceptible manner. Triggered by the last words of a letter from Kane that Thatcher reads aloud while facing the camera ("I think it would be fun to run a newspaper"), an Offenbach-style "gallop" (Bernard Herrmann's term) accompanies the banker's increasingly indignant reactions to a series of *Inquirer* headlines, and comes to an end just as Thatcher puts a question to Kane in what is already the next sequence: "Is that really your idea of how to run a newspaper?" Thatcher's near-yell concludes a musical development, which it endows with a rebound effect, an unforeseen extension. After the virtuosity of the preceding montage, another lightning-speed progression and a striking example of *Citizen Kane*'s constant bombardment of the viewer's senses prevents the audience from catching its breath. The "gallop" is thus symmetrically enclosed on either side by two lines spoken by Thatcher that answer each other. Another stunning musical cue, the "can-can scherzo" (again, Herrmann's terminology), is played behind the reflections of Kane, Leland, and Bernstein as they gaze into a *Chronicle* display window showing a photograph of that newspaper's staff of reporters. The nondiegetic music ends by blending with the diegetic sound of a flashbulb, and the camera pulls back to show the same *Chronicle* team, now purchased by the *Inquirer*, being photographed for an identical shot six years later. After a *pizzicato* swell of strings, the sound of the flash-bulb explosion intermingles with an E played simultaneously by the violins and the percussion, which brilliantly concludes the scherzo. This sound, which occurs between two of Kane's lines, also separates the point at which he appears to be still speaking to Leland and Bernstein ("Well, tonight, six years later, I got my candy, all of it") from the moment when he unambiguously addresses the assembled reporters ("Welcome, gentlemen, to the *Inquirer*"). The effect here is similar to the one in the earlier sequence involving Thatcher, when the line "Is that really your idea of how to run a newspaper?" pinpoints the moment at which Thatcher proves to be speaking no longer to himself but to Kane.

Two of the film's most abrupt transitions are executed by distorted sounds. The theme music that concludes "News on the March" is distorted by the sudden stopping of the projector, which breaks off to reveal the noise of people coughing and moving about in a projection room; the music seems to disintegrate, not only into the sound of its own subsiding, but also into the ambient sounds that lead up to the journalists' conversation. Likewise, at the end of the cacophonous musical montage that sums up Susan's musical tour of the United States, Susan's loss of her voice and the consequent silencing of the orchestra that accompanied her causes her song to dissolve into mere noise. This transformation segues into the sound of her labored breathing after her suicide attempt, and the succession of the two sounds creates a strong link between them.

As Jim Gettys exits down the stairs of the love nest after his confrontation with Kane, the latter screams three times at his opponent that he will send him to Sing Sing. Kane's last "Sing Sing," already muffled when we cut to the outside of the house, is silenced ("Sing Si—") when Gettys shuts the front door, and then is immediately mocked by an auto horn honking from somewhere offscreen—actually, two honks so close together that they give the illusion of a single sound whose intensity and tone resemble Kane's voice and reduce it to a kind of squeak. Despite the absence of any sounds of car engines, this honking horn is instantly offset by others, which are softer but just as deftly inserted. As Gettys and Emily exchange formalities in the doorway ("Have you a car, Mrs. Kane?"/"Yes, thank you."/"Good night."/ "Good night"), two distinct horns can be heard. The first has the tone of a clarinet: high-pitched and prolonged, it coincides with Gettys's first line. The second, on a much lower pitch, serves as punctuation after Emily's "Yes, thank you." Again, a shrill honk emanates from the first hypothetical car. This D is then followed by an instrumental C of the same intensity, which can be interpreted as a final honking horn. The horn "music," which is stripped of any musical line, chromatically strings together the conjunct notes to the initial D. It does not make itself known as music, however, until the first brass *crescendo* passage of nondiegetic orchestral score, which seems to follow it and grow out of the street noise.

The interplay of sounds becomes even more complex in two of the most striking series of transitions, each ending with what Peter Cowie has dubbed a "lightning mix"[9]—a technique through which one character's line of dialogue, thanks to a particularly conspicuous cut, is completed in another place (and, generally, at another time) by another character. Thus when the young

Kane sourly wishes Thatcher a "Merry Christmas," Thatcher completes the statement seventeen years later with "And a Happy New Year," and as the camera pulls back we see that he is dictating a letter to his secretary. Likewise, Leland's campaign speech in support of Kane is interrupted after the words, ". . . who entered upon this campaign . . ." and completed by Kane's own speech, ". . . with one purpose only." The candidate's voice is amplified by the immense reverberations of Madison Square Garden, sweeping away the less powerful voice of his friend.

In these two cuts, a sense of coherence seems to derive from our perception of two parts of a sentence as one whole, according to its meaning and its melodic curve. But in both cases the abrupt second part of the sentence entirely obliterates the first, and the two elements seem more opposed than joined. Paradoxically, the lightning mix is a technique that separates the elements it is supposed to connect. To create a seamless or inevitable effect, it needs the presence of other sound sources and other scenes that can be fitted into a chain of transitions. Thus we have three scenes leading up to Thatcher's "Happy New Year": the scene of young Charles's departure for New York, suggested by the sound of train whistles and the image of a snow-covered sled; the scene of young Charles being offered a sled as a Christmas present from Thatcher; and the scene of Thatcher dictating a letter to his secretary. At the end of the first scene, after the noise of the train has waned and given way to Herrmann's music and the moaning of wind, we hear the chiming of small bells. This nearly musical sound[10] is followed by the sound of wrapping paper being torn from a gift and then, after a short pause, by Thatcher's "Well, Charles, Merry Christmas." The third scene, showing Thatcher dictating the New Year's wish, not only completes the child's resentful "Merry Christmas" but also abruptly cuts off the jingling bells, so that it creates a combined effect of disruption and continuity.

The second example, in which a temporal ellipsis is stressed with mounting strength and conspicuousness, brings four shots and three transitions into play: Susan singing upon Kane's request; Susan continuing to sing a few months later in a more luxurious apartment while accompanying herself on a better piano; Leland's campaign speech; and Kane's speech. The ellipsis between the first two shots is quite discreet: Rossini's aria, *Una voce poco fa*, from *The Barber of Seville*, continues as if nothing has happened, but in Italian rather than in English. The transition from one language to the other is skillfully carried out as the "o" of the second "Lindor" is sung:

> *Yes, Lindor shall be mine*
> *I have sworn it for weal or woe*
> *Yes, Lindor*
> *Lo giurai, la vincerò.*[11]

The ticking of a wall clock in Susan's new apartment beats approximate time to the embellished rhythm on the eighth notes, and fills in the lull between the end of the aria and the beginning of Kane's solitary applause. This applause, before being taken over by the more generous clapping of the small group assembled around Leland, coincides with the regular sounds of the clock. The ticking thus seems to set a rhythm both for Kane and for the group of potential voters. The applause of Leland's audience stops independently during his final words (between "who entered" and "this campaign"), but continuity with the next shot is soon reinforced by a quick burst of applause from Kane's audience at Madison Square Garden. The lightning mixes are thus strongly marked by the breaking off of a sound: in the first mix, tiny Christmas bells; in the second, applause. They are further characterized by the presence of a large range of sounds of which the last sound becomes a strong culmination.

The dense interpenetration of dialogue, music, and sound effects that prevails in *Citizen Kane* is made possible only by the virtual elimination of a fourth element, silence. Despite (or because of) its relative absence, this silence must be considered an important sonic element in its own right. It participates in the meaningful interweaving of sounds in the film, as we can hear in its rare uses, most of which are linked to the Rosebud mystery.

Citizen Kane arises from silence. After the opening logo and signature sound effects of the production company (the letters "An RKO Radio Picture" are spelled out in Morse code), no sound accompanies the two title cards and the black screen that precede the first measures of Bernard Herrmann's score. The film's initial segment is in fact bracketed by silence: the absence of sound at the beginning is answered by an equivalent absence at the end, just before the cry "News on the March!" Notice also that the nondiegetic music in this prologue stops abruptly when a light in one of Xanadu's windows goes out. This interruption, while irrational in one sense, is also necessary, its primary function being to balance the entire prologue with two points of accentuation. Had Kane's final whisper been surrounded by two phrases of atmospheric background music, the effect would have been quite different, lacking in surprise or shock. As it stands, the unexpected sound shift at the climax makes us feel the utter inevitability of the unfettered "Rosebud."

In the last minutes of the film, we encounter two more stretches of silence, which symmetrically frame Kane's ransacking of Susan's room after her departure. The first image of Raymond's story has barely appeared on screen when we hear the sudden scream of a cockatoo, which fluffs its feathers and flies away.[12] The cockatoo's cry is followed by the sound of Susan's footsteps fading into the distance, and by the butler's footsteps approaching down Xanadu's hallway. These effects give way to a moment of silence, into which the viewer/listener is almost brutally thrust. Kept in reserve for such a long time, this silence imparts a maximum intensity to the shot in which Raymond watches Kane's motionless silhouette at the other end of the exaggeratedly long hallway. The silence persists while Kane, overwhelmed, stands without reacting. Tension is then suddenly released by the explosion of his unbridled fury—the only point of the film at which sound effects are permitted to completely dominate the foreground of a scene. These sounds progressively mount in intensity before subsiding again into silence. First we hear a discreet click as Kane closes a suitcase on Susan's bed, and then a crash as he lifts the suitcase and throws it across the room; a series of more violent but still isolated sounds follows, as when Kane successively throws three more suitcases to the floor and rips off the bedspread, pulling it toward himself. A *crescendo* ensues as Kane upsets and pulls out lamps, paintings, mirrors, furniture. Then a momentary pause, filled only by the sound of heavy breathing as Kane looks around for whatever might be left for him to destroy. This is followed by the *decrescendo* of the last few objects he overturns; next comes a fragment of silence when he sees the glass snowstorm paperweight and grasps it in his hands, and, finally, some faint sounds when he steps on a broken chip of porcelain and staggers against a small table. The final pivot of the narrative, the "Rosebud" uttered by Kane in a whisper as he holds the paperweight in his hand, is again framed by silence—a silence of surrender and resignation, barely disturbed by the echo of Kane's footsteps as he enters the corridors of Xanadu only to depart in turn from the film.

This final silence, though necessarily less pronounced than the one leading up to the destruction of Susan's room, is by no means without structural importance. The two Rosebuds whispered by Kane and placed nearly two hours apart in the film are treated in similar fashion. In the opening segment, "Rosebud" is framed by a brief silence. A few moments before the silence descends, snowflakes whirl on the screen, the nondiegetic music discreetly comes to an end, and we hear a delicate and barely audible tinkling of small bells. Always associated with snowflakes, these bells briefly reappear and blend with Herrmann's music when it returns after Kane has uttered his last word. The sound of the first whispered "Rosebud" is therefore preciously set in a triple encasement: the nondiegetic music, the effect of bells, and the silence. The second "Rosebud" is similarly surrounded by a double layer of sound and silence. Just as the coldness of many of the sounds, including the musical elements, in *Citizen Kane* is suggestive of glass or of the paperweight Kane associates with Rosebud, so the embedding of one sound into others is suggestive of something placed in a bubble or a glass cocoon. Meanwhile, the dissipation and dispersion of sound corresponds less to a jigsaw puzzle than to the scattered shards of a broken glass ball.

Although each sound element of the film constitutes its own network, voices, music, sound effects, and silence have no independence in *Citizen Kane*. Rather, they combine to endow the film with a carefully planned sound structure. The sonic bridges that link the sequences together permit the film to flow, like the gold of the Colorado Lode, "in an unending stream," and even the smallest sequence constitutes a unit in which every sound contributes to the whole as a result of its placement, its volume, and its relation to other sounds. *Citizen Kane* contains not a single moment at which the demand on our attention is left to the image alone. This being the case, no element of the sound design can be modified without compromising the film as a whole. While a dubbed version of *The Magnificent Ambersons* has been created in France by rerecording not only the dialogue but also the sound effects and music score, no sound translation has been attempted in the case of *Citizen Kane*. The unhappy result of such a translation can be observed in the dubbed German, Spanish, and Italian versions of the film, which destroy the intermingling of the dialogue as well as the interplay of the voices with the sound effects and the music—so much so that in more than one transition, the producers of the Italian version had to cut a number of shots in order to eliminate untranslatable sound-image relationships. *Citizen Kane* is, par exellence, a film impossible to dub; its web of sounds is too perfectly woven to allow for the removal of a single thread.

Notes

This essay was translated by Hope Wasburn. It is reprinted with slight modifications from a book written in collaboration with Jean-Pierre Berthomé, and it greatly benefited from his remarks.

1. This essay does not deal with Herrmann's score because the book from which it is taken also contains a lengthy chapter on the film's music. That chapter can be found in English translation in Ronald Gottesman, ed., *Perspectives on "Citizen Kane"* (New York: Hall, 1996).

2. The only scene to intermingle these three different arrangements of lines, one of the longest and also one of the climaxes of the film, is the only scene to depend almost entirely on dialogue. It is the

virtuoso four-voice confrontation in the love nest at 184 West 74th Street, during which Susan, unable to get a word in, repeatedly asks, "What about me?" while Kane, Emily, and Gettys sort out their futures and hers without taking her presence into account.

3. Charles's war cries refer to Andrew Jackson, pioneer of American independence and champion of individual rights. Even more transparently, they refer to the Civil War: "The Union forever!"

4. Old Hickory was Andrew Jackson's nickname.

5. Robert L. Carringer, *The Making of Citizen Kane* (Berkeley: University of California Press, 1985), p. 104, reveals that "this extremely resonant whispering sound was created in the rerecording console by combining two separate tracks of Welles's voice with different reverberation times."

6. According to Joseph Cotten, who explains in several accounts how the director had put him into a state of extreme fatigue in order to appear inebriated, Welles put to good use an accidental slip of the tongue that occurred during shooting.

7. Careful not to resort to the standard sound effects in the RKO sound library, Welles specially invited Harold Essman, one of his radiophonic sound-effects engineers, to come from CBS in order to add some of the most unusual sound effects during postproduction.

8. "Diegetic sound" refers to any sound (such as the crashing of furniture around Bernstein as he enters the *Inquirer* office) that appears to come from the story space itself; "nondiegetic sound" refers to any sound (such as orchestral background music) that comes from outside the story space.

9. In *The Cinema of Orson Welles* (New York: Barnes, 1997).

10. Although its exact timing has been changed, it is indicated in Herrmann's score.

11. The singing of "Lindor" is not drawn out in Rossini's score, which has long been overembellished by virtuoso singers. Here, its protraction allows *Sì, Lindoro mio sarà* to be translated simply as "Yes, Lindor."

12. The bird call cuts into the last word of Raymond's narration ("Like the time his wife left him"), but, as in many other similar cases (the collapse of a stack of furniture, or a door slamming in Xanadu), it comes after the intrusive consonant, so that the word is implicitly completed.

The Politics of Magic

Orson Welles's Allegories of Anti-Fascism

MICHAEL DENNING

◆ ◆ ◆

The Aesthetics of Anti-Fascism

THE RHETORIC OF FASCISM and anti-fascism runs throughout Welles's career. "Our *Julius Caesar* gives a picture of the same kind of hysteria that exists in certain dictator-ruled countries of today," a Mercury press release asserted of the 1937 modern-dress production. The most famous scene in the Mercury *Julius Caesar* was the killing of Cinna the poet (played by Norman Lloyd) by the mob. One critic wrote that it was "a scene which for pure power and sinister meaning has never been surpassed in the American theatre"; "not even the Group Theater in all their frenzy against dictators," another wrote, "ever devised a more thrilling scene than that in which the poet, Cinna, is swallowed up by an angry mob." "It's the same mob," Welles told the *New York Times*, "that hangs and burns Negroes in the South, the same mob that maltreats the Jews in Germany. It's the Nazi mob anywhere." When Welles went to Hollywood two years later, his first project, the unfinished film of *Heart of Darkness*, was, in his own words, "a parable of fascism": "the picture," he told his assistant Herbert Drake, "is, frankly, an attack on the Nazi system." Three decades later, Welles told Peter Bogdanovich that *Touch of Evil* (1958) was "if anything *too clearly* antifascist." But, Welles continued, "the French are convinced it's the absolute proof that I'm a fascist."[1]

It is not surprising to discover that during Welles's brief career as a political commentator his great theme was fascism. Touring the United States in 1944 and 1945, he lectured on "The Survival of Fascism" and "The Nature of the Enemy." These lectures do not reveal Welles to be a profound or original political theorist; rather, they should be interpreted as a compendium of political narratives and metaphors by which Welles and his Popular Front audiences understood fascism. Thus, they offer a way of understanding the lineaments of the anti-fascist aesthetic that informs Welles's plays, broadcasts, and films. Fascism, for Welles and for the Popular Front, was a matter of politics *and* aesthetics.

Welles elaborated several tangled and contradictory accounts of fascism. The first, which might be called the gangster theory of fascism, had long been part of Popular Front common sense: a classic instance was Dashiell Hammett's *Red Harvest*. As Welles tells the story:

> A group of industrialists finance a group of gangsters to break trade-unionism, to check the threat of Socialism, the menace of communism or the possibility of democracy. . . . When the gangsters succeed at what they were paid to do, they turn on the men who paid them. . . . [T]he puppet masters find their creatures taking on a terrible life of their own.

This story reminds us that anti-fascism was not simply an *international* politics for the Popular Front. Welles, like many of his contemporaries, saw a continuum between European fascism and domestic fascism, between Hitler and Hearst, the Brown Shirts and the Black Legion. When Welles became a political commentator in 1945 and 1946, he regularly wrote and spoke about the

dangers of American fascism, warning that "even the uncondi-
tional surrender of the Axis will not automatically destroy the
fascist principle."[2]

However, Welles's fictions rarely drew directly on this account
of industrialists hiring gangsters. Rather, Welles was more apt to
draw on a second definition: "What is Fascism? . . . In essence it is
nothing more than the original sin of civilization, the celebration
of power for its own sake." The confrontation with power for
power's sake—the touch of evil in Welles's moral universe—was
the core of *Heart of Darkness*, Welles's "parable of fascism" (which,
though never filmed, was twice produced by Welles as a radio
play). Welles's scenario not only moved the story to Latin America, but translated the imperialist boundary between civilization
and the jungle to a boundary between civilization and fascism.
This fascination with the face of power also informed both of
Welles's characteristic—and apparently contrary—genres: the revived classic and the pulp thriller, each of which is central to
Popular Front anti-fascism.[3]

Welles's revival of the classics was not only an act of preser-
vation in the face of fascism, a defense of civilization against bar-
barism. For Welles, the Elizabethan tragedies and histories of
Shakespeare and Marlowe offered a critique of fascism's worship
of power, and their giant protagonists paralleled the "great dictators" of modern times. *Julius Caesar*, the Mercury manifesto asserted, "might well be subtitled 'Death of a Dictator.' . . . In our
production the stress will be on the social implications inherent
in the history of Caesar and on the atmosphere of personal greed,
fear and hysteria that surround[s] a dictatorial regime." "Welles
played Brutus," Alfred Kazin recalled:

> and Brutus was a liberal intellectual in a shabby overcoat
> plotting against Caesar, who was a Fascist dictator in a garish
> Middle European military uniform; Brutus was the nervous
> thread of the action, he was the conspirator, the assassin,
> the general, the suicide, whose movements incarnated the
> disturbance of our time.[4]

The tale of the "great dictator" haunted the Popular Front imagination, informing Chaplin's *The Great Dictator* (1940) and Peter Blume's surrealist history painting, *The Eternal City* (1937), with its grotesque portrait of Mussolini growing out of a classical landscape. These narratives drew not only on the fascist dictators Hitler, Franco, and Mussolini, but on the flamboyance and popular notoriety of the "robber barons" like J. P. Morgan, the Du Ponts' Liberty League, and William Randolph Hearst; the fear and loathing of radio demagogues like Father Charles Coughlin and Huey Long; and the fascination with the giant protagonists of the Soviet Revolution and its aftermath—Lenin, Stalin, and Trotsky. Though Welles played the dictator's foil in *Julius Caesar*—he was Brutus to Joseph Holland's Mussolini-like Caesar—he more often played the giant figure himself: he was, as he told BBC interviewer Leslie Megahey, a "king actor," one who had to play authoritative roles. Welles's roles combine a political demonology with overtones of Shakespearean tragedy, gothic supermen, and, with his heavy makeup, horror movie monsters.[5]

Welles's gigantic hero-villains were both fascinating and repulsive, tricksters that disobeyed any straightforward political logic. As a result, they were the subject of continual political controversy. Welles himself told a reporter that "Caesar was a great man. Why present him otherwise just because the play is anti-Caesar? That is . . . the error of left-wing melodrama, wherein the villains are cardboard Simon Legrees."[6] Two years earlier, Welles had played a ruined capitalist driven to suicide by the 1932 bank failures in Archibald MacLeish's *Panic*. One performance of *Panic* was followed by a debate, sponsored by the radical New Theater League and the *New Masses*, over the political significance of the play's focus on the individual tragedy of the capitalist, McGafferty. A similar controversy erupted before the 1938 Mercury production of *Danton's Death*, as the Mercury company argued about the parallels between the conflict of Robespierre and Danton and that of Stalin and Trotsky: as a result of Marc Blitzstein's objections, the script was eventually revised.

Welles's great dictators turned up not only in his classical revivals but in his pulp thrillers, the series of *film noir* melodramas that included *Journey into Fear* (1943), *The Stranger* (1946), *Lady from Shanghai* (1948), the film and radio versions of *The Third Man* (1949, 1951), *Mr. Arkadin* (1955), and *Touch of Evil* (1958). "More or less voluntarily, you know," Welles later remarked, "I've played a lot of unsavory types. I detest Harry Lime, that little black market hustler, all of these horrible men I've interrupted. . . . Quinlan [in *Touch of Evil*] is the incarnation of everything I struggle against, politically and morally speaking." But Welles's performances always had an element of sympathy with the devil: "in melodrama, one's sympathy is drawn forcibly to the villain." He was, he admitted, "more than the devil's advocate": "in becoming these characters, I transfigure them by giving them the best I have. But I detest what they are." The fascination and repulsion evoked by Hearst, Morgan, Hitler, Mussolini, Stalin, Trotsky, and Roosevelt gave Welles's tycoons and dictators their political edge for Popular Front audiences.[7]

Welles's thrillers were not only the core of his film work but were also part of a distinctive genre of Popular Front anti-fascism. Beginning with the spy novels of Eric Ambler and Graham Greene, the espionage thriller with its international intrigues proved particularly amenable to the anti-fascist aesthetic. Anti-fascist politics were often international, mobilizing support for the Spanish Loyalists as well as anti-fascist exiles and resistance movements, and the spy thriller—once an imperial genre—was one of the few popular forms that narrated international plots. Eric Ambler's villains, Alfred Hitchcock wrote in 1943:

> are big business men and bankers; the cheap scum of the low cafés of the ancient Continental city; the professional, suave, well-heeled gangsters whom we have learned to recognize as the incipient chiefs of Gestapos and fascist conspiracies. In brief, they are not only real people, they are actually the kind of people who have generated violence and evil in the Europe of our time.

Eric Ambler himself later remarked that he had taken the "right wing" and often "outright fascist" thriller and turned it "upside down," making "the heroes left wing and Popular Front figures."[8]

The espionage genre was quickly adopted by Popular Front directors and screenwriters as a way to combine Hollywood formulas and anti-fascist politics. The only Hollywood film made about the Spanish Civil War, *Blockade* (1938), was a spy story. Written by Communist screenwriter John Howard Lawson and directed by left-wing émigré William Dieterle for liberal producer Walter Wanger, *Blockade* attempted to combine, as Lawson later noted, "the story of the woman trapped into spying for the fascists" with mass crowd scenes influenced by Soviet cinema. Espionage melodrama also dominated Hollywood's only prewar anti-Nazi film, Warner Brothers' semidocumentary *Confessions of a Nazi Spy* (1939) (written by John Wexley and starring Edward G. Robinson), as well as left-wing wartime thrillers like Lillian Hellman's *Watch on the Rhine* (1943), in which an anti-fascist refugee is pursued by Nazi agents in Washington; *Hangmen Also Die* (1943), Fritz Lang's film about the killing of Heyrich (written by Wexley from a story by Brecht); and *The Fallen Sparrow* (1943), in which John Garfield played a Spanish Civil War veteran hounded by Nazis in New York (based on Dorothy Hughes's popular thriller). The most enduring of these thrillers was of course *Casablanca* (1942) (written in part by Mercury scriptwriter Howard Koch), in which Humphrey Bogart played the cynical and reluctant American—who had fought for the Spanish Loyalists—drawn into the anti-fascist war.[9]

When Welles arrived in Hollywood in 1939, he was immediately drawn to the anti-fascist thriller; after all, he was a veteran of pulp radio, having played Lamont Cranston, the millionaire playboy who is secretly the mysterious foe of evil, the Shadow. Welles's earliest Hollywood projects included two adaptations of Popular Front spy novels: *The Smiler with a Knife* by Nicholas Blake (the pseudonym of poet C. Day Lewis) and *The Way to Santiago* by Arthur Calder-Marshall. Day Lewis had edited and Calder-Marshall had contributed to an influential British anthology, *The Mind in Chains: Socialism and the Cultural Revolution.* Welles's screenplay of *The Smiler with a Knife* transplanted Day Lewis's story of British fascists to the United States, depicting an American S.S. (Stars and Stripes) led by "rich people with too much time on their hands."

Welles's screenplay of *The Way to Santiago* was the tale of a man who awakes with amnesia and finds himself among Nazi spies in Mexico.[10]

Neither of these projects was filmed, but one of the earliest Mercury films was an adaptation of an Eric Ambler thriller, *Journey into Fear*, produced and designed by Welles. The first and best of several Hollywood adaptations of Ambler, it was a version of his distinctive plot: the innocent abroad who gets entangled against his will in a sordid web of espionage. Joseph Cotten plays the engineer—"a ballistics expert who has never fired a gun"—who finds himself the target of Nazi assassins; he is initiated into the world of international intrigue by the Turkish secret policeman, Colonel Haki, played by Welles. A fast-paced, low-budget film, *Journey into Fear* is one of the earliest *films noir*; its pervasive paranoia is heightened by nighttime settings, low-key lighting, expressionistic camera angles, and the scratchy 78 that becomes the assassin's signature. The film ends with a virtuoso struggle on a hotel balcony, the first of Welles's increasingly baroque endings.

The tension and interplay between Joseph Cotten's naive engineer and Welles's powerful and threatening secret policeman was to serve as the narrative fulcrum for many of Welles's productions: Cotten's Leland and Welles's Kane in *Citizen Kane*; Edward G. Robinson's Nazi hunter and Welles's Nazi in *The Stranger*; Cotten's pulp writer and Welles's criminal black marketeer in Carol Reed's *The Third Man*; Robert Arden's young con man and Welles's shadowy tycoon in *Mr. Arkadin*; and Charlton Heston's narcotics detective and Welles's corrupt policeman in *Touch of Evil*. The narrative of *The Stranger*, in which Edward G. Robinson finds the escaped Nazi, played by Welles, teaching at a Connecticut boarding school, was not only part of the genre of postwar anti-fascist thrillers—like Hitchcock's *Notorious* (1946) and John Wexley and Edward Dmytryk's *Cornered* (1946)—but also drew directly on Welles's postwar political writings against resurgent fascism: "the phony fear of Communism is smoke-screening the real menace of renascent Fascism," he wrote in his *New York Post* column.[11]

Like Graham Greene, who called his thrillers "entertainments" to distinguish them from his serious "novels," Welles did not approach his thrillers with the aesthetic ambitions of *Citizen Kane* or *The Magnificent Ambersons*. As a result, *Journey into Fear, The Stranger* (1946), and Welles's extraordinary performance as Harry Lime in the film of Greene's "entertainment" *The Third Man* have often been discounted by critics (and by Welles himself) as simply studio products. However, just as Greene was to discover that the line between "novel" and "entertainment" blurred, so Welles was to become increasingly ambitious in his thrillers: *Lady from Shanghai*—in which Welles adopts the guise of Bogart and Garfield's Popular Front proletarian, complete with service in the Spanish Civil War—*Mr. Arkadin*, and *Touch of Evil* all join pulp plots to virtuoso filmmaking.

In these films, the political content seems overshadowed by the formal showmanship. Critics who have discounted Welles's politics have generally suggested that this showmanship is more important than his politics or his plots. "The great directors all had great personal stories to tell," Norman Lloyd, a Mercury Theater actor, once noted, "but not so with Welles." For Lloyd, *Julius Caesar* was the definitive Mercury production because of its "supreme theatricality." There is no doubt that the originality of Welles and the Mercury lay in their combination of the resources of theater, film, and radio to develop a repertoire of expressionistic devices and special effects. Among these are compositions in depth (not only in the cinematography of *Citizen Kane* and *The Magnificent Ambersons*, but in the distorted extensions of the stage apron in *Dr. Faustus* and the tilting of the stage away from the audience in *Julius Caesar*); the bare, nonnaturalistic sets; the use of radio sound effects in both film and theater, including the adaptation of radio's cross-fade into the famous "lightning mix," where a temporal and scenic shift is glued by continuity of sound; the elaborate lighting effects; the fondness for the omniscient voice-over and first-person narration (the Mercury radio program was originally called "First Person Singular"); filmic montage editing on the stage; and the play on the conventions of news reporting.[12]

However, one cannot so easily separate Welles's showmanship

from his politics. The magic of theater, film, and radio was not, for Welles, merely a formal device. Since Welles understood fascism as itself a form of showmanship, his exploration of that showmanship became a reflection on fascism, the other side of his anti-fascist aesthetic. "Showmanship is fundamental to the fascist strategy," Welles argued, "and the chief fascist argument is the parade":

> Inspiration for the showmanship of fascism comes from the military, the old dumb-show of monarchy and mostly from the theater. In Germany, the decor, the spectacular use of great masses of people—the central myth itself was borrowed from grand opera. In Italy, the public show, the lavish props, the picturesque processions were taken from the movies. Even the famous salute, the stiff arm up-raised, comes not from history, but from Hollywood. Surely one of the most amusing footnotes in all the chronicles of recorded time is that Hitler and Mussolini stole their showmanship from Richard Wagner and Cecil B. DeMille!

Welles in turn stole *his* showmanship from the Nazis. "Orson dictated clearly and exactly the look he wanted," the pioneering Mercury lighting designer Jean Rosenthal recalled of the spectacular lighting of *Julius Caesar*: it was "a very simple look based on the Nazi rallies at Nuremberg. . . . The up light was taken entirely from the effect the Nazis achieved."[13]

Welles was not alone in his fascination with the rhetoric of fascism; the German Marxist Walter Benjamin had argued in 1936 that "the logical result of Fascism is the introduction of aesthetics into political life," to which "Communism responds by politicizing art." In the United States, Benjamin's counterpart was the Popular Front cultural critic Kenneth Burke, whose writings on the great dictators included a 1935 analysis of the "Great Demagogue" in Shakespeare's *Julius Caesar*, a detailed reading of Peter Blume's *The Eternal City* in 1937, and a famous address to the 1939 American Writers' Congress on "The Rhetoric of Hitler's *Battle*." "This book is the well of Nazi magic," Burke wrote, "crude magic, but effective. A people trained in pragmatism should want to inspect this magic." Welles and the Mercury Theater attempted to turn the magic of the Nazis against them.[14]

Just as Welles's portrayals of his grotesque hero-villains were always ambiguous, so too was his deployment of the magic and showmanship of the mass media, not least in the celebrated panic caused by the radio broadcast of "The War of the Worlds" on 30 October 1938. "The War of the Worlds" is a particularly interesting example of Welles's anti-fascist aesthetic, because it was entirely a "formal" triumph; it has no "political" content or plot. Institutionally, the Mercury Theater's radio program was an example of the contradictory compromises between Popular Front struggles and the culture industry. A campaign in the early years of the New Deal to nullify broadcasting licenses and reallot frequencies with a quarter of them going to "educational, religious, agricultural, labor, cooperative, and similar non-profit associations" had been defeated by the broadcasting industry, but the networks agreed to create their own "public service" programs, using unsponsored air time to lend an image of prestige and cultural uplift to the radio. CBS's "Columbia Workshop" was the first of these "sustaining" programs, and it sparked a brief renaissance of radio drama, where experiment and innovation were subsidized, and poets and playwrights addressed a mass audience. In the summer of 1938, CBS brought "an entire theatrical institution to the air": the Mercury Theater on the Air. Welles and the Mercury arrived at CBS, as they would later arrive at RKO studios, as a prestige property, with a license to innovate.[15]

Welles and his collaborators took the forms of radio drama seriously; "radio," Welles said, "is a popular, democratic machine for disseminating information and entertainment." They began by adapting popular classics into first-person radio narratives: "Dracula" and "Treasure Island" were their first two programs. "The War of the Worlds" broadcast was at first glance nothing special, though it departed from the usual format by prefacing the long first-person narrative of the survivor, Professor Pierson, with the mock news broadcast of the Martian invasion. Its structure resembles the later *Citizen Kane*, but unlike *Kane* the persuasiveness of the newsreel overwhelmed the pedestrian narrative that followed, triggering a panic. According to sociologist Hadley Cantril's analysis of public opinion polls about the panic, six million people heard part of the broadcast, and over a million of them believed it was a real news broadcast and were frightened by it. The panic came to figure, for writers, politicians, and journalists, the power and dangers of the still relatively new mass culture of broadcasting. For some, Welles was as irresponsible as the right-wing radio demagogues; for others, the program was a salutary warning. For Welles and the Mercury Theater, the panic represented not only national notoriety, but the other side of the people's theater, of this "popular, democratic machine": the lure and danger of hypnotizing an audience.[16]

Cantril's study, a landmark work in mass communications research, offered several explanations of the panic. Some were formal, stressing the program's effective illusion of real-time duration by the extended cuts to the music of Ramon Raquello and his orchestra between news bulletins; others appealed to the peculiarities of radio, whether to the common experience of tuning in late and missing the frame, or to the authority the conventions of special on-the-spot bulletins had acquired in the recent war crisis of the early fall of 1938. However, the central explanation pointed to the audience, arguing that "it was the people who were closest to the borderline of economic disaster who were most apt to take the program as news." For Cantril, working-class people, particularly those with religious beliefs, had little "critical ability."[17]

However, listeners like Sylvia Holmes, a black woman from Newark who assumed that the invasion by Martians that the radio reported was actually an invasion by the Nazis with a terrifying new weapon, were not misreading the broadcast. For not only does the actual broadcast play down the Martian identity of the invaders—a "critical" listener like Sylvia Holmes could easily dismiss the Martian stuff as the mistake of the clearly distressed radio announcer—but the drama was based on the conventions of the anti-fascist radio dramas to which Welles himself had contributed. "The War of the Worlds" did not have to be an explicit "parable of fascism" because its very form was part of the anti-fascist aesthetic.[18]

The central device of "The War of the Worlds," the use of the radio announcer as a character, had been created in the experimental radio dramas depicting fascist invasions and air raids. As one critic has noted, unlike the radio serial—"The Shadow," for example—where "everything that happens, happens in front of the mike as a result of the dialogue, thus evoking the illusion that the characters are in control of the plot," the new radio dramas foregrounded the announcer. There was little dialogue and the action took place off-mike, beyond the control of the announcer-reporter. Welles's first major radio appearance had been as one of these fictional announcers in the April 1937 "Columbia Workshop" production of Archibald MacLeish's thirty-minute verse drama, "The Fall of the City." Produced in an armory with a cast of two hundred drama students for the crowd, "The Fall of the City" was a critical and popular success, inaugurating the Popular Front genre of serious radio drama and making Welles one of its representative voices. Welles's announcer witnesses the fall of an unnamed city to a conqueror, and his climactic narration of the arrival of "the conqueror" foreshadows the description of the Martians: "We can't see for the glare of it. . . . Yes! . . . Yes! . . . / He's there in the end of the street in the shadow. We see him! / He looks huge—a head taller than anyone / . . . They cover their faces with fingers. They cower before him. / They fall." When his visor opens, there is no face: "The helmet is hollow! / The metal is empty! . . . I tell you / There's no one at all there: there's only the metal." But the people respond to his raised arm, the fascist salute: "The people invent their oppressors: they wish to believe in them," the announcer concludes. "The city is fallen."[19]

Welles also used this form for the Mercury radio broadcast of "Julius Caesar" in September 1938: deprived of the Nuremberg lights and his stark stage design, Welles recruited the radio news commentator H. V. Kaltenborn to "report" the play, using passages from Plutarch's history. Moreover, just three days before "The War of the Worlds" broadcast, Welles listened to another of these anti-fascist dramas, the "Columbia Workshop" production of MacLeish's "Air Raid." "Air Raid"'s announcer, played by Mercury actor Ray Collins, reported the attack on a fictional European border town. "You are twenty-eight miles from the eastern border: / You are up on top of a town on a kind of a tenement," the announcer said over continuous static and a background of women's voices. The program ends with the roar of planes and machine guns: "We hear them: we can't see them. / We hear the shearing metal: / We hear the tearing air." Again, the broadcast was a critical and popular success, featured in *Time* magazine. In the spring of 1939, Norman Corwin's "They Fly through the Air" continued the Popular Front "air raid" genre. A CBS broadcaster noted in 1939 that "we have been flooded with scripts about bombing planes—not entirely, we believe, because of the success of MacLeish's 'Air Raid' or Corwin's 'They Fly through the Air,' but because of the fact that people are conscious of bombing planes these days." The technological terror of fascist air raids in Spain as well as Hitler's March 1938 invasion of Austria was the subtext for these pervasive invasion and air raid narratives: the most famous was not a radio show but Picasso's huge mural *Guernica*, painted for the 1937 Paris World's Fair in the wake of the 28 April 1937 fascist bombing of the city of Guernica.[20]

The Martian broadcast is thus best understood as one of these anti-fascist air raid stories. It may seem ironic that a tale of Martian invasion should cause a panic, rather than the more "realistic" dramatizations of air raids. In fact, the persuasiveness of the Martian broadcast lay not simply in the Mercury's technical mastery of the conventions of news broadcasting but also in its depiction of the failure of radio. If the panic demonstrated radio's power, "The War of the Worlds" narrative emphasized the limits of mass communication. Though Cantril argued that the susceptibility of listeners was demonstrated by their uncritical faith in the authority of scientists, radio announcers, and military officers, in fact the broadcast repeatedly shows the inability of any of these authorities to comprehend the invasion, whether the radio reporter Carl Phillips who "can't find words" or the scientist Pierson whose wordy explanations explain nothing. Moreover, the Martians "avoid destruction of cities and countryside," attacking the means of communication and transportation. This "fall of the city" takes place not with the crowd prostrate in front of the conqueror's salute but on top of Broadcasting Building. "This may be the last broadcast," the announcer says, and the mock broadcast ends with the radio operator's haunting "2X2L calling CQ. . . . Isn't there anyone on the air?" It is precisely radio's inability to generate a mass resistance to the Martians that is the heart of the broadcast.

The Martian panic generated the "live, participating-audience" the Mercury manifesto had promised, but not in the way it intended. The magic and showmanship of "The War of the Worlds" seemed closer to the fascist demagogues and to Hearst's propaganda than to the "popular, democratic machine" the Mercury imagined. It captured the contradictions of anti-fascist culture: at once trying to create a "people's culture" with the new means of communication, while fearing that the "people" constituted by the apparatuses of mass culture were less a participating audience than a dispersed series of panicked individuals. This dialectic between the people and the apparatus became the heart of the Mercury's masterpiece, *Citizen Kane*.

Citizen Kane's Anti-Fascist Newsreels

Citizen Kane combined the two fundamental elements of Welles's anti-fascist aesthetic: the portrait of the great dictator and the reflection on showmanship and propaganda. The wit and tragedy of the story of the yellow journalist Kane are produced by the jokes, fulminations, drunken diatribes, and soapbox rhetoric about the mass media. The first line that Kane speaks (after the deathbed "Rosebud") is an allusion to the Martian panic: "Don't believe everything you hear on the radio." Lest our gullibility persist, Leland says of Rosebud, "I saw that in *The Inquirer*. Well, I've never believed anything I saw in *The Inquirer*." Unlike the other of Hollywood's now-forgotten tycoon "biopics," Kane's story becomes a hall of mirrors in which the cultural apparatus sees itself.

This gives Welles's portrait of Charles Foster Kane its rich and contradictory character. On the one hand, *Kane* certainly was an attack on William Randolph Hearst. Welles's "sympathies were," as a *New Masses* writer noted, "with the opponents of either alien or native fascism," and for Welles and the Popular Front Left, Hearst was an emblem of American fascism, a powerful capitalist who was also a visible demagogue. His public statements supporting Hitler and Mussolini were notorious, and his newspapers were rabidly antilabor. He had led the attack on the 1934 San Francisco general strike and continued to hound the ILWU leader Harry Bridges. His papers were the major antagonist of the left-wing Newspaper Guild. As a result, the Popular Front press regularly attacked Hearst: there were Anti-Hearst rallies and a National People's Committee against Hearst.[21]

This picture of Hearst was by no means limited to Communist militants. "Out of the westcoast haze comes now and then an old man's querulous voice," Dos Passos wrote in *U.S.A.*'s portrait of Hearst, "hissing dirty names at the defenders of civil liberties for the working mans; / jail the reds, / praising the comforts of Baden-Baden under the blood and bludgeon rule of Handsome Adolph." The Wisconsin sociologist Edward A. Ross wrote:

> Hearst, with his twenty-seven newspapers, his thirteen magazines, his broadcasting stations and his film studios is a greater menace to the lovers of American institutions than any other man in the country. In the last three years it has become evident that he has an understanding with European Fascist leaders and is using his vast publicity apparatus to harry and discredit those who stand up for American democracy.

Citizen Kane's depiction of Hearst was deeply indebted to this anti-Hearst sentiment, and particularly to Ferdinand Lundberg's muckraking biography, *Imperial Hearst* (1936). When Hearst tried to suppress *Citizen Kane*, the Popular Front rallied to Welles's defense, with the League of American Writers campaigning for the film's release. "If you've never seen a picture before and never see another, if you have to picket your neighborhood theater until they show it to you in desperation (because although this week it was shown to the press its release is not yet assured) see *Citizen Kane*," Molly Castle wrote in the left-wing newsweekly *US Week*.[22]

However, Welles's Kane, like his other great dictators, elicited sympathy for the devil. For some Popular Front critics, this was the film's strength. "Welles does not merely show us one aspect of the man and pound on it," Cedric Belfrage argued in the *Clipper*:

> He comes not to praise nor to indict Kane, but to reveal him. . . . The result is that a profound pity is stirred up in the audience, and the indictment is not of a man but of environments and social and economic factors which make him what he becomes . . . the might and majesty and profits of dark yellow journalism—exposed by *Kane* so effectively, because so humanly and with such inspired craftsmanship.

Others were more wary: "Citizen Welles becomes so fascinated by the lonely vortex of sad violence and failure of the flesh into which he hurls his main character, that Citizen Kane is lost," Muriel Draper wrote in *Direction*. "The life and death connection between the man as editor of a paper that affects the daily lives of millions of people who read it, is volatilized in the cocoon of personal conflict and frustration he spins about himself." Writing decades later, John Howard Lawson maintained that even though

> *Citizen Kane* inherits the class consciousness of the thirties in its portrait of a millionaire who is a prototype of American fascism, . . . the film treats Kane with ironic sympathy, ignoring the implications of his conduct. It recognizes the dark forces in American society but avoids a direct challenge to these forces.[23]

Welles himself articulated this ambivalence. "Kane is a detestable man," Welles told the *Cahiers du Cinéma* interviewers in 1958, "but I have a great deal of sympathy for him so far as he's a human being." On other occasions, Welles's sympathy seemed to outweigh his horror: he once suggested that his disagreement with screenwriter Herman Mankiewicz over the character "probably gave the film a certain tension: that one of the authors hated Kane and one of them loved him." For Mankiewicz, Kane was simply Hearst: "in his hatred of Hearst," Welles remarked, he had the "point of view of a newspaperman writing about a newspaper boss he despised." But for Welles, who had never worked in newspapers, Kane was always more than Hearst. Welles had far closer connections to Henry Luce, the publisher of *Time, Life*, and *Fortune*, and Luce is, I will suggest, as important to *Citizen Kane* as the aged Hearst. Indeed, *Citizen Kane* might best be seen as a combination of two different films: what we might call "Citizen Hearst" and "Citizen Luce."[24]

"Citizen Hearst" is the historical film inside *Kane*, Welles's rendition of the decline and fall of the Lincoln republic, an American version of the Shakespearean history plays that haunted him. Like the trilogies of Dos Passos and Josephine Herbst, *Citizen Kane* returns to the 1870s (it opens in 1871) to show the rise and fall of a boy brought up by a bank. The scene in which Mrs. Kane, played by Agnes Moorehead, gives up her son to the banker Thatcher remains one of the most powerful in the film. Its elements—the echo of the dying Kane's snowy glass globe, the boy yelling "The Union forever," the fairytale of the boarder who leaves the "worthless stock" that founds the copper-mine fortune, the unexplained estrangement of Kane's parents, and the sled that will be Rosebud—condense the story of Kane's lost childhood into that of the republic itself. The tremendous visual and narrative energy in the scenes of the 1890s and the Spanish-American War underline the ironic legacy that Kane's, and America's, fortune proved to be. The arc of Kane's career follows that of the United States: "News on the March" superimposes "1929" over factory closings, intoning "for Kane, in four short years, collapse."

The story of the Lincoln republic also informed Welles's second film, *The Magnificent Ambersons*, the tale of a family torn between the genteel tradition and the world of the automobile—Fordism. "The magnificence of the Ambersons began in 1873," Welles's voice-over tells us. "Their splendor lasted all the years that saw their Midland town spread and darken into a city." "The whole point," Welles later said, "was to show the automobile wrecking it—not only the family but the town." Welles's vision of the decline and fall of the Ambersons was as bleak as Dos Passos's *Big Money*, and its ending was too harsh for RKO. The eight-minute final reel, with Joseph Cotten's visit to Agnes Moorehead in a cheap boardinghouse and Welles's concluding voice-over—"Ladies and gentlemen, that's the end of the story"—was cut. "Everything is over," Welles recalled in an interview, "her feelings and her world and his world." Welles's "U.S.A." trilogy comes to an end with *The Stranger*, in which the Lincoln republic is figured as a New England town, complete with folksy general store, white church, and prep school. The town unwittingly adopts an escaped Nazi as teacher and son-in-law (he marries the daughter of a Supreme Court justice): he is, metaphorically, one of them. Despite its macabre evocation of Americana, however, it has little historical resonance, and becomes one of the pulp thrillers that came to supplant Welles's "history plays."[25]

Neither *The Magnificent Ambersons* nor *The Stranger* succeeds in uniting social content with formal experiment. In *The Magnificent Ambersons*, the narrative of the automobile inventor (played by Joseph Cotten) remains relatively peripheral, with the striking exception of the virtuoso scene cross-cutting between the sleigh and the automobile in the snow. As a result, the confrontation between the inventor and the Ambersons is locked in a static, if sometimes frenzied, family romance. In *The Stranger*, the only magic the Welles character exercises is his repair of the town's medieval clock, and that is little more than an excuse for one of Welles's characteristically baroque endings. In *Kane*, however, the film's magic is a reflection on Kane's magic.[26]

In this respect, *Kane* is no longer Hearst, for Welles was not particularly interested in the magic of newspapers. "Not one glimpse of the actual content of his newspapers is afforded us," the *New Masses* critic complained in an exaggerated but not inaccurate comment. It was the radio newsreel, "March of Time," that taught Welles and his Mercury colleagues the craft of radio drama. "I'd been years on *The March of Time* radio program," he told Peter Bogdanovich. "Every day. It was a marvelous show to do. Great fun, because, half an hour after something happened,

we'd be acting it out with music and sound effects and actors.
. . . One day they did as a news item . . . the opening of my production of the black *Macbeth*, and I played myself on it. And that
to me was the apotheosis of my career — that I was on *March of
Time* acting *and* as a news item." *Citizen Kane*'s real subject is the
newsreel, whose magic it mocks and mimics.[27]

If "Citizen Hearst" is the historical film inside *Kane*, "Citizen
Luce" is *Kane* as newsreel. The first account of Kane's career is
given by an imitation newsreel, "News on the March," which was
edited by RKO's newsreel editors to approximate the real thing.
Welles's model was Henry Luce's film newsreel (also called "March
of Time"), which had been widely praised, on the Left as well as
in the mainstream press, for its innovative showmanship and politics. When Welles argued in *Friday* that the film was *not* about
Hearst, he emphasized its connection to "March of Time." "*Citizen
Kane* is the story of a search by a man named Thompson, the
editor of a news digest (similar to *The March of Time*) for the meaning of Kane's dying words." In *Kane*'s projection room scene, the
Luce figure, Rawlston, is lit as a conductor.[28]

Unlike "The War of the Worlds," however, in which the formal
trick of imitating a news broadcast was far more interesting than
the narrative that followed, *Citizen Kane* trumped its mock newsreel with its own magic, its own showmanship. The film is not
an homage to the newsreel but a critique of it; it implicitly offers
a richer and truer way of seeing Kane and his world than that
of the newsreel. *Kane*'s response to the newsreel and its ideology
takes three forms: the virtuoso newsreel, composition in depth,
and the moving camera. The first, the virtuoso newsreel, is em-
bodied in the several scenes, usually lit in high contrast, with a
highly foregrounded montage, that narrate the triumphs of
young Kane. These scenes use the staple of the newsreel, flashing
newspaper headlines, to remarkable effect, as in the sequence
where the increasingly irritated Thatcher reads the headlines con-
demning the traction trust. The newsreel's use of still photographs is then elaborated in the cut from the still of the reporters
to the photographing of the same reporters six years later. Many
of these sequences are narrated by Bernard Herrmann's music,

which uses popular dance forms to create, as he wrote, "a kind of ballet suite in miniature." This part of the film is less a critique of the newsreel than a virtuoso riff on its forms.

The second filmic response to the newsreel is the composition in depth, the use of deep-focus cinematography, wide-angle lenses, deep sets with ceilings, in-camera matte shots, careful attention to sound effects, and avoidance of shot/reverse-shot cutting and conventional close-ups to create a sense of an elongated space in which actors revolve in an elaborate dance, moving from light to shadow and occasionally into a ballooned foreground presence but never out of focus. This composition marks moments of crisis that the commercial newsreel is unable to narrate: the boardinghouse scene; the confrontation between Kane, Gettys, Emily, and Susan; the two scenes with the drunken Jedidiah Leland. Depth of field becomes the correlative of a historical and psychological depth that escapes the shallow, foreshortened newsreel.

The third response to the newsreel is perhaps the most ambiguous, calling attention to itself while masking its supposed agent. This is the invasive camera that displaces the supposed representative of the viewer, the journalist Thompson. As Peter Wollen has noted, "the decision to use sequence-shots in the framing story is clearly a decision not to use classical field reverse field cutting, and thus to de-emphasize the role of Thompson, the narratee. Thompson only appears as a shadowy figure with his back to the camera." The obscured narrator combined with the moving camera produce the visual equivalent of a Mercury trademark, the Wellesian voice-over. Unlike the relatively static camera of the newsreel, the film's camera ignores No Trespassing signs, dissolves through skylights into nightclubs, through steel doors into the sanctum of the Thatcher Library, and into the flames to reveal Rosebud. The magic of *Citizen Kane*'s "newsreels" is, therefore, not simply showmanship and formal experiment but, like the radical newsreels of the Film and Photo League and the staged Living Newspapers of Joseph Losey and Nick Ray, an attempt to transform and refunction the newsreel.[29]

"Citizen Luce," however, haunts more than *Kane*'s newsreels.

Life's still photography was, as Robert Carringer has noted, one of the models for Gregg Toland's cinematography, and *Fortune*'s feature on San Simeon lay behind the design of Kane's Xanadu. Moreover, Welles had come into contact with Luce through the poet Archibald MacLeish, and *Citizen Kane* draws on the relationship between Luce and MacLeish for its portrait of Kane and Leland. Luce and MacLeish were both Yale graduates: Luce was the innovative young editor, MacLeish the slightly older modernist poet. In 1929, Luce persuaded MacLeish to join the staff of *Fortune*, and MacLeish became a major contributor of social commentary. His *Fortune* essays, though never collected, are as much classics of depression reportage as Edmund Wilson's *American Jitters*. At the same time, MacLeish moved to the left. His 1935 play, *Panic*, which starred the nineteen-year-old Welles, brought MacLeish into the radical theater: "the New Theatre–New Masses gang turned up Saturday night," he wrote to Dos Passos, "it was superb. A better audience I have never seen & the symposium afterwards, with Lawson & Burnshaw & V. J. Jerome & myself (with the grippe), was exciting as hell. I have never had such a sense of *audience* before." MacLeish began writing for *New Theatre* and became active in Popular Front organizations.[30]

Welles's performance in *Panic* led MacLeish to suggest him for the part of the announcer in his 1937 radio drama, "The Fall of the City." A few months later, MacLeish took part in the unsuccessful negotiations with the Federal Theater Project over *The Cradle Will Rock*. When they failed, MacLeish joined Welles on stage at *The Cradle*'s historic opening, delivering an impromptu speech after the production. When the Mercury Theater was established in the fall of 1937, Welles and Houseman appealed to MacLeish for money, and he arranged a meeting with the Luces: Luce contributed $2,500 to the Mercury, a figure that echoes the one with which Kane tries to pay off Jed Leland. Soon after, in May 1938, Welles was featured on the cover of *Time* magazine.[31]

By 1938, however, MacLeish had grown increasingly critical of *Time*'s coverage of the Spanish Civil War, and he resigned from *Fortune*. In a long and anguished letter of July 1938, he accused Luce of betraying his journalistic ideals:

I don't know you very well these days. . . . I wish some things had gone differently with you. . . . Maybe what I mean is that I wish you hadn't been so successful. Because it's very hard to be as successful as you have been and still keep your belief in the desperate necessity for fundamental change. I think what you have done amazing and I give you all credit and all honor for it. It would have been very easy for you to forget everything you believed true when you were twenty. . . . But I don't know—you were meant to be a progressive. . . . You were meant to make common cause with the people—all the people. . . . You would have been very happy inside yourself as one of the leaders in a democratic revolution in this country. . . . Maybe I'm wrong. It's presumptuous to guess about another man's happiness but I think you would have been. I think you hate being rich. . . . I think you would have liked to write *The People Yes*.

We don't know if Welles ever saw this letter, but he may well have talked to MacLeish about Luce. For MacLeish's ambivalent disillusionment with Luce seems to inform *Citizen Kane* as much as Mankiewicz's hatred for Hearst. Certainly MacLeish's account of the conflict between Luce's wealth and his populism is echoed throughout the film, and particularly in the conflict between Leland and Kane.[32]

"You talk about the people as though you owned them," the drunken Leland tells Kane. "As though they belong to you. As long as I can remember, you've talked about giving the people their rights as if you could make them a present of liberty, as a reward for services rendered . . . You used to write an awful lot about the workingman." Kane's tragedy, of course, is not simply that he sold out his Declaration of Principles; from the beginning he had told Thatcher that there were two Kanes: the crusading publisher defending the "decent, hard-working people" and the owner of Metropolitan Transfer stock who knows exactly the extent of his holdings. Rather, the tragedy is the loss of his magic, his inability to tell the people what to think, the taking of "the love of the people of this state away from" him. It is the shift from the self-confidence of the exchange with Emily—"Really, Charles, people will think . . ." "What I tell them to think"—to the frustration of his response to Susan's music teacher—"The people will think. . . ." "People will think. You're concerned with what people will think, Signor Matiste? I may be able to enlighten you a bit. I'm something of an authority about what people will think. The newspapers, for example." "Such men as Kane," Welles once said, "always tend toward the newspaper and entertainment world. They combine a morbid preoccupation with the public with a devastatingly low opinion of the public mentality and moral character."[33]

Ironically, this dialectic—morbid preoccupation with the public together with a low opinion of the crowd—ran throughout the Mercury's own productions. As "The War of the Worlds" broadcast demonstrated, the other side of Welles's fascination with propaganda and media manipulation was an inability to imagine a popular resistance to it. Even the anti-fascist *Julius Caesar* had, as the *New York Times* critic noted, "the somewhat ambiguous effect . . . of implying that there is no use rebelling against a fascist state." The *Daily Worker* had criticized its "slanderous" picture of the masses swayed by a demagogue. Welles's crowds were more often lynch mobs than strikers.[34]

Citizen Kane has few crowd scenes: Welles avoided both the crowd scene and the close-up, which had been, as Walter Benjamin suggested, film's great perceptual advances. Traces of the crowd may be seen: the sight gag of the stagehand holding his nose at Susan's performance, and the street cleaner sweeping up the debris of the election campaign. Moreover, the existence of the crowd is suggested by a variety of technical tricks. These tricks include the elaborate use of lights, sound, and painted sets to produce the effect of crowds without hiring large numbers of extras. Robert Carringer has emphasized the technical success of these tricks: shooting into the lights in the opera scene to suggest but not show a large audience; and carefully rerecording the soundtrack of the Madison Square Garden rally to suggest the noise if not the presence of the crowd. These techniques were in part the result of budgetary constraints. The Mercury productions had always lacked money for extras, and the painted hall and audience in *Kane*'s Madison Square Garden scene had its origins in the cyclorama of skulls in *Danton's Death*, where the revolutionary mob was suggested by five thousand Halloween masks glued to canvas. But these magical, disembodied crowds take on an ideological meaning as well; the illusions of the political rally and the opera house yield a curiously hollow phantasmagoria where the people are an effect of the apparatus.[35]

Luce also became an important ally in the struggle over *Kane*. According to Welles, he was "one of the first people to see the movie—in New York. He and Clare Luce loved it and roared with laughter at the digest. . . . They saw it as a parody and enjoyed it very much as such—I have to hand it to them. He saw it as a joke—or *she* saw it as a joke and he had to because she did." Luce "ordered his staff to unleash their guns to get the film released," *Variety* reported. *Time* published a laudatory article on the film, and *Life* did a feature spread, using photographs taken by Toland to illustrate the technical accomplishments of the film, including its "pan focus."[36]

Welles's connections to Luce and MacLeish were, for the New York intellectuals around *Partisan Review, Politics,* and *Dissent,* symptoms of the Popular Front's middlebrow character. For them, Welles's appearances in *Time* and *Life* were of a piece with his antifascist politics, his dramatizations of thickly plotted bestsellers by Booth Tarkington, his revivals of Victorian classics like *Treasure Island* and *Dracula* on "highbrow" radio, and his modernizations of Shakespeare. "Mr. Welles, to judge from his interpretations of *Macbeth, Dr. Faustus,* and *Caesar,* has the idea an Elizabethan play is a liability which only by the most strenuous showmanship, by cutting, doctoring, and modernizing, can be converted into an asset," Mary McCarthy wrote in *Partisan Review,* "Mr. Welles's method is to find a modern formula into which a classic can somehow be squeezed. In the case of *Macbeth,* the formula was *The Emperor Jones*; for *Dr. Faustus* it was a Punch and Judy show; for *Caesar* it was the proletarian play." For McCarthy and the *Partisan* critics, the Mercury Theater, far from being a genuine experiment in radical or avant-garde art, was, like the cultural front generally, a political disguise for kitsch, a middlebrow travesty of the aesthetic experience.[37]

There is no doubt that the Mercury Theater was always on the edge of the new "middlebrow" culture which, as Joan Shelley Rubin has suggested, modernized the genteel tradition for the world of mass communications and consumption. The entrepreneurs of middlebrow culture abandoned the genteel tradition's traditional hostility to the lively and disreputable arts in order to regulate and "improve" them. The Mercury shared the strategies and techniques of such middlebrow institutions as the Book-of-the-Month Club, NBC's radio symphonies, and radio's cultural commentators like Yale English professor William Lyon "Billy" Phelps. The Mercury recordings of Shakespeare were, like Penguin's paperback classics and the "great books" of Robert Hutchins and Mortimer Adler, an attempt to popularize and to market high culture.[38]

However, the anatomists of "midcult" like Mary McCarthy and Dwight Macdonald missed the social contradictions at the heart of middlebrow culture. For the middlebrow was not only a form of cultural "uplift"; it was also a form of plebeian self-improvement, and could carry radical democratic energies. Perhaps the most powerful and persuasive defense of the autonomy, legitimacy, and, one might even say, greatness of middlebrow taste has been mounted by Pierre Bourdieu, the sociologist of culture. Middlebrow culture, Bourdieu argues, is the culture of the autodidact. The autodidact is one who takes the game of culture too seriously and is thus liable to know too much or too little, condemned to amassing cultural information which is to legitimate culture "as his stamp collection is to an art collection, a miniature culture." The culture of the middlebrow is always a culture of pretension, "divided between the tastes they incline to and the tastes they aspire to." The middlebrow consumer buys the cut-rate cultural product because it is "cheaper and creates the same effect." So middlebrow culture consists of "accessible versions of avant-garde experiments or accessible works which pass for avant-garde experiments, [and] film adaptations of classic drama and literature." By this definition, the Mercury productions are clearly middlebrow.[39]

However, for Bourdieu, these tastes are not "bad" taste, but are rather the signs and weapons of class conflict, an embattled attempt at distinction by people with little cultural capital. The middlebrow is a tragic hero, able neither to live by culture nor to live without it. It is not surprising that the aesthetics of the Popular Front should have a middlebrow accent. The Popular Front alliance was made up of classes and peoples in transition: second-generation workers caught between the immigrant cultures of their parents and the Americanist culture of high school, radio, and the movies; children of working-class families finding white-collar employment in the expanding industries of leisure and entertainment; women entering the wage-labor world of the wartime industries and the expanding service sector. For these young workers, culture itself was a labor, an act of self-enrichment and self-development. The very terms and values of cultural capital were in flux in the age of the CIO, and this created the space for both high culture popularizers, plebeian avant-gardes, and the arts that were not quite "legitimate"—jazz, cinema, photography, science fiction, detective stories, folk music—all of which thrived in the cultural front.

Citizen Kane was not only an emblem of the culture of the Popular Front; its working-class heroine, Dorothy Comingore's Susan Alexander, spoke in its middlebrow accent. The girl Kane finds in the gutter is shrill, not "high class," a seller of sheet music misplaced as a diva, a Stella Dallas lost in Xanadu. "You know what Charlie called her," Leland tells the reporter. "He said she was a cross-section of the American public." Despite the rhetoric of the workingman that Leland invokes, Kane always thought of "the people" as female. The older editor objects to Kane's newspaper on the grounds that it will print "the gossip of housewives," and the key scene of Kane winning the love of the people establishes them as women: his dance with the chorus girls who sing the Charlie Kane song, a scene that includes one of the few kisses in the film. *Citizen Kane* recodes politics in sexual terms, as Kane's public life is displaced by his private life.[40] Moreover, in spite of the cruel jokes—the line called out at the end, "Twenty five thousand bucks. That's a lot of money to pay for a dame without a head," is surely some kind of filmic parapraxis—Susan triumphs: "everything was his idea, except my leaving him," something that not even Leland can claim. When scored with a jazz band rather than an operatic orchestra, she can break with Kane and tell her story to Thompson. "The last ten years have been tough on a lot of people," Thompson tells her. "Aw, they haven't been tough on me. I just lost all my money." Popular Front audiences recognized Comingore's Susan Alexander as one of their own: Comingore was featured in the Popular Front picture weekly, *Friday*, and the *New Masses* critic wrote that she was "the most astonishing young actress since Garbo was a pup." An active member of the Sleepy Lagoon Defense Committee in 1943, Comingore married Communist screenwriter Richard Collins. After their marriage ended, Collins became an informer, and Comingore was blacklisted for refusing to name names in 1951.[41]

The destruction of Comingore's career paralleled the collapse of the Mercury Theater's unstable mixture of the Luce papers and the people's theater, as the brief alliance of Luce and Welles ended. On 17 February 1941, a few weeks before *Citizen Kane* was released, Luce's own manifesto, "The American Century," appeared in *Life*. It was a statement of war aims and a vision of an imperial United States exporting capitalism and the American way of life to the postwar world. If "Mr. Luce's prediction of the American century will come true," Welles later wrote, "God help us all. We'll make Germany's bid for world supremacy look like amateur night, and the inevitable retribution will be on a comparable scale." By 1944, Welles was speaking out against Clare Luce, who had become a right-wing, anti–New Deal congresswoman from Connecticut; she in turn attacked Welles as part of "the whole Broadway-Browder axis." Having gone from theatrical angel to red-baiter, she was no longer laughing at *Citizen Kane*.[42]

Notes

1. Mercury press release quoted in Barbara Leaming, *Orson Welles: A Biography* (New York: Penguin, 1986), p. 170. Unnamed critic quoted in John Houseman, *Run-Through: A Memoir* (New York: Simon and Schuster, 1972), p. 317. *Catholic World* quoted in Richard France, ed., *Orson Welles on Shakespeare: The W.P.A. and Mercury Theatre Playscripts* (New York: Greenwood, 1990), p. 105. Welles quoted in Simon Callow, *Orson Welles: The Road to Xanadu* (New York: Viking, 1995), p. 324. Orson Welles and Peter Bogdanovich, *This Is Orson Welles* (New York: HarperCollins, 1992), p. 212.

2. Orson Welles, "Survival of Fascism," speech at Modern Forum, Wilshire Ebell Theater, 4 December 1944, p. 4, in Orson Welles Manuscripts, Lilly Library, Indiana University, Box 5 f12. Welles, "The Nature of the Enemy," 22 January 1945 speech in Orson Welles Manuscripts, Lilly Library, Indiana University Box 4 f26. p. 3.

3. Welles, "The Nature of the Enemy," p. 4.

4. Quoted in Houseman, "Again—a People's Theatre," *Daily Worker*, 18 September 1937, p. 7. Kazin, *Starting out in the Thirties* (Boston: Little, Brown, 1965), p. 119.

5. "With Orson Welles," Turner Network Television, 1990: this was a version of the 1980 BBC production. "The Orson Welles Story," directed and produced by Alan Yentob and Leslie Megahey.

6. Welles quoted in James Naremore, *The Magic World of Orson Welles* (Dallas, Tex.: Southern Methodist University Press, 1989), p. 12.

7. "Interview with Orson Welles," *Cahiers du Cinéma*, 1958, translated and edited in Terry Comito, ed., *Touch of Evil* (New Brunswick, N.J.: Rutgers University Press, 1985), pp. 205–7.

8. Alfred Hitchcock, introduction to Eric Ambler, *Intrigue* (New York: Knopf, 1943). Joel Hopkins, "An Interview with Eric Ambler," *Journal of Popular Culture* 9 (Fall 1975): 286. For a more extensive discussion of the Popular Front spy thriller, see Michael Denning, *Cover Stories: Narrative and Ideology in the British Spy Thriller* (London: Routledge and Kegan Paul, 1987), pp. 59–90.

9. John Howard Lawson, *Film: The Creative Process* (New York: Hill and Wang, 1964), p. 126.

10. Screenplay quoted in Brett Wood, *Orson Welles: A Bio-Bibliography* (New York: Greenwood, 1990), p. 157.

11. Welles quoted in Naremore, *The Magic World of Orson Welles*, p. 117.

12. Lloyd quoted in Richard France, *The Theatre of Orson Welles* (Lewisburg, Pa.: Bucknell University Press, 1977), pp. 55, 106.

13. Welles, "The Nature of the Enemy," p. 13. Jean Rosenthal, *The Magic of Light* (New York: Theatre Arts Books, 1972), p. 22.

14. Walter Benjamin, "The Work of Art in the Age of Mechanical Reproduction" [1936], in *Illuminations* (New York: Schocken, 1969), pp. 242–43. Kenneth Burke, "The Rhetoric of Hitler's *Battle*," in his *The Philosophy of Literary Form: Studies in Symbolic Action* (1941; rpt., Berkeley: University of California Press, 1973), pp. 191–92. See also "Anthony in Behalf of the Play" and "Growth among the Ruins" in the same collection.

15. Welles's experience in the Federal Theater Project and in radio's world of sustaining programming led him to argue that Hollywood too should have its "experimental" studios: "It is too bad that there is no money spent in Hollywood for experiment. If you take any other large industry—General Electric, chemistry, automobiles—you spend at least ten per cent—maybe twenty per cent—of your profits on a laboratory where experimentation is done. There is not one cent spent by anybody in Hollywood for experiment." Orson Welles, lecture to motion picture students of New York University, 20 October 1942, p. 2, in Orson Welles Manuscripts. Lilly Library, Indiana University, Box 5 fl.

16. Welles quoted in Naremore, *The Magic World of Orson Welles*, p. 13. Hadley Cantril, *The Invasion from Mars: A Study in the Psychology of Panic* (1940; rpt., New York: Harper and Row, 1966), pp. 47–63.

17. Cantril, *The Invasion from Mars*, p. 157. Cantril's elaborate attempt to explain why working people and poor people were more likely to be frightened is based on an unexamined metaphor, the word "insecurity," which insecurely conflates economic and psychological insecurity. At one point, Cantril writes that the answers to one question "reflect the basic insecurity of over half the population." The question from the Gallup Poll, however, only asked how long the respondent could survive without relief if he lost his job. The rest of the explanation depends on an elaborate opposition between "critical ability" and "susceptibility-to-suggestion-when-facing-a-dangerous-situation." "Critical ability" is defined as "a general capacity to distinguish between fiction and reality or the ability to refer to special information which is regarded as sufficiently reliable to provide an interpretation." For Cantril, critical ability knows no escape: "If critical ability is to be consistently exercised, it must be possessed by a person who is invulnerable in a crisis situation and who is impervious to extraneous circumstances." Behind this argument lay a deep contempt for working-class culture: "Dull lives may be cheered with bright clothing or gaudy furniture, harassed breadwinners may become fixtures at the local beer hall, worried housewives may zealously

participate in religious orgies, repressed youths may identify themselves for a few hours with the great lovers or gangsters of the silver screen. There are many socially accepted ways of escape from the responsibilities, worries, and frustrations of life—the movies, the pulp magazines, fraternal organizations, and a host of other devices thrive partially because their devotees want surcease from their woes." Though Cantril explicitly distances himself from those who "condemn 'the masses' in wholesale fashion," his conclusions echo them. Cantril, *The Invasion from Mars*, pp. 155, 130, 117, 149, 161.

18. Sylvia Holmes is quoted in Cantril, *The Invasion from Mars*, pp. 53–54.

19. Eckhard Breitinger, "The Rhetoric of American Radio Drama," *Revue des langues vivantes* 44 (1978): 229–46. Archibald MacLeish, *The Fall of the City: A Verse Play for Radio* (New York: Farrar & Rinehart, 1937), pp. 31–33; my quotation follows the radio broadcast, which differs slightly from the published text.

20. Archibald MacLeish, "Air Raid," in his *Six Plays* (Boston: Houghton Mifflin, 1980), pp. 102, 120. Douglas Coulter, preface to his collection *Columbia Workshop Plays: Fourteen Radio Dramas* (New York: Whittlesey House, 1939), p. xvi.

21. Emil Pritt, "Orson Welles and Citizen Kane," *New Masses* 4 (February 1941), p. 27.

22. John Dos Passos, "The Big Money," in *U.S.A.* (New York: Modern Library, [1938]), pp. 476–77. Edward A. Ross, "How to Smash Hearst," *Champion of Youth*, in FBI, "Welles," exhibit 94. For the League and *Citizen Kane*, see Charles Glenn, "News, Views, Gossip from Filmland Capital," *Daily Worker*, 21 January 1941, p. 7; and Charles Glenn, "Hollywood Writers Say No to War Maneuvers," *Daily Worker*, 23 January 1941, p. 7. Molly Castle, " 'Citizen Kane': Tops from Every Angle," *US Week* 1 no. 8 (3 May 1941), p. 17.

23. Cedric Belfrage, "Orson Welles' *Citizen Kane,*" *Clipper* 2, no. 3 (May 1941), pp. 13, 12. Muriel Draper, "Citizen Welles," *Direction* 4, no. 5 (Summer 1941), p. 11. Lawson, *Film: The Creative Process*, p. 139.

24. "Interview with Orson Welles," *Cahiers du Cinéma*, p. 204. Welles quoted in Callow, *Orson Welles*, p. 494.

25. Welles and Bogdanovich, *This Is Orson Welles*, pp. 114, 490, 130.

26. Many critics have missed this, separating the film's formal techniques from its content. "There are far too many trick camera angles," Joy Davidman argued in *New Masses*, "too many fantastic combinations

of light and shadow, indicating an incomplete translation of Welles' famous stage technique into screen terms. Frequently he lets his showmanship run away with him, preferring to astound rather than to convince." For formalist critics, this showmanship was the heart of the film. "All Welles's tricks, as they are often contemptuously called—the lightning mixes, the stills which come to life, the complex montages, the elasticity of perspective, the protracted dissolves, the low-angle camera movements—are what still gives the film any interest," Peter Wollen argued in a classic interpretation of *Citizen Kane*. "Nobody, after all, has ever made high claims for its 'novelistic' content, its portrayal of Kane's psychology, its depiction of American society and politics in the first half of the twentieth century, its anatomy of love or power or wealth. Or, at any rate, there is no need to take such claims seriously." Davidman, "Citizen Kane," *New Masses*, 13 May 1941, p. 28. Peter Wollen, "Introduction to *Citizen Kane*," in his *Readings and Writings* (London: NLB, 1982), p. 60.

27. Welles and Bogdanovich, *This Is Orson Welles*, p. 74. Welles told Barbara Leaming a similar story, except that he played himself in a "March of Time" show about *The Cradle Will Rock*; Leaming, *Orson Welles*, p. 628. The incident he remembers may actually be the 22 March 1935 "March of Time" show, in which he recreated part of his stage performance of *Panic*.

28. Welles, "*Citizen Kane* Is Not about Louella Parson's Boss," *Friday*, 14 February 1941.

29. Wollen, "Introduction to *Citizen Kane*," p. 52.

30. Robert Carringer, *The Making of "Citizen Kane"* (Berkeley: University of California Press, 1985), pp. 50–51, 75. R. H. Winnick, ed., *Letters of Archibald MacLeish, 1907–1982* (Boston: Houghton Mifflin, 1983), p. 275.

31. On the Luces' financial involvement with the Mercury, see Houseman, *Run-Through*, pp. 304–5. "Marvelous Boy," *Time*, 9 May 1938, pp. 27–31.

32. Winnick, ed., *Letters of Archibald MacLeish*, p. 293.

33. Welles quoted in Callow, *Orson Welles*, p. 497.

34. Quoted in Callow, *Orson Welles*, p. 338.

35. Carringer, *The Making of "Citizen Kane*," pp. 81, 105.

36. Welles and Bogdanovich, *This Is Orson Welles*, p. 74. *Variety* quoted in Callow, *Orson Welles*, p. 549. "Orson Welles," *Life*, 26 May 1941, pp. 108–16. The key figure seems to have been *Life* editorial assistant Richard Pollard, to whom Welles wrote: "If anybody is responsible for 'Citizen

Kane' being released, I think it is you.... You have been so interested that it is difficult for me to remember you are not with us in the Mercury Theatre. I wish you were." Orson Welles, letter to Richard Pollard, 15 May 1941, in Time Inc. Archives.

37. Mary McCarthy, "February 1938: Elizabethan Revivals," in her *Sights and Spectacles, 1937–1956* (New York: Farrar, Straus and Cudahy, 1956), p. 17.

38. For accounts of the middlebrow culture of modern times, see Joan Shelley Rubin, *The Making of Middlebrow Culture* (Chapel Hill: University of North Carolina Press, 1992); James Sloan Allen, *The Romance of Commerce and Culture* (Chicago, Ill.: University of Chicago Press, 1983); and Joseph Horowitz, *Understanding Toscanini: How He Became an American Culture-God and Helped Create a New Audience for Old Music* (Minneapolis: University of Minnesota Press, 1987).

39. Pierre Bourdieu, *Distinction: A Social Critique of the Judgement of Taste* (Cambridge, Mass.: Harvard University Press, 1984), pp. 329, 326, 323. The classic critique of middlebrow culture is Dwight Macdonald, "Masscult & Midcult," in his *Against the American Grain: Essays on the Effects of Mass Culture* (New York: Random House, 1962).

40. See also Beverley Houston, "Power and Dis-Integration in the Films of Orson Welles," *Film Quarterly* 35, no. 4 (Summer 1982), p. 9, who notes that "for 'people,' of course, read women.' "

41. Davidman, Citizen Kane, p. 28. Victor S. Navasky, *Naming Names* (New York: Penguin, 1981), p. 227.

42. Welles quoted in Naremore, *The Magic World of Orson Welles*, p. 116. W. A. Swanberg, *Luce and His Empire* (New York: Scribner's, 1972), p. 221.

Citizen Kane

From Log Cabin to Xanadu

LAURA MULVEY

◆ ◆ ◆

ALTHOUGH THE idea of embarking on a new analysis of the
most written-about film in film history is daunting, I am
using *Citizen Kane* for a specific and experimental purpose. That
is, I want to speculate about certain areas of overlap between
psychoanalysis and history and use the film, as it were, as a guinea
pig. I have two further excuses for this project. First, although
the history in question here is primarily that of the United States,
I have tried to approach that history from a European perspective
which, I feel, illuminates aspects of the film that have been over-
looked. Second, I am applying the film theory and criticism of
my generation to this film, which has been put through the mill
by each generation of critics since it appeared in 1941. The main
influences on my thought have been psychoanalytic theory and
feminism, and both have strongly inflected my analysis of *Citizen
Kane*. Although the presence of feminism in this essay may not
be obvious at first glance, the principles of feminist film theory
have not only molded my way of thinking about cinema in general, but have necessarily informed my approach throughout this

particular analysis. My approach is experimental in another way: it is a feminist analysis of a film that is not, on the face of it, appropriate for a feminist analysis.

However, *Citizen Kane* is about an enigma, and the enigma is refracted through a text that creates a strong appeal in its spectator to read clues and to decipher meanings. The film creates an active, self-conscious form of spectatorship and one that is not founded on a polarization of gender (that is, an active spectator positioned as masculine in relation to an eroticized feminine spectacle). One of the ways in which *Citizen Kane* seems strikingly anti-Hollywood is the absence of the glamour effect generated by a female star. Welles's own towering presence on the screen provides a magnetic draw for the spectator's eye and leaves little space for sexualized voyeurism. This displacement opens up a space for a different kind of voyeurism, that of curiosity—both the perhaps prurient desire to crack the secret of a life and also a kind of detective work, a reading of cinematic signs that carries on alongside and finally transcends that of the diegetic investigator. So, liberated from its conventional erotic obsession with the female figure, cinematic voyeurism—displaced—is replaced by a different currency of exchange between screen and spectator.

Feminist film theory has always been preoccupied with the question of decipherment—first and foremost, of course, the decipherment of unconscious meanings invested in images of women. It is in this light that the appropriation of psychoanalytic theory by feminist film theory should be understood. Psychoanalytic theory is, itself, a means of decoding symptoms: symptoms that have evaded the processes of censorship in the conscious mind, with the original material then disguised by the unconscious mind through its own particular linguistic processes of condensation and displacement. Freud, searching for analogies to describe the language of the unconscious, cited the hieroglyph and the rebus. Without implying any literal identity between the cinema and the unconscious, critics have pointed out that the cinema, sliding between the visual and the verbal and in the very looseness of its "language," can also be compared to the hieroglyph and rebus. And meanings created through image, gesture, object, camera movement, and so on can be transferred onto subsequent repetitions or similarities (of image, gesture, object, camera movement, and so on), displacing or condensing their resonances to forge links in the proverbial chain of sliding signifiers. *Citizen Kane* exploits these formal aspects of film in a story/scenario that is itself about its main protagonist's unconscious. I have broken down the overlap between psychoanalysis and history into three separate levels:

1. *Citizen Kane*'s narrational strategy and its exploitation of the cinema's hieroglyphic potential to create a space for a deciphering spectator. I will argue that this form of spectatorship has historical and political significance.
2. The psychoanalytic content of the story, as reflected in its narrative structure, patterns, and symmetries. I will argue that these themes are organized around gender and also reach out to wider American mythologies that have a social significance for an immigrant society.
3. The historical background and the political crisis at the time when the film was made, refracted through a psychoanalytic frame of reference.

Citizen Kane's polemical edge was directed at contemporary politics. The film's politics were not only eclipsed over the course of the years, but were glimpsed only through innuendo and implication even at the moment of its release. And then, its critical reputation as one of the great films of all time detached it further from its politics and left it floating, as it were, in the discourse of pure film criticism. The Hearst references were understood, at the time and since, as personal and scandalous rather than as political. Not only will I be attempting to right this balance, but I will also argue that the film's politics include psychoanalysis, and that only through the application of psychoanalytic theory can its politics truly emerge into visibility. Then themes of Oedipal conflict and fetishism come into play, not only within the story itself, but to reflect back onto the historical conflicts from which the film emerged.

Psychoanalytically oriented critics may have been intimidated by Pauline Kael's famous and triumphant citation of Orson Welles's apparently dismissive description of the film's psychoanalytic themes as "dollar-book Freud." However, Welles's remark, taken in context, seems less dismissive.[1] At the time when *Citizen Kane* was attracting widespread attention as a portrait of newspaper tycoon William Randolph Hearst, Welles issued a careful press statement about his film. He drew attention to its psychological themes in an attempt to generalize the personal into the political. He discussed Kane's separation from his mother, his subsequent parenting by a bank, and the significance of the sled Rosebud, which

> in his subconscious . . . stood for his mother's love which Kane never lost. In his waking hours, Kane certainly forgot the sled and the name which was painted on it. Case books of psychiatrists are full of these stories. It was important for me in the picture to tell the audience as effectively as possible what this really meant. . . . The best solution was the sled itself. . . . It was necessary that my character be a collector—the kind of man who never throws anything away.[2]

Faced with the skepticism and, indeed, disappointment of the assembled press over this psychoanalytic emphasis, Welles made his infamous and oft-quoted remark about "dollar-book Freud." My intention here is to restore some of the depth inherent in the "Freud" and to take Welles, in the spirit of his own analysis, beyond the level of the "dollar book." At the same time I shall try to unravel the intricate interweaving of the quite obviously factual references to Hearst with their by and large fictional psychoanalytic underpinnings and, finally, to speculate about the wider ideological significance of both.

Although I shall return to the film's politics at the end of this essay, I want to place the film historically before embarking on the theoretical sections of my analysis. Some dates: work started on the *Citizen Kane* script in February 1940, during the "phony war" period that followed the German invasion of Poland in 1939. While scripting continued in the spring and early summer, the

German offensive moved across Europe; *Citizen Kane* went into production on 29 June, during the bleakest moments of the war, between the fall of France in May and the battle of Britain, which stretched out, in a last stand against Hitler, from July to September 1940. As Europe appeared to be falling inexorably to fascism, the battle between involvement and isolationism was bitterly engaged in America. When *Citizen Kane* opened in New York in May 1941, Pearl Harbor was still six months away. Not only was the question of the war in Europe the burning public issue at the time, it was also of passionate personal importance to Orson Welles. He was deeply committed to Roosevelt, the New Deal, and the struggle against fascism, but was also deeply influenced by European culture. Hearst, on the other hand, had always been a major exponent of isolationism, particularly where Europe was concerned. He had broken with the Democrats over Wilson's involvement of the United States in World War I and with the Republicans over, among other things, Hoover's support for the League of Nations. Although the historical and political background is hardly visible on an explicit level, I shall attempt to argue that its presence is distinctly discernible through the film's imagery and in its metaphoric allusions.

I

Now: the inscription of a mode of spectatorship. The film—as has been often pointed out before—challenges conventional relations between screen and spectator. But, most crucially, it uses the language of cinema to create a mesh with the language of the psyche. The enigma in *Citizen Kane* goes beyond the content level of the Rosebud mystery to a level of form, presenting the spectator with a film text that is aesthetically constructed around visual clues that appeal to an active, curious spectator who takes pleasure in deciphering enigmas and interpreting signs. Music also plays its part. Bernard Herrmann wrote about the necessity for musical leitmotifs in *Citizen Kane*:

There are two main motifs. One—a simple four-note figure in brass—is that of Kane's power. It is played in the very first two bars of the film. The second is the Rosebud motif. A vibraphone solo, it first appears during the death scene at the very beginning of the picture. It is heard again and again throughout the film under various guises, and if followed closely, is a clue to the ultimate identity of Rosebud itself.[3]

Curiosity has to have an object, an enigma to arouse it. In *Citizen Kane*, the central enigma of Kane himself is neatly encapsulated in, or displaced onto, Rosebud, which then becomes the focus of the journalist/investigator's quest. But the enigma is never solved for the characters within the fictional world on the screen, either through the protagonist's investigation or through the witnesses' testimony. Welles separates the spectator from the diegetic world of the screen and upsets our normal assumption that the story's resolution will be provided by its characters' transcendent understanding. In this way the film avoids the conventions of the hermetically sealed narrative usually associated with the Hollywood cinema. It opens up and marks another kind of narrational strategy, which breaks down the barriers between the screen and the auditorium, moving, as it were, out of the diegetically contained third person and into the second-person mode of address.

By its very use of inconsistency and contradiction, the film warns the audience against any reliance on the protagonists as credible sources of truth and, ultimately, deflects understanding, away from character, away from a dramatic interplay between people and their destinies. In *Citizen Kane* the audience can come to its own conclusions, but only if the viewers break through the barrier of character as the source of meaning and start to interpret clues and symptoms on the screen as might a detective or a psychoanalyst. Once the characters fall into place as just one element in an intricately patterned web, the film's own internal consistency and logic, independent of character, come clearly into focus. In this sense the film as a whole, as a text, sets up an enigma, and through its formal mode of address, through its use of the camera, it also sets up the clues to its decipherment. The clues spread through the story on the screen, hidden in the varied elements that make up a film: camera movements, objects, gestures, events, repetitions, mise-en-scène. Among these elements, the characters are only one more link in the chain, another piece in the jigsaw puzzle. So *Citizen Kane* upsets our usual sense of hierarchy in storytelling, in which the ratio between people and things tends to be organized along an anthropomorphic bias. The spectator is left to "figure out" what is going on (beyond, in Lucy's famous words to Linus, "Rosebud's his sled") and to pick up hints at messages that are quite clearly not delivered by Western Union.

The film's opening sequence sets up the relationship between camera and spectator and invokes the spectator's investigative gaze through a collaboration with the investigation of the seeing camera rather than with the unseeing character. When the title *Citizen Kane* fades from the screen and the film's initial image takes its place, the audience is swept into the story with an interdiction and a camera movement. A sign saying "No Trespassing" can easily be seen through the murky lighting, and a wire fence fills the screen, barring the way forward. This sign, although rationalized through its place on the gate of the Xanadu estate, directly addresses the audience. Everyone knows that prohibited space becomes immediately fascinating and that nothing arouses curiosity more than a secret. And in response, after barely even pausing on the first image, the camera cranes up and over the top of the fence, moving forward through a series of lap dissolves over the grounds of neglected grandeur, toward a fairytale castle on the top of a hill. There is no grounding of the camera here. It is freed from an establishing character's presence, literally approaching the gate on the ground. The space is simply that of the screen and the frame and the gravity-defying movement of the camera.

The camera's movement functions both literally and figuratively. It establishes a place and a mystery but it also gives a visible rendering of the opening of a story as an opening of a narrative space. The space of the story is depicted as an enclosed place from which the audience is excluded, and the camera's effortless passage from outside to inside acts like a magic eye, opening a way into the storyteller's world and imagination. The end of the film reverses the camera movement, so the space that opened up the story is symmetrically closed, returning the audience to its original position, outside the wire fence, ultimately back into the auditorium, the same as the viewers were, but different for having undergone the experience of the previous two hours.

There is an echo, in this narrating camera, of the grand experiment that Welles had planned for his first Hollywood project, the adaptation of Conrad's *Heart of Darkness*. That project grew out of the Mercury Theater's radio series "First Person Singular," in which novels built around a narrating "I" were adapted for dramatic performance and combined with the storyteller's voice-over. *Heart of Darkness* had been one of these productions. To transform the first-person narration into the new medium, cinema, Welles wanted to shoot the film with the camera as the eye of the "I," using a subjective camera throughout, the kind later used by Robert Montgomery in *The Lady in the Lake*. The difficulties involved in shooting the film in this way greatly inflated the *Heart of Darkness* budget, and the project was shelved. The film was to have been introduced by a prologue in which Welles would give an an illustrated lecture on subjective camera and explain directly to the audience that the camera's point of view was also theirs. Robert Carringer, in his book *The Making of "Citizen Kane,"* says:

> To Welles's explanatory narration, the camera would adopt the points of view, successively of a bird in a cage, a condemned man about to be electrocuted, and a golfer driving a ball. Then it would take Welles's point of view from the screen, looking into a movie audience made up entirely of motion picture cameras. In the final shot, an eye would appear on the left side of a black screen, then the equals sign, then the pronoun I. The eye would wink, and a dissolve would lead to the opening shot of the film.[4]

The opening of *Citizen Kane* offers an infinitely more sophisticated version of a subjective camera. Because the camera's look is not associated with a character, a literal first-person participant in the story, it takes on, rather, the function of narrator outside the world of the story. While it still assimilates and represents the audience's eye as the members look at the screen, it also sets up an invocation to decipher. Later in the film the shadowy presence of Thompson, the investigating journalist, acts as a surrogate for the audience's curiosity, carrying the narrative forward and precipitating the film's flashbacks to the past. He is never, however, given the transcendent look that is marked by a character's assimilation to a subjective camera.

Because the overt solution to the Rosebud enigma only appears in the film's closing seconds, many important signs and clues set up earlier in the film will, more likely than not, have gone unnoticed in a first viewing. *Citizen Kane* has, built into its structure, the need to think back and reflect on what has taken place in the main body of the film as soon as it finishes. And when the camera tracks into the furnace and supplies the missing piece of the jigsaw puzzle, it throws everything that has led up to that moment into a new relief. Those whose curiosity has been truly engaged by the film find themselves wanting to see it again. The next and subsequent viewings are bound to be experienced quite differently from the first. There is, in a sense, a didactic metaphor at play here. The film's "active spectator" is forced to look back at and reexamine events as though the film were suggesting that history itself should be constantly subjected to reexamination. Not only should history never be accepted at face, or story, value, but also, from a political perspective, it should be detached from personality and point of view and be rediscovered, as it were, in its materiality and through the decoding of its symptoms. This inscribed return to the past to decode the film as history overlaps with the question of the unconscious and its enigmas.

The sled, for instance, functions as lost object and as screen memory, and, being literally buried in the snow, it is both hidden and preserved, perfectly in keeping with Freud's picture of memory within the unconscious. The little glass ball that contains the log cabin and snow scene makes three appearances, one at the very beginning of the film, Kane's death scene; one at the end, when Susan leaves him; and one in the middle, when they meet for the first time. Because the glass ball belongs to Susan, it first appears in the chronology of Kane's story when she does, that is, in the middle of the film, during Leland's turning-point narration. Kane meets Susan in the street, at a crossroad, and she stops, as it were, in its tracks, Kane's journey back into his past. He explains to her:

> You see, my mother died, a long time ago. Well, her things were put in storage out West. There wasn't any other place to put them. I thought I'd send for them now. Tonight I was going to take a look at them. A sort of sentimental journey.

This scene includes the second of the only two times in the film that Kane mentions his mother. And this nostalgia for his past also reintroduces the theme of motherly love and ambition:

SUSAN: I wanted to be a singer. That is, I didn't. My mother did. . . . It's just—well you know what mothers are like.
KANE: Yes. You got a piano?

(Susan herself comments perceptively at the end of her narration, "Perhaps I should never have sung for Charlie that first evening.") The glass ball is distinguishable on Susan's dressing table, to the left-hand side of her reflection in the mirror. Neither of the characters draws attention to it, nor does the camera, but there it sits, like a narrative time bomb awaiting its moment, the observant spectator to pick up and take note.

These are just some instances of the way in which the film links motifs through objects. The semiology of the objects offers the spectator an aesthetic opportunity to return to and reread the text and to puzzle out its configurations retrospectively. The end returns the viewer to the beginning; there is both the formal symmetry (the camera's exit through the fence) and the unanswered questions that are left hanging in the smoke rising from Xanadu's chimney.

II

The next area of overlap between psychoanalysis and history lies inside the film, starting with the narrative structure of the film and its organization around thematic symmetries. The personalized nature of the flashbacks and their general adherence to chronology overshadow and disguise the film's underlying dramatic structure, which divides into two parts, cutting across the chronological biography and the narrations of the different witnesses with a broad, dominating, binary opposition. Kane's rise and decline separate the two parts narratively, but his relation to male and female worlds separate the two parts thematically. The Thatcher and Bernstein stories tell of Kane's dramatic rise to triumphant success. Susan's and Raymond's flashbacks tell the story of his disgrace and withdrawal. The first two stories are set in the competitive, public, all-male world of newspaper reporting; Susan's and Raymond's narratives are set in the spectacular, cultural, and feminized world of the opera and Xanadu. The turning point comes in Leland's narration, which deals with Kane's love life and political life, and the increasingly inextricable relationship between the two. The turning-point effect is accentuated by the fact that the world of politics is sandwiched between Kane's meeting with Susan and their marriage.

Kane's defeat in his campaign for governor marks the apex of the rise-and-fall structure and switches the movement of the story. Kane invests all his financial and emotional resources into Susan's career in opera so that, in terms of the film's symmetry, the opera, Salaambo, balances the newspaper, the Inquirer. While the Inquirer's triumph led to Kane's first marriage and to politics, Salaambo's collapse leads to the claustrophobic grandeur of Xanadu. Kane's major enterprise is concentrated on buying and importing art treasures to construct an appropriate environment for his retreat into an isolated domesticity with Susan.

The scene of Kane's childhood separation from his parents could be described as the film's "primal scene." It enacts, in dramatic form, the two psychoanalytic motifs that determine the later development of the plot and divide it into its two parts: the child's closeness to his mother and his instinctive aggression against his surrogate father. The first, male-dominated section of the film tells the story of the radical, Oedipal Kane continuing to battle against his surrogate father. The second, Susan-dominated section of the film shows him isolated from public life and fetishistically amassing things, attempting to fill, as it were, the void of his first loss, his separation from his mother.

The Thatcher flashback covers, in three scenes, the whole span of Kane's career, from the first meeting in the snow, to Thatcher's rage at Kane's campaigns against capitalist corruption, to the stock-market crash and Kane's bankruptcy. The last lines in the sequence are:

THATCHER: What would you like to have been?
KANE: Everything you hate.

When Kane, as an old man, gives his uncompromising answer to Thatcher's question ("Everything you hate"), this one line suddenly illuminates the Oedipal element in Kane's political behavior. The line, the last of the Thatcher episode, links back not only to Kane's violent reaction to Thatcher at their first meeting, but also to the *Inquirer*'s campaigns against everything for which Thatcher stands. To fight against Thatcher, the banker and old-fashioned capitalist, Kane espouses the cause of those who suffer at the hands of privilege, using as his weapon a new form of capitalist enterprise, that is, the mass-circulation newspapers known in the United States as the "yellow press." But, in implying that this radical stand has an unconscious, Oedipal origin, the film throws doubt on the altruism of Kane's politics and implies a personal agenda concealed behind the overtly political principles.

When Kane first attacks Thatcher, he uses the sled as a weapon; his aggression is directed at the adult male who is threatening to, and who will, separate him from his mother:

MOTHER: Mr. Thatcher is going to take you on a trip with him tonight. You'll be leaving on number ten.

FATHER: That's the train with all the lights on it.

CHARLES: You goin' Mom?

THATCHER: Oh no. Your mother won't be going right away, Charles, but she'll . . .

CHARLES: Where'm I going?

The scene is credible only from a psychoanalytic point of view. The characters' motivations and attitudes are not rational or explicable. Only the threatening nature of the doubled fathers, and their incompatible violences, give the scene cohesion.

This scene splits the image of the father into two opposed aspects, but both pose a threat to the child. While the biological father threatens the son with physical violence, the surrogate father threatens him with separation from his mother. The scene ends with the mother and son clinging to each other, the mother protecting her child against his father's violence, the child holding on to her love and staring resentfully offscreen at his substitute father, who proposes to introduce him to a new cultural and symbolic order. The child is suspended between two psychological phases, wavering on the threshold between a pre-Oedipal love for his mother and rivalry with his father and the post-Oedipal world in which he should take his place within society, thereby accepting separation from his mother and acknowledging the authority of his father. The scene is played with the irrationality and condensation of the unconscious. The characters act out their psychic roles without regard for verisimilitude, and the snow-covered landscape with its remote log cabin is an appropriate setting for this psychic moment. Kane never crosses the threshold between the pre- and post-Oedipal, remaining frozen, as it were, at the point of separation from his mother and, from then on, directing his Oedipal aggression at his surrogate father. The child, from then on, is in conflict with the Symbolic Order.

There is a symbolic father who represents the demands of culture and society and necessarily disrupts the mother and child's unity. A child's closeness to its mother creates a sphere of physical and emotional completeness, simultaneously an eden and a strangulation, a place of safety from which to escape, and, once escaped, a place of longing that cannot be regained. There is a before and an after. The sphere of maternal plenitude gradually gives way to social and cultural aspirations represented by the father's social and cultural significance. This process may never, as in the case of Charles Foster Kane, be satisfactorily achieved. If Mr. Kane represents a pre-Oedipal father, Thatcher personifies the father who should teach the child to understand the symbolic systems on which social relations rest and which replace the physical, unmediated bond between mother and child. Both money and the law are products of a social order based on abstract principles and symbolization. Money transcends the physicality of a literal exchange of objects and substitutes an abstract system of value. The law transcends the literal and physical relations between people and places them within a timeless system of morality. The scene inside the log cabin polarizes Kane's split father figures on each side of these symbolic systems. One represents poverty, failure, and ignorance, while the other represents wealth, success, and education. When Mrs. Kane signs her son away to the world of culture and social advancement by means of a legal agreement and in return for money, she seems to acknowledge the inevitability of a transition that only the mother, she seems to imply, can ever understand and, then, only mourn. The child's mourning returns, in the manner of the repressed, through symptoms that perpetuate an original trauma. He will become fixated on *things* and the accumulation of objects, rejecting the abstract complexities of capital, exchange, and the circulation of money.

The real father, who is left behind in the "before" that the log cabin stands for, complains, "I don't hold with signing away my boy to any bank as guardeen just because we're poorly educated." His speech and dress are rough and diametrically opposed to Thatcher, whose clipped legalistic language and dark suit come from a world without room for emotion. That world is about order, in the sense of both regulation and hierarchy, without which money cannot become capital. Mrs. Kane's correct gram-matical speech and her dark dress are iconographically closer to Thatcher than to her husband. She understands some abstract cultural necessity while her husband ("I want you to stop all this nonsense, Jim") in his naïveté does not. The scene in the log cabin places Thatcher and Mrs. Kane together on the right-hand side of the frame, sitting at the table with the documents, while Mr. Kane hovers anxiously, and unstably, on the left side. In this famous scene of deep-focus photography, Charlie is playing out-side, as seen through the window—within the divide. Within the Oedipal conflict, it is the mother's role to give up her child. To hold on to him would be to keep him in the netherworld of infancy, cultural deprivation, and impotence, and would prevent his departure on the journey toward greatness, toward the White House, as it were. In *Citizen Kane*, the transition is too abrupt and painful, and is never resolved.

The last shot of the separation scene holds for a long time on the abandoned sled now covered by the snow, while a train's whistle sounds in the distance. As I mentioned earlier, in Freud's theory of the unconscious, a memory that is apparently forgotten is also preserved, to return, if called on, at a later date. The snow, with its connotations of both burying and freezing, perfectly evokes this metaphor. The memory can be recovered when some-thing happens to make the mind delve into the depths of time and the unconscious, just as the memory of Rosebud is revived for Kane by the little glass snowstorm and log cabin he finds when Susan leaves him. The mise-en-scène is no more rational than the characters' actions. The remote, snow-covered country-side and the little log cabin create a phantasmic landscape that introduces American myth into the psychoanalytic metaphor, and the action combines melodramatic gesture with the rudi-mentary elements of Oedipal drama.

When the serial father figures who stood in his way—Thatcher, Carter, and the *Chronicle* (the lawyer/banker, non-populist/liberal journalist, yellow-press magnate)—have been de-feated by the Kane *Inquirer*, there is a party/celebration that also marks Kane's passage from youth to maturity. At this point, toward the middle of the story, a triumphant happy ending seems to be a foregone conclusion. Happy endings are, in popular culture, immediately preceded by marriage, the rite of passage that marks a transition from youthful irresponsibility to patriarchal authority. The party, almost like a stag party (the original script included a brothel scene that was ultimately cut, at the request of the Hays Office), leads immediately to Kane's engagement. When he appears with Emily Monroe Norton, Bernstein's narration ends on a triumphant note. He understands that Kane's marriage opens the way for his next step up the ladder toward the presidency:

Miss Townsend (awestruck): She's the niece of the President of the United States!
Bernstein: President's niece, huh! Before he's through she'll be a President's wife!

Kane's campaign as the Independent candidate for governor is a stepping-stone on the way to the White House. (The "News on the March": "The White House seemingly the next easy step.") In American mythology, the iconography generated by the White House complements the iconography of Kane's childhood. In his trajectory from the poverty and obscurity of a remote Colorado log cabin to fabulous wealth one step from the White House, Kane encapsulates a populist cliché of the American political dream. Like a version of the old Whittingtonesque folktale of trans-class mobility, "from a log cabin to the White House" is a story cum icon of American mythology. The United States, as the land of equality and opportunity, promised to put the old folktale within reach of all the European rural and urban poor who crossed the Atlantic. William M. Thayer called his biography of President James Garfield *From Log-Cabin to the White House*[5] to emphasize the parallels between Garfield's trajectory and that of President Lincoln, both born to poor pioneer families "in the wilderness," both called to the highest office in the United States. In a short article,[6] Freud suggested that the story of a young man's journey to seek his fortune could be the basic model of the daydream, but he also points out that it integrates the erotic fantasy with the ambitious fantasy. The young man achieves power and riches through marriage to the daughter of an important man who will pass on his position to a worthy son-in-law. Kane's first marriage illustrates the close ties between the love or erotic element of this daydream story and the theme of power through marriage and inheritance through the wife. His marriage to Emily Monroe Norton, the president's niece, puts him, as it were, in line to succeed the president, just as, in Freud's bourgeois version, a father-in-law leaves a business to his daughter's husband or, in the folktale version, the hero is rewarded for his heroism with the princess's hand in marriage, thereby inheriting her father's kingdom.

But Kane himself, or perhaps more precisely Kane and his unconscious, sabotage the happy ending. So, ruined by success, his future narrative path leads not from a log cabin to the White House, but from a log cabin to Xanadu. Susan and the theme of fetishism take over from Oedipal struggle. And although Kane tries for a while and with an increasingly rhetorical and empty sense of desperation, to turn Gettys into a father/monster, he lapses back into the personal, unable to come to terms with the symbolic implications of political and thus patriarchal power. The *Inquirer* and its campaigns fall into the background when Kane's personal struggle against Thatcher becomes subsumed into a circulation battle against the *Chronicle*, which, in turn, is subsumed into political ambition. In the sixteen years covered by the breakfast-table montage, the fairytale promises of Bernstein's narration fade away. The film and Kane's life then both reach a crossroads. By the time he starts on his political campaign, Kane's radical, Oedipal, populist politics are a thing of the past, and slogans about the "cause of reform" against Tammany Hall look increasingly like an investment in his own dictatorial personal power. Both Leland, explicitly, and Gettys, implicitly, accuse him of not being able to distinguish between the personal and the political.

It is during the *Inquirer* party that Kane's collecting mania is first mentioned, as if, once his struggle with his surrogate father has faded, this symptom could perpetuate the scene of separation in the snow in his unconscious. So this symptom, which in the future will take on manic proportions, appears chronologically before his relationship with Susan and before his self-exile from the male world of power and politics into the female world of fantasy and fetishism. This massive accumulation of things relates back, metonymically, to the original lost object, the sled, and the traumatic loss represented by the object, his mother. At the party Bernstein mentions, for the first time, Kane's new habit of collecting statues:

BERNSTEIN: Say, Mr. Kane, so long as you're promising there's a lot of statues in Europe you ain't bought yet—
KANE: You can't blame me Mr. Bernstein. They've been making statues for two thousand years and I've only been buying for five.

There is, however, an Oedipal as well as a fetishistic element here. Kane's collecting obsession fits in with his rebellion against the frugal principles of careful investment and return for which Thatcher stands. The third and last scene between Kane and Thatcher includes this dialogue:

THATCHER: Yes, but your methods. You know, Charles, you never made a single investment. You always used money to—
KANE: To buy things. To buy things. My mother should have chosen a less reliable banker.

The Protestant ethic of productive capitalism stands in diametrical opposition to the wasteful consumption of capital through the accumulation of useless things. Kane is not interested in productive capital ("Sorry but I'm not interested in goldmines, oil wells, shipping, or real estate") and the abstract, symbolic concepts of money and exchange. He cashes in his capital and turns it into concrete objects. In the second part of the film, and especially in the construction of Xanadu, Kane takes spending to obsessive levels, being unable even to unpack the vast amount of stuff he accumulates. At the same time, as evidenced in the last scene at Xanadu, he has never thrown any object away. The things of a lifetime lie strewn about, higgledy-piggledy, and the camera tracks across them, allowing the audience to recognize particular objects that have figured in earlier scenes, and to find the original object, the sled, Rosebud. This massive accumulation of things is set in the context of a lifetime that has attempted to freeze and preserve a traumatic moment of loss. Held in the timelessness of the unconscious, the things relate to each other metonymically, reaching back, longingly and through displacement, toward the original lost object, which screens the memory of loss itself. Into the midst of these fetishized objects, the film introduces a personification of fetishism into its story line.

I argued earlier that the film does not entice the spectator into voyeuristic complicity by means of a depiction of femininity as spectacle. When Susan's erotic qualities and performing abilities enter the scene, the audience is not involved with Kane's gaze. Susan produces an effect of distanciation, and Kane's estimation of his love object is wildly at odds with reality. From the first moment that Susan sings at the parlor piano, the audience finds listening to her painful. But for Kane her voice is the source of true fascination. As he fetishizes Susan's inadequate voice into a precious and valued object, he blinds himself to what he knows and invests all his emotional and financial resources in a deluded belief. He transforms Susan into a highly stylized and produced object. For the opera, her small, inadequate singing voice is dressed up and embellished in an elaborate costume crowned with two enormous blond plaits and a top-heavy headdress. Her legs moving across the stage appear incongruously vulnerable and detached from her body. Confusion swirls around Susan, the presentation of the opera, and the culture it attempts to mimic.

At the same time, the review Kane finishes for Leland indicates that, in some way, he perceives the situation realistically. Fetishism, according to Freud's theory, bears witness to the human psyche's ability to separate knowledge and belief. The woman's body may be traumatically misperceived as castrated, and thus the knowledge of sexual difference itself is disavowed, and belief in the missing object is then preserved by a substitute idealized object. Nevertheless, psychoanalytic theorists since Freud have argued that fetishism is a structure of which the castration model need only be one example. Fetishistic disavowal and substitution can represent other kinds of traumatic loss. In the Kane "case study," the child's separation from his mother is traumatic and need not be literally or mechanically tied to castration anxiety. However, the substitution of an object (the sled) for the mother, subsequent objects (Kane's things), and, finally, another woman (Susan), all bear witness to the structures of disavowal, substitution, and displacement.

Fetishism holds time in check. It is fixated on a thing that artificially resists the changes that knowledge brings with it. The object links back to the original scene and substitutes for it. Freud argues that the fetish functions as a screen memory. The fetish interjects an object between memory and the actual traumatic moment. At the same time the object also marks the place of the lost memory it masks. Freud describes a screen memory as a "witness, simultaneously precious and insignificant, where something that must never be lost may be hidden and preserved."[7] This image evokes the little sled (simultaneously precious and insignificant) buried in the snow (hidden and preserved).

The fact that Kane's collecting is directed exclusively toward European things brings a wider cultural and historical metaphor into the scene. The statues he collects are European in origin and imported into his collection. They prefigure the opera and its European origin, by means of which Susan is transformed into a living fetishized fantasy. Everything is then concentrated in Xanadu itself. And the scenario of the opera and the scenario of Xanadu, while being constructed out of culture and antiquity, end up as pastiches. Although they have a veneer of European antiquity and culture, they are empty, shell-like constructions that Kane never even attempts to understand.

III

I now want to introduce the third level of the overlap between psychoanalysis and history: the political context in which the film was made. It is here that the figure of William Randolph Hearst arises with full force as the main object of Orson Welles's attack. The question of Hearst, of course, added a further level of enigmatic encrustation to the film. Hearst himself contributed the first dramatic, public chapter of *Citizen Kane*'s extracinematic history in the vendetta waged by the Hearst press against the film just before and after its release. At the end of a private screening of the film, the columnist Louella Parsons, accompanied by her chauffeur and two Hearst lawyers, stormed out, furious at what she had seen; only the chauffeur stopped to say to Welles that he enjoyed the picture (Brady, 278). Hearst not only attempted indirectly to sabotage the release of the film but attacked Orson Welles politically. Welles's radio program "His Honor the Mayor" in CBS's "Free Company" series was reported in the Hearst press, sometime after the broadcast but coincidentally with the release of *Citizen Kane*, to have been condemned by the American Legion as "an appeal for the right of all subversive fifth-column groups to hold anti-American meetings in the public hall of an American city," and because "the name itself, 'Free Company,' sounds suspiciously Communistic." Frank Brady, in his book *Citizen Welles*, describes the subsequent government surveillance:

> Welles never knew that a number of Hearst sympathizers began reporting Orson's activities to the FBI as potentially dangerous to the national interest. . . . In a report by a special FBI agent to J. Edgar Hoover, it was noted: "It should be pointed out that this office has never been able to establish that Welles is an actual member of the former Communist Party or the present Communist Political Association; however, an examination of Welles's activities and his membership in various organizations reflects that he has consistently followed the Communist Party line and has

been active in numerous 'front' organizations." (Brady, 292–93)

Welles fought back with reiterated denials that Hearst was the model for Kane, responding politically to political attacks, with psychoanalytic explanations to economic sabotage, and later through anecdotes and humor. One of the last denials appeared, strangely, in his introduction to Marion Davies's book *The Times We Had*, published in 1975:

> Xanadu was a lonely fortress and Susan was quite right to escape from it. The mistress [Marion Davies] was never one of Hearst's possessions. . . . she was the precious treasure of his heart for more than thirty years until the last breath of life. Theirs was truly a love story. Love is not the subject of *Citizen Kane*. . . . If San Simeon had not existed it would have been necessary for the authors to invent it.[8]

In the face of the Hearst campaigns and their undoubted ability to damage Welles professionally and to damage him through political innuendo, there is no doubt that he had to deny the importance of the Hearst model for Kane after the event. Debate, however, continued over the origin of the Hearst model in the context of rival claims over the authorship of *Citizen Kane*. John Houseman describes Herman J. Mankiewicz's interest:

> Total disagreement persists as to where the Hearst idea originated. The fact is that, as a former newspaper man and an avid reader of contemporary history, Mank had long been fascinated by the American phenomenon of William Randolph Hearst. Unlike his friends on the left, to whom Hearst was now an archenemy, fascist isolationist and a red baiter, Mankiewicz remembered the years when Hearst had been regarded as the working man's friend and a political progressive. He had observed him later as a member of the film colony—grandiose, aging and vulnerable in the immensity of his reconstructed palace at San Simeon.[9]

In the years before Welles went to Hollywood, Hearst's vast empire was barely staving off financial collapse. In 1937 his financial affairs were removed from his direct control and put in the hands of a conservation committee, and he was forced to auction off some of his art collection. In March 1939 his financial difficulties were the subject of a *Time* magazine cover story, and around the same time Aldous Huxley's Hearst novel, *After Many a Summer Dies the Swan*, was published. In *Citizen Welles*, Frank Brady describes a dinner, at which Welles was present, held to celebrate the publication of Huxley's book, and at which the model for the portrait and the consequent impossibility of turning the novel into a film were discussed (Brady, 219). Hearst was, therefore, in the news during the months before the conception of *Citizen Kane*. It was when "the miraculous contract had three and a half months to run and there was no film in sight" (in John Houseman's words) that the Hearst idea was floated somewhere between Welles and Mankiewicz. But when Welles, who was definitely on the Left, decided in 1940 to use Hearst as the basis of his first film, he was interested in more than the story of a grand old man of capitalism who was running out of time and money.

Orson Welles had come of age, as it were, and had risen to be an outstanding figure in American theater at a time when extraordinary opportunities had been created by the New Deal's cultural policy, as orchestrated through the Works Progress Administration. Welles first attracted widespread attention with his production of *Macbeth* for the Negro Theater Project in Harlem, of which John Houseman was, at that time, a director. Welles and Houseman were later commissioned by the Federal Theater to run their own company, which they named after its WPA number, Project #891. Welles, returning to the United States from Europe in 1934 at the age of nineteen, was formed intellectually and professionally by the Popular Front and the theater of the New Deal. Welles and Houseman then founded their own, independent Mercury Theater and published their manifesto in the Communist party newspaper, the *Daily Worker*. Welles's growing reputation as an actor and director was established at a new level by his Mercury productions. Their success brought offers from CBS radio, for which Welles was already working, and the formation of the Mercury Theater of the Air. One of their regular

Sunday evening radio adaptations, broadcast on Halloween 1938, "The War of the Worlds," put Welles on the front pages of newspapers across the United States and led George Schaefer of RKO to invite Welles and the Mercury company to Hollywood. In spite of his outstanding qualities as an actor and director, it is always possible that his career would not have taken off in such meteoric style if it had not been for the unprecedented, and unrepeated, opportunities offered by the WPA. This would add a personal element to Welles's political commitment to Franklin Roosevelt, borne out by Welles's continued support for him throughout the years, support the president publicly acknowledged. In 1944 Roosevelt chose Welles to run a radio campaign to sell war bonds, and that year Welles devoted himself to campaigning for the president's reelection; he was invited to the White House for the reelection celebration. In 1944 Roosevelt even encouraged Welles to stand as a candidate for senator in California.

Hearst had moved from reluctant support for Roosevelt as the Democratic presidential candidate in 1932 (only at the last moment and under enormous pressure, when it became clear that his candidate, John Garner, had no hope of victory) to outright denunciation of him for the rest of the 1930s. Hearst was far from in retreat from political activity during the New Deal period. His hostility toward Roosevelt escalated critically regarding new tax legislation that penalized the super-rich in 1935 and union protection legislation that led to conflicts with his own editorial staff during the mid-1930s, after they organized through the American Newspapers' Guild. Hearst's increasingly vituperative move to the right was also a symptom of a generalized political polarization during this period, instanced not only by Upton Sinclair's candidacy for the governorship of California but by the longshoremen's strike in 1934, to the defeat of which Hearst contributed through behind-the-scenes politics as well as newspaper pressure. But polarization in American politics was also marked by international association, on both the Left and the Right. Toward the end of 1934 the *San Francisco Examiner* published, without editorial comment or detachment, three articles by Nazi propagandist Goebbels. And the Hearst papers' red-baiting campaigns, prototypical of anti-Communist McCarthyism of the postwar period, escalated in the same year. In 1936 his antagonism toward Roosevelt put Hearst back in the Republican camp. He contributed $30,000 to the Republican campaign and said, "The race will not be close at all, Landon [the Republican candidate] will be overwhelmingly elected and I'll stake my reputation as a prophet on it."[10]

The Hearst papers were instructed to refer to the New Deal as the "Raw Deal." William Stott describes how the newspapers reached a low ebb of credibility:

> Throughout the early thirties the press managed to ignore or belittle evidence of a depression. In the 1936 Presidential campaign, more than 80 per cent of the press opposed Roosevelt, and he won by the highest percentage ever. During the campaign and for years after, many newspapers, including major syndicates, went beyond all legitimate bounds in an effort to disparage the President and the New Deal. And, as Roosevelt warned the editors, the press lost by it. Public opinion polls in the late thirties suggested that 30 million Americans, nearly one American in three, doubted the honesty of the American press.[11]

Hearst's deep involvement with public and political affairs during the 1930s, and his active support for the Right, present a problem for any attempt to analyze *Citizen Kane* in terms of Welles's own political position. Kane retires from politics after his personal disgrace and political defeat, and the film thus avoids almost any reference to the contemporary political scene and its immediate antecedents. Nonetheless, this apparent lapse has important implications. It allows the Hearst model to be molded into a narrative that has its own self-sufficiency, its own symmetries, and wider metaphorical significance. The split in the narrative between male and female spheres achieves sharp relief as an aesthetic structure in its own right; Kane retreats from public life into a private world of his own making. Furthermore, the psychoanalytic and metaphoric aspects of the film's themes gather a strength that moves beyond the individual into wider mythological issues. The Hearst model is, thus, of importance for *Citizen Kane* not only in its accuracy but in its deviations. In its accuracy it comments on a major and recognizable political figure of the far Right from the political perspective of the liberal Left. Mankiewicz used Ferdinand Lundberg's hostile biography *Imperial Hearst* for his source material so precisely that Lundberg brought a suit for plagiarism against *Citizen Kane* in 1948. The accuracies are obvious. They include the silver-mine fortune; concentration of political power through a popular press that exploited jingoism, sex, and violence; the Hearst papers' part in the Spanish-American War; Hearst's aspiration to the presidency and tangles with Tammany Hall; his collecting mania and his construction of San Simeon; his poaching of archrival Pulitzer's staff from the *World*; his relationship with Marion Davies. The deviations are concentrated particularly at the beginning and end of *Citizen Kane*, in Kane's humble birth in a log cabin, his separation from his mother, and his relation with, and separation from, Susan Alexander. There was no precedent in the Hearst-Davies model for Susan's humiliating failure as an opera singer and attempted suicide, or in the breakdown of their relationship. Hearst and Davies lived happily together, unmarried, until his death in 1951. These deviations are the basis for a psychoanalytic reading of the film.

The insertion of a psychoanalytic explanation for the famous Hearstian puzzle makes *Citizen Kane* seem particularly iconoclastic. The fictional unconscious that the film constructs may well amount to nothing more than sophisticated mischief making. It could be that it seemed amusing to find unconscious motivations for the eccentricities of a recognizable, aging, and reactionary public figure. After all, the political problem that Hearst represents, radical youth giving way to conservative old age, is a cliché in a society that pioneered adolescent revolt as a rite of passage into responsible citizenship. But the war in Europe and the alignment in the United States of Left and Right around isolation or involvement throw light both on the appeal that a Hearst-based script would have for Welles and on the wider implications of its psychoanalytic undertone.

By the time Welles and the Mercury players arrived in Hollywood, Hearst was a major opponent of the entry of the United States into the war in Europe. For the Left, the threat of fascism was actual and urgent. The Mercury Theater had staged a production of *Julius Caesar* in which Caesar was portrayed as a contemporary fascist surrounded by Black Shirts; the production was lit to create a Nuremberg look, in the aftermath of the infamous Nazi rally. In the eyes of the Left, the powerful tycoon's press campaigns to keep America from joining the struggle against fascism was tantamount to support for fascism. While he was vacationing in Germany in 1934, Hearst had visited Hitler, and the German press had quoted Hearst's approving and friendly remarks, which Hearst later claimed had been misquoted. But the famous lines spoken by Kane during an interview included in "News on the March" are the only trace of contemporary politics in *Citizen Kane*:

I have talked with the responsible leaders of the Great Powers—England, France, Germany, and Italy. They are too intelligent to embark upon a project that would mean the end of civilization as we now know it. You can take my word for it, there will be no war.

And alongside the commentary, "No public man whom . . . Kane himself did not support . . . or denounce. Often support . . . and then denounce," the fictional newsreel shows Kane appearing on a balcony with Hitler. The penultimate draft of *Citizen Kane* links Kane more explicitly to fascism through his son, who grows up to become a Nazi and is killed in a raid on an armory in Washington, D.C. So although the film is set in an earlier moment in American history, the choice of Hearst as the subject of Welles's film was still politically relevant in the late 1930s. Right-wing opposition to Roosevelt had emerged as a new and real threat in the context of fascism.

From the perspective of the New Deal and antifascist politics, Hearst presented an appropriate subject for the first Mercury production in Hollywood. However, the political references to Hearst are overshadowed by the psychoanalytic undertones of the fictional character Kane. But the condensation of the real-life political and fictional psychoanalytic traits carry their implications into a psychoanalytic attack on the politics of right-wing populism. This is where the film is daring. It could be that the furor over the question of whether or not the film was a portrait of Hearst distracted critics and commentators from what the film was implying about the political and personal bankruptcy of the American Right. The film continually reaches out toward a mythological level, appropriating quite obvious, even hackneyed, psychoanalytic tropes to cut corners between character and metaphor.

The image of Kane at the end of the film serves as an allegorical warning about the fate of European-American relations. As I noted at the beginning of this essay, the film was made during the bleakest period of the war, when Roosevelt was becoming more and more convinced of the need for America to get involved in the conflict. Welles's portrayal of Kane is an apt image of the destiny that isolationism would bring in its wake. Kane is shown as an old man, lonely and alone, literally isolated in the enormous, claustrophobic castle he has constructed as a fantasy world against the world outside, no longer involved with it, and incarcerated inside his own mausoleum. This image seems to represent the isolationist policies of the Hearst press; and Xanadu, through its blatant similarity to San Simeon, is one of the most transparent references to Hearst in the film.

Robert Carringer, in *The Making of "Citizen Kane,"* analyzes the designs of RKO's art director, Perry Ferguson, for Xanadu, showing how the Great Hall at Xanadu was based closely on a photograph of the Great Hall at San Simeon. Carringer notes:

> The Hearstian element is brought out in the almost perverse juxtaposition of incongruous architectural styles and motifs—Gothic along the far wall, Venetian Baroque in the loggia, Egyptian on the landing (including a sphinx on a plinth!), vaguely far Eastern figures along the staircase. (Carringer, 54)

Such a confusion of cultures points to a confusion of history and the ordering of time—and also to the confusion of populist politics. If Kane, and by implication Hearst, is stuck in a fetishistic inability to understand or acknowledge the processes of history, the film seems to hint that this disorder has a psychoanalytic origin. And, also by implication, the isolationist stance is a sign of a repressed, unworked-through Oedipal trajectory that has been prematurely broken off, leaving the subject tied to a "frozen" memory of loss. In Freudian terms, a child's edenic relation to his or her mother may be represented metaphorically by antiquity, the place of ancient origin, the "old world." It is striking that no Hollywood genre, and relatively few individual films, deal with migration across the Atlantic. It is almost as if this passage, from the Old to the New World, was a taboo subject in American popular culture. In *Citizen Kane*, however, the Old World is presented ambivalently. It contains a threat of paternal violence within the "before" of the before-after divide between the mother's exclusive and dependable love and the child's Oedipal journey into the outside world of ambition. For both these reasons the "old world" is in danger of lying outside history, subject to repression. At the moment of fascist threat, Welles seems to suggest a psychoanalytic metaphor to explain the dilemma facing the Euro-American collective psyche. At the same time, the film's formal appeal cuts across a purely psychoanalytic rhetoric and refuses to represent only its dilemma. The film addresses the discernment of those spectators who can figure out an enigma without the help of a narrator/commentator. The spectators, in the last resort, will piece together the history of the film's protagonist in its closing moments and then, if their curiosity has really been engaged, will review and retell the film by tracing and linking together the clues and symptoms that conceal, but preserve, its meaning. In doing so, they would be directed not only toward the figure of the newspaper magnate and his hold over national narrative, but also toward their own ability to read cinematic images and even, perhaps, toward the entanglement of contemporary politics with past, historical trauma.

There is a kind of poetic justice in Welles's and cinematographer Gregg Toland's use of deep focus in a film that attacks Hearst.

The magnate of newspapers and old-style movies is depicted in a new style of cinematography pioneered by the newspapers' new rival, the photo-magazines. And, on the level of sound, Welles made maximum use of his own experience in radio, the medium beloved by Roosevelt, to create a texture that had never been heard before in the Hollywood cinema. And although the deep-focus look had been previously pioneered in Hollywood, the politics of *Citizen Kane* juxtaposes it, perhaps even coincidentally, with the cinematic aesthetics of other Left cinemas of the 1930s and 1940s. In the view of André Bazin, the deep-focus cinematography of Jean Renoir's Popular Front movies in the 1930s in France returned in the Italian neorealist and leftist cinema of the postwar period. For Bazin, engagement between spectator and screen in *Citizen Kane* was an effect of its composition, and formed a triptych with the Popular Front cinema on the one hand and that of neorealism on the other. Dramatic juxtapositions are composed within the frame, and a shot then lasts long enough for the spectator to work out the relationships between the characters and to extract the poetic and emotional implications of the scene. Bazin argued that this kind of composition gave the spectator's eye and mind an autonomy and freedom that both montage and the cutting conventions of commercial cinema (especially after the coming of sound) denied.

From my own, European point of view, Bazin's inclusion of *Citizen Kane* in his political/aesthetic argument always seemed anomalous and to privilege aesthetics over politics. However, looking again at *Citizen Kane*, in the context of the New Deal in the United States and of the conflict between an extreme Right and an attempted Popular Front in both the United States and Europe, Welles's perhaps intuitive approach to cinema finally fits with Bazin's intuitive triptych.

Notes

1. Frank Brady, *Citizen Welles: A Biography of Orson Welles* (New York: Doubleday, 1989), 285; hereafter cited in text as Brady.

2. In Dilys Powell, "The Life and Opinions of Orson Welles" (London) *Times*, 3 February 1963.

3. Bernard Herrmann, "Score for a Film," in *Focus on "Citizen Kane,"* ed. Ronald Gottesman (Englewood Cliffs, N.J.: Prentice-Hall, 1971), 70.

4. Robert Carringer, *The Making of "Citizen Kane"* (Berkeley: University of California Press, 1985), 11; hereafter cited as Carringer.

5. William Makepeace Thayer, *From Log-Cabin to the White House: Life of James A. Garfield, Boyhood, Youth, Manhood, Assassination, Death, Funeral* (New York: Alden, 1883).

6. Sigmund Freud, "The Relation of the Poet to Day-Dreaming," in *On Creativity and the Unconscious: Papers on the Psychology of Art, Literature, Love, Religion*, translated by Joan Riviere et al. (New York: Harper and Row, 1958), 44–54.

7. Sigmund Freud, "Fetishism," in *The Standard Edition of the Complete Psychological Works*, vol. 21 (London: Hogarth, 1961).

8. Marion Davies, *The Times We Had* (New York: Bobbs-Merrrill, 1975).

9. John Houseman, *Unfinished Business* (London: Chatto and Windus, 1986), 223.

10. W. A. Swanberg, *Citizen Hearst* (London: Longman, 1965), 477.

11. William Stott, *Documentary Expression in 1930s America* (Oxford: Oxford University Press, 1973), 79.

Citizen Kane

PETER WOLLEN

❖ ❖ ❖

To WRITE ABOUT *Citizen Kane* is to write about the cinema.
It is impossible to think about this film without thinking
about its place in film history. Most critics, despite Welles's own
unhappy relations with Hollywood, have seen him primarily
within the framework of the American narrative cinema. Pauline
Kael talks about the 1930s newspaper picture and builds up the
role of Herman Mankiewicz, a hardcore Hollywood scribe if ever
there was one. Charles Higham talks of a "wholly American
work," Andrew Sarris of "the American baroque," and they leave
no doubt, I think, that where the cinema is concerned, for them
America = Hollywood. And, from the other side, an enemy of
Hollywood such as Noël Burch places Welles in relation to Elia
Kazan, Robert Aldrich, Joseph Losey, and Arthur Penn and con-
demns *Kane* for simply displaying an amplification of traditional
narrative codes that it does nothing to subvert.

Against this mainstream trend, of course, we have to set the
massive influence of André Bazin. For Bazin, *Kane* and *The Magnificent Ambersons* were crucial moments in the unfolding of the

cinema's vocation of realism. Together with the work of Jean Renoir and William Wyler, *Kane* represented a rediscovery of the tradition of realism, lost since the silent epoch (Louis Feuillade, Erich Von Stroheim, F. W. Murnau). *Kane* looked forward to Italian neorelaism and, had Bazin lived longer, his interest would surely have turned to *cinéma vérité* and the new developments in documentary that followed the invention of magnetic tape, the lightweight recorder and camera, and the tape join. (Indeed the strain of "technological messianism" in Bazin's thought must surely have taken him in this direction.)

For Bazin, of course, the crucial feature of *Citizen Kane* was its use of deep focus and the sequence-shot. Yet one senses all the time, in Bazin's writings on Welles, an uneasy feeling that Welles was far from sharing the spiritual humility and self-effacement, or even the democratic mentality, which marked for Bazin the "style without style," the abnegation of the artist before a reality whose meaning outruns that of any artifact. It is easy to forget that, on occasion, Bazin talked about the "sadism" of Welles, of his *rubbery* space, stretched and distended, rebounding like a catapult in the face of the spectator. He compared Welles to El Greco (as well as to the Flemish masters of deep focus) and commented on his "infernal vision" and "tyrannical objectivity." But this awareness of Welles the stylist and manipulator did not deflect Bazin from his main point. Fundamentally, his enthusiasm was for the deep-focus cinematography which Welles and Gregg Toland introduced with such virtuosity. It was on this that Welles's place in film history would depend.

Yet a third current has been felt recently, again often more implicit than explicit. . . . [I]t is possible to place *Kane* as a forerunner of *Last Year at Marienbad*, a film that pointed the way toward the breakdown of unilinear narration and a Nietzschean denial of truth. It is in this sense too that we can understand Borges' praise of *Kane* as a "labyrinth without a center" *Kane*'s perspectivism (leading so easily to nihilism), its complex pattern of nesting, overlapping, and conflicting narratives, puts it in a particular tendency within the modern movement, which has its origins perhaps in Joseph Conrad or William Faulkner and its most radical exponents in Luigi Pirandello and the further reaches of the French new novel.

And of course, this tendency, whose origins are in literature, has begun to spread into the cinema, especially in France, through the influence of writers—Marguerite Duras, Alain Robbe-Grillet—who have worked on films, even become filmmakers.

The oddest of these three versions of *Kane* is undoubtedly Bazin's. So flexible, so generous in many respects, Bazin was nevertheless able at times to restrict and concentrate his vision to an amazing degree. Obviously he felt the influence of expressionism (which he hated) on *Kane*, but he simply discounted it—or tried to justify it by pointing to the exaggeration and tension in the character of Kane, a kind of psychological realism, similar to the way in which he defended the expressionist style of a film about concentration camps (in the same vein, Christian Metz remarks how the formal flamboyance of *Kane*, the film, parallels the flamboyant personality of Kane, the man). In general, however, Bazin simply hurried on to his favorite theme—the importance of deep focus and the sequence-shot.

The key concepts here for Bazin were those of spatial and temporal homogeneity and of dramatic unity. It is almost as if the theatrical scene was the model for Bazin's theory of the cinema. Of course, he believed that filmed theater should respect the scene and the stage. Beyond that, it seems he believed in a *theatrum mundi*, which it was the calling of the cinema to capture and record—there is a sense in which all cinema was for him filmed theater, only in neorealism, for instance, the world was a stage, the players were living their lives and the dramatist, who gave meaning to the action, was God himself. No wonder then that for him the artist, in Annette Michelson's phrase, was "artist as witness" and the whole of reality the offering of an "Ultimate Spectacle." Indeed, Bazin writes that in Italy daily life was a perpetual commedia dell'arte and describes the architecture of Italian towns and cities as being like a theater set.

Bazin always laid great stress on the theatricality of Orson Welles. He saw Welles as a man of the theater and talked about the sequence-shot as a device for maintaining the primacy of the actor. "An actor's performance loses its meaning, is drained of its dramatic blood like a severed limb, if it ceases to be kept in living, sensory contact with the other characters and the setting. Moreover, as it lasts, the scene charges itself like a battery."

Bazin justifies the sequence-shot and deep focus for three reasons: it maintains the dramatic unity of a scene, it permits objects to have a residual being beyond the pure instrumentality demanded of them by the plot, and it allows the spectator a certain freedom of choice in following the action. In *Kane* it was the first which was uppermost. The second was important to Bazin—he talks about the door handle of Susan Alexander's bedroom, in the sequence after the suicide attempt, and goes on to describe the cold feel of copper, the copper or indented enamel of a door handle, yet we must feel that this is his own projection, reverie almost (in the Bachelardian sense) which has little relevance to *Kane*. As for the third reason, Bazin recognizes that Welles directs the spectator's attention through lighting and movement as imperiously as any editor at times, but he remains aware of the potential ambiguity of the sequence-shot and, of course, links this to the ambiguous portrayal of Kane's character.

Yet, with the advantage of hindsight, we can see that Bazin's love of the sequence-shot has been strangely betrayed by the filmmakers who have subsequently used it. Who do we think of? Andy Warhol, Michael Snow, Jean-Luc Godard, Jean-Marie Straub, Miklos Jancso. There are links of course—Straub reveres Bazin's hero, Robert Bresson; Godard was deeply marked by Roberto Rossellini—but clearly the sequence-shot has been used for purposes quite different from those foreseen by Bazin. Some of these filmmakers have stressed the autonomy of the camera and its own movement, rather than the primacy of the actors or the drama (Jancso, Snow); others have used the sense of duration to derealize the imaginary world of the film (Godard); others have been interested in duration as a formal feature in itself (Warhol). Straub, probably the closest to Bazin in his insistence on authenticity, on a refusal of guidance for the spectator's eye, has nonetheless put his Bazinian style to purposes very different from those Bazin himself could have envisaged.

It is worth noting that most of the sequence-shots in *Citizen Kane* are, in fact, used in the framing story rather than the flashbacks, in the scenes in which Thompson talks to each of the interior narrators. The average length of a shot in *Citizen Kane* is not particularly long because of the number of short shots that exist both in the newsreel sequence and in the numerous montage sequences which Welles uses, mostly as transitions. The decision to use sequence-shots in the framing story is clearly a decision not to use classical field/reverse-field cutting, and thus to deemphasize the role of Thompson, the narratee. Thompson only appears as a shadowy figure with his back to the camera. It is hard to separate decisions on length of shot and editing from decisions on narrative structure. By shooting Thompson in this way Welles precludes any spectator identification with the character who, from the point of view of information and focalization, is the spectator's representative in the film.

In the last analysis, what concerned Bazin was dramaturgy (even if, as with the neorealists, he could speak of a "dramaturgy of everyday life"), and he tended to assume the need for characters and a continuous narrative line. He simply thought that psychological truth and dramatic configurations would reveal themselves more fully if there was a minimum of artistic intervention. He remained hostile throughout to experimental film (for him Von Stroheim was the great experimentalist and Welles, of course, can easily be perceived as an avatar of Von Stroheim) and thought of theater and the novel as the models with which cinema should be compared. There too he tended to have conventional tastes—he aligns himself with Sartre's condemnation of Mauriac, but seems also to accept without question Sartre's positive tastes: John Dos Passos, William Faulkner, Ernest Hemingway—and clearly was not interested in the literary revolution inaugurated by Gertrude Stein and James Joyce.

Yet the example of contemporary filmmakers has shown that the long take and the sequence-shot tend to undermine the primacy of the dramaturgy: duration becomes a stylistic feature in itself and, far from suppressing the filmmaking process, the sequence-shot tends to foreground it. At most, the sequence-shot can be associated with a Brechtian type of dramaturgy, based on tableaux. In fact this tendency can be seen even in *Citizen Kane*, where it is disguised by the movement in and out of the framing story and the complex character of the transitions. Bazin thought that the principal function of the cut should be that of ellipsis, but within the kind of rhythm built up by a series of long sequence-shots, the cut automatically plays a role as caesura rather than as ellipsis alone.

Although Bazin talked mainly in terms of traditional dramaturgy and the realistic essence of photography (photochemical transfer of *presence* from the world to the film) his writings seem now almost to be—or at least to conceal—a theory of time in the cinema, hence a theory of *absence*. What strikes us with the long take is not so much that the image is there, but that it is *still* there. Bazin talks about time in terms of length, lasting, duration. The type of montage he liked least was the "accelerated" montage he associated with Abel Gance. Indeed, he is at pains to point out how montage sequences in *Kane* are equivalent to the frequentative, the imperfect—designating continuous or repeated actions—rather than being accelerated montages of the Gance type. One feels that by the same token, his suspicion of Sergei Eisenstein was not simply a dislike of abstraction but a dislike of the short duration of Eisenstein's shots: exactly the feature that attracted Stan Brakhage. Montage in the classical sense, by stressing relations between shots rather than relations between objects in the shot, produced a dialectic of loss and absence, difference and division, rather than of presence, continuity, and unity.

Time in the cinema involves at least two—perhaps three—realms of time. There is the imaginary time of the story and there is the real (with reservations) time of the film—story time, screen time, and also perhaps production time, filmmaking time. (Certainly it is the introduction of filmmaking time as a conscious category which marks the films of directors such as Godard-Gorin and Dziga Vertov. Of course, filmmaking time can be phantasmatically incorporated into imaginary time, as with François Truffaut's *Day for Night*.) Between these different realms of time there is a series of differential relations—relations which can be analyzed through the concepts of duration, order, and frequency, as developed by Gérard Genette in his work on literature. We should note also that, as the cinema is constituted at present, screen time is determinate and fixed—it can be calculated by the number of frames and constant (standard) speed of projection. This was not always the case—silent films were projected at variable speed, so that the projectionist was somewhat like the performer of a piece of music, who, to a certain extent, can vary tempo and duration. In the future, when films are watched through video recorders, we can envisage a screen time more like that of book reading, with a spectator who pauses, hurries through, replays, turns back to refresh the memory.

In most films—Hollywood films particularly—story time is longer than screen time and hence the basic operational figures are those of compression and ellipsis. In contrast, independent and experimental films have tended to suppress imaginary time entirely and to work with screen time alone, often with great complexity, or else they have chosen to move toward isochronicity (Warhol) or, through repetition, for instance, to have story time shorter than screen time (Bruce Conner). Independent films, too, have tended to have screen time either of shorter (down to one frame) or longer duration than Hollywood films (Snow, Jacques Rivette, Warhol, *Scottie's Endless Movie*, of indefinite duration, because never completed). In general terms, we can say that Hollywood cinema has tended to suppress consciousness of screen time, to transport the spectator into the realm of the imaginary, but here again it is easy to think of exceptions in which time is organized in a very complex or idiosyncratic way—Alfred Hitchcock's *Rope*, Raphael-Donen's *Two for the Road*, and, of course, *Citizen Kane*.

The most obvious feature of *Kane* in this context is the flashback structure, which involves duration, order, and frequency. Kane's life as a whole is narrated twice (newsreel, memories) and one section of it, the opera sequence, twice by different interior narrators. In a sense, there is a third narration—the tracking shot over the accumulation of objects in the great hall of Xanadu, which passes over the residue of different periods of Kane's life in inverse order, culminating with the sled preserved from early childhood. Order is also affected by the movement in and out of the framing story and the variations from unilinear order within the flashbacks. Duration is clearly involved in the compression of Kane's life into roughly two hours of screen time, through the selection of key scenes (Bazin's sequence-shots, or near-sequence-shots) and complicated transitions between them.

Fundamentally, the flashback structure of *Kane* is a variation on the classical detective story format. Every detective story is in fact two stories: the story of a crime and the story of an investigation. The crime story revolves around a mystery, a secret, and the investigation story ends with the revelation of the secret and the narration of the crime story. Thus the investigator is presented first as a narratee, who listens to the fragmentary, misleading, or limited versions of various witnesses, participants in the crime story, and then must piece these together into a coherent story, which he finally narrates. (Or he may elicit a confession, in which case he remains in the role of narratee, whose function has been not to tell the story, but to hear it by inducing or compelling someone else to tell it, whether witness or criminal.)

Kane follows this pattern of the twofold story, the second ending with the narration of the first, but with a number of crucial differences and variations. First, of course, we must point out that the investigator—Thompson, a journalist rather than a detective—never himself discovers the clue which would enable him to reveal the secret and tell the story of Rosebud. The secret is revealed by the filmmaker to the spectator alone. Within the imaginary world of the film story, the enigma is never solved. It remains insoluble. However, it is solved for us. In effect, there is a second framing narrative—the prologue and the epilogue to the film—which is narrated by the filmmaker(s), the implicit or inscribed author.

This secret—the secret of Rosebud's identity—is not, of course, the answer to the riddle set by a crime, which always involves discovering the identity of a criminal, casting one of the characters in the investigation story as protagonist in the crime story. However, almost all the "evidence" narrated to Thompson by Thatcher (via the written word), Bernstein, and the others is set in a time period after the crucial event, the loss of the sled, rather than before it, as is usual in a crime story, in which the secret is that of the ending rather than the beginning. Most of the interior narration, in the flashbacks, has no direct bearing on the secret. In fact, the narrators typically begin by denying any knowledge of Rosebud. The structure of *Kane* is that of a biographical portrait, from different points of view, set within an investigation story. This is the opposite of the type of investigation story in which the personality of the detective becomes more important than the solution of the crime. Here the investigator is almost anonymous: it is the personality of Kane that dominates. In effect, also, there is a play on the problem of identity: who or what was Rosebud? Who or what was Kane? In Hitchcockian terms, Rosebud is the MacGuffin around which the narrative pivots, but which is of structural rather than informational significance.

Each level of narration in the film is in a different register and has a different kind of time structure. The investigation story proper—the series of interviews which Thompson has—lasts for about a week. We are shown the interviews themselves—or rather their beginnings and ends—principally in sequence-shots, but bookended or introduced by an insert or short establishing sequence. The story time omitted—the time in which Thompson travels from one interview to another, for instance—is marked elliptically by dissolves. At times, we return to the framing story within a flashback, presumably to cover a difficult transition. Apart from the opening sequence in the screening room and the closing sequence in Xanadu, Thompson is always shown subordinated to the interior narrators—in the inserts which introduce interviews he is sometimes absent (the famous crane shots through the El Rancho skylight) or scarcely present (the shot of the hospital under the bridge). Even the "interview" with Thatcher, which cannot show Thatcher live, is dominated by sculpture and paintings which portray him.

The flashbacks themselves are almost in chronological order, and it is interesting to note that the major ellipses exist *within* rather than *between* flashbacks. Between Leland's narration and Susan Alexander's there is overlap and repetition; there is a minor ellipsis between Bernstein's and Leland's and direct continuity between Susan Alexander's and Raymond's. The flashbacks, which make up the bulk of the film, show the most varied types of time organization. Following Genette, we can distinguish five types of relation between story and screen time in respect of duration. These exist both at the level of the shot and at the level of the sequence:

1. *Elongation.* Screen time greater than story time.
2. *Summary/abbreviation.* Screen time less than story time.
3. *Scene.* Screen time and story time the same.
4. *Stasis.* Screen time continuous. Story time discontinuous.
5. *Ellipsis.* Story time continuous. Screen time discontinuous.

These categories provide an alternative approach to that of Christian Metz and the classification of types of syntagma, which are also defined largely in terms of temporal and spatial relationships between the diegesis, the story, and the screen. Both the "autonomous shot" and the "scene" (in Metz's sense) fall within the category of "scene" (in Genette's sense), one with spatial discontinuity of field of view, the other without. The ordinary sequence displays minor ellipses, the episodic sequence major ellipses; in fact, one of the difficulties with Metzian analysis is deciding when a minor discontinuity becomes major. An important difference, which also produces problems, is that Metz assumes that the narrative is discontinuous and that the story can be readily divided and demarcated into actions or events, each of which is a unity. While this may be true logically (though this is very uncertain once the Proppian realms of fairytale are left behind) it does not follow that a logical caesura will be coterminous with a chronological break, marked by an ellipsis. *between* syntagmas, while other ellipses, *within* syntagmas, lack the same logical status.

In any case, the flashbacks in *Kane* contain a number of interesting temporal features. The mini-sequence (two shots linked by

a dissolve) of snow falling on the sled, after young Kane's departure with Thatcher, is an example of summary or abbreviation, a
variant on the classical calendar-leaves shot. The famous breakfast
montage is an example both of spatial continuity with major temporal discontinuity and also of repetition with variation within
the story time. There are two examples of freeze frame/photo-
graphed still (stasis). The first, the still of journalists at the *Chronicle* coming to life when they join the *Inquirer*, plays on both the
duration of stills (passage of time) and their nonrepeatability
(ironic repetition; same image, different time and circumstance).
The second, when the door of Kane's "love nest" freezes into a
press photograph, after the departure of his wife, takes up the recurrent theme of the contrast between the emblematic public image, frozen and apparently objective and determinate, and the flu-
idity/subjectivity and indeterminacy of the life which lies behind.

A further category of filmic time is found both in the flashbacks and, more obviously, in the newsreel sequence: the shot
Bazin calls "frequentative" and Genette "iterative." For instance,
the shot in the newsreel of the paper running through the press
signifies not a particular incident in the story time, but a repeated
process. Paper runs through the press every day. This usage,
which approaches the symbolic, depends partly, however, on context—introduced within what Metz calls the "bracketing syntagma"—and partly on our familiarity with the look of stock
shots and library material. Welles and Toland also attempted to
simulate filmmaking time in the newsreel by making some of the
footage look old, in the same way that Godard and Raoul Cou-
tard shot *Les Carabiniers* to simulate the look of silent orthochro-
matic stock.

Finally, there are the prologue and epilogue. Here the major
time phenomenon is symmetry. The film begins with a series of
shots dissolving into each other—the dissolve establishes an element of continuity in screen time, lacking with the cut; it is
rarely used to signify a purely spatial change in the field of vision—beginning outside the fence of Xanadu, passing the No
Trespassing sign, then approaching the house, high up, as though
with a crane shot. The end is similar, though not quite identical,

as we leave Xanadu, again in a series of dissolves, pass the No Trespassing sign, and end outside the fence once more. Symmetry, of course, is a figure that combines order with repetition: the same shots are repeated, but in inverse order. In fact, the whole of *Kane* is marked by symmetry—the crane shots in and out of El Rancho, for instance, or, perhaps more subtle, the way in which the sequence of Kane's rage, the destruction of Susan Alexander's bedroom, is bookended by two quasiinserts: the screeching cockatoo and the empty series of receding mirror images.

In an essay, "On the Problems of Symmetry in Art," Dagobert Frey observes, "Symmetry signifies rest and binding, asymmetry motion and loosening, the one order and law, the other arbitrariness and accident, the one formal rigidity and constraint, the other life, play and freedom." Without necessarily seeing the question in such clear-cut terms, there is an apparent tension in *Kane* between the formal symmetry of the film and the themes of the irreversibility of biographical time and the shifting perspectivism which led Borges to his description of it as a "labyrinth without a center." In fact, *Kane* reflects the old contrast between the order, permanence, and certainty of art and the disorder, transiency, and uncertainty of life. Despite everything Pauline Kael or François Truffaut have said about the "journalistic" quality of *Kane*, its formal structure alone demands that we approach it as art. (In this respect we can compare Welles with Samuel Fuller—another director of whose films it is appropriate to talk in terms of "layout" or "headline shots," but who seems less insistent on his own identity as an artist.)

Truffaut, always fundamentally a conservative critic—as he has shown himself to be a conservative filmmaker—has said that "if *Citizen Kane* has aged, it is in its experimental aspects." It seems to me that precisely the opposite is true. All Welles's "tricks," as they are often contemptuously called—the lighting mixes, the stills which come to life, the complex montages, the elasticity of perspective, the protracted dissolves, the low-angle camera movements—are what still gives the film any interest. Nobody, after all, has ever made high claims for its novelistic content, its portrayal of Kane's psychology, its depiction of American society and politics in the first half of the twentieth century, its anatomy of love or power or wealth. Or, at any rate, there is no need to take such claims very seriously. It seems quite disproportionate for Noël Burch to submit them to his acute dissection and attack, as he himself seems to half-acknowledge.

Indeed, the pro-Hollywood defense of *Kane* is quite pathetic in its lack of ambition. (*Kane*, after all, is widely held to be the greatest film ever made.) Pauline Kael begins with hyperbole— "the one American talking picture that seems as fresh now as the day it opened"—but soon descends to dub *Kane*, in a famous phrase, "a shallow work, a *shallow* masterpiece." The shallowness does not worry her, however, because it is what makes *Kane* "such an American triumph," and then we discover its triumph lies in "the way it gets its laughs and makes its point." She assimilates *Kane* to the tradition of the well-made Broadway play, translated into the 1930s comedy film, with all its astringency and sense of pace and fun. Other critics do not really claim much more— Charles Higham talks of a "masterpiece," but also "epic journalism"; once again, we get the insistence on the "American" quality of Welles and *Kane*, ironic in the light of the original intention to call *Citizen Kane, The American*: energy, grandeur, and emptiness.

The truth is that the content of *Citizen Kane* cannot be taken too seriously. Yet it had an enormous impact—largely because of its virtuosity, its variety of formal devices and technical innovations and inventions. In themselves, of course, these are purely ornamental, and the dominant aesthetic of our age is one that rejects the concept of ornament—the ruling aesthetic of our day is one of expressionism or functionalism or symbolism or formalism, seen as a complex process of problem solving rather than as wit or decoration. Welles is usually described in terms of baroque or expressionism, sometimes the gothic, but this seems to reflect the ponderousness of his themes. His interest in formal devices and technical ingenuity places him closer to mannerism, to a conscious appreciation of virtuosity and the desire to astonish.

It is this "mannerist" aspect of Welles that is still significant— not the dramatic unity which deep focus and the long take make possible, but the long take and deep focus as formal features in themselves. Similarly, it is not the theme of time—youth, memory, age—that is of any interest, but the devices used to organize time within the film. Many of these point the way toward a quite different kind of use—contemporary filmmakers' variations on the long take, Robbe-Grillet's variations on the freeze frame/still. *Kane* remains an important film historically, not within the terms it set itself, or those within which it has been mainly seen by critics, but because, by a kind of retroactive causality, it is now possible to read there an entirely different film, one that Welles probably never intended. *Citizen Kane*, we can now say, was a milestone along the road that led, not to a reinvigoration of Hollywood, nor a novelistic complication of narrative, nor the unfolding of the realistic essence of film, but toward the expansion and elaboration of a formal poetic that would transform our concept of cinema entirely, toward film as a text that is a play with meaning rather than a vehicle for it.

Out of the Depths

Citizen Kane, *Modernism, and the Avant-Garde Impulse*

PAUL ARTHUR

◆ ◆ ◆

There's no art
To find the mind's construction in the face.
—*Shakespeare*, MACBETH

O RSON WELLES, who was seldom at a loss for an artistic opinion, complained in a 1965 interview: "I see that there are directors, full of future, sensitive, who explore new themes, but I see no one who attacks form, the manner of saying things."[1] The attitude expressed here is familiar, a combination of bitterness at creative opportunities lost and a disdain for those not seizing their moment in the light to reflect upon the nature of the medium. Admittedly Welles tried on many public masks besides that of intrepid formal investigator. Yet a twinned and on the surface seemingly discordant impulse haunts his public statements, and indeed his creative output, virtually from the beginning. Writing in 1938, at the pinnacle of his trek through the New York theater world, he asserts that the "business" of a director is "to make his playhouse a kind of magic trick in which something quite impossible comes to be."[2] What manner of aesthetic system binds a belief in magic with an "attack" on form? The key, perhaps, is to be found at the crossroads of what is meant by the "impossible."

There is, I would suggest, a consistent and intricate negotiation in Welles's work between the aims of seduction and those of demystification, illusion and anti-illusion, and in another register, popular entertainment and modernist rigor. More blatantly, the imprint of a radical, avant-gardist vision can be tracked across Welles's theater pieces and films, and it runs far deeper than frequent critical claims for "innovation" or "rule breaking." The vision constitutes, in fact, a historically and culturally specific practice rooted in European cinematic and theatrical avant-gardes of the 1920s and anticipatory of the American filmic movement launched in the years following and in part spurred by the release of *Citizen Kane*. Like many other strands in his manifold achievement, Welles's proclivity for modernist didacticism is most exactingly and excitingly realized in his initial film—a project so inclusive in its inventory of genres and styles and formal tropes, so double-edged in its quotient of retrospection and prophecy, that it functions as a kind of textual Xanadu.

Cast as the notorious "boy genius" poised between two careers and (at least) two media, at the cusp of a fateful decade, it is hardly accidental that Welles steers his first encounter with what he called Hollywood's "train set" on a collision course with the demands and the prerogatives of *both* mass culture and so-called high culture. Utilizing the dramatic props of a standard biopic to, among other things, deflect attention from reflexive "difficulty," he dons an elite armature of modernism as a means to distance his work from "crass" commercial ploys. When the smoke clears, as it does at the end of *Citizen Kane*, we are left not with scattered wreckage but a mirage, held in place by the force-field of a singular narrative and, paradoxically, by the open-endedness of its message. This is aesthetic sleight of hand of the first order, and it will be the task of this essay to expose the mechanics of the trick and provide a broader setting in which those mechanics acquire previously unsounded significance.

I

The response to *Citizen Kane*, especially in daily press reviews but also in longer and more studied assessments, was straightforward in its attribution of an "experimental" impulse. For example, Anthony Bower of the *Nation* cited Russian and German expressionist precedents and praised Welles as perhaps the first Hollywood director "really to exploit the screen as a medium." Cedric Belfrage called the film's techniques "a revolution, and a major one."[3] Appositely, critical reservations tended to focus on Welles's "undisciplined" or "excessive" visual display, which, as Bosley Crowther put it, "worked against the logic of his story."[4] Regardless of their final judgment, commentators shared an inference that the director consciously set out to forge a new cinematic language, one that would transcend and inherently critique dominant conventions of the period. Of course, such response was abetted by all the publicity surrounding the film, by Welles's reputation and artistic pronouncements, and furthered by collaborators such as Gregg Toland with his bristling account of "How I Broke the Rules."[5] In François Truffaut's elegant retrospective view, the burden of *Kane*'s "declaration of love for the medium" was to "summarize forty years of cinema while taking the opposite course of everything that had been done."[6]

It should come as no surprise then that Welles's unquestioned originality prompts comparison with figures understood to be at the cutting edge of literary or visual culture. His approach is placed in the company of Proust, Faulkner, Kafka,[7] and loosely analogized with the procedures of abstract expressionist painting and serial music.[8] Although the gesture of linking Welles and his film to "highbrow" elements might in its historical context fulfill a number of ideological functions—including the campaign by arbiters of the 1940s to promote a native culture as the equal of European masters, culminating in the Cold War logic of, for example, "The Triumph of American Painting"[9]—there is little doubt that the occasion of *Citizen Kane* provided ammunition for those seeking broad acceptance of cinema as a credible art form.

That Welles was ideally suited as an avatar of cinematic parity with the other arts was due not only to his talent for self-aggrandizement but to his genuine knowledge of and contact with a range of European experimentalists; Brecht, Cocteau, and Eisenstein are but three names in Welles's (not always harmonious) circle of acquaintances.

Moreover, unlike most of Hollywood's theatrical expatriates such as Ben Hecht, Welles had made a substantial contribution to the revitalization of American stagecraft. Preparing the ground for critical reception to *Kane*, the Mercury Theater engendered a parallel controversy over bravura formalism versus theme or content. Individual productions were praised or damned for their experimental bias, their supposed willingness to sacrifice clarity of interpretation for spectacular effect. Thus the presentation of *Horse Eats Hat* devolves into "surrealist slapstick," and *Danton's Death* is seen as "self-consciously avant-garde." Welles's methods are compared, favorably or unfavorably, to innovators such as Piscator and Meierhold, and so on.[10] Long-time collaborator John Houseman characterized the source of his "magic" as an "ability to stretch familiar elements of theatrical effect far beyond their normal point of tension."[11] Richard France, author of the sole monograph on Welles's theatrical career, concludes that "the uniqueness of a Welles production is that its form, not its content, carries his meaning," a decidedly modernist tendency.[12]

Extrapolating from second-hand reports, from drawings and photographs, three points are worth making about the specific ways in which the theater productions "called attention" to themselves. First, Welles seemed to organize individual plays around a single concept, expressive device, or *coup de théâtre* that served as a visual emblem for his interpretation of the text. For instance, in *Danton's Death* a huge wall of Halloween masks, variously lit for different scenes, anchored the theme of accumulating horror, a literal architecture of death.[13] For the ill-fated Shakespearean adaptation *Five Kings*, a revolving stage partitioned into separate playing areas gave spatial form to the idea of history as a continuous transformative flow of location and event.

Another facet to Welles's stage technique involved an emphasis on the material, even site-specific, conditions of the theater apparatus—lighting grid, curtain, wings, backstage area—in the creation of spectacle. That is, he seemed to possess a coextensive desire to startle an audience with "impossible" visions and to foreground the materials from which a spectacular effect was crafted, mixing a "delight in sharing an illusion [with] the mechanics of illusion."[14] He appears to have sought the means by which to break through the fourth wall convention of invisibility while erecting in its place, on the foundation of acknowledged artifice, a renewed sense of wonder. What must have inevitably suffered in this transaction was the viewer's mental identification with character, and this lapse was indeed a frequent source of critical denunciation.

While it is difficult to be more concrete about theatrical techniques, one might plausibly assume that Welles extended the foregrounding of materials to other creative endeavors. Recordings of the famous 1938 "War of the Worlds" radio broadcast demonstrate that Welles seized on both the rhetorical conventions and physical conditions of the medium to draw the listener into a web of illusion. In early portions of the broadcast numerous references to the current time and location of a speaker give a veneer of authenticity played off against the ensuing rapid compression of time and space. Similarly, an exaggerated insistence on first-person direct address ("Ladies and gentlemen . . .") gets turned against itself as the action intensifies and characters lose control of their measured speech and the assurance of a securely distanced audience ("Hello, is anyone there . . . ?"). Even more telling, and more formally inventive, is the use of enacted mechanical breakdowns: microphone feedback, interruptions of speech by ambient noise, long static-filled silences. Precisely those awkward material conditions that radio attempts to disguise or elide— among them the dramatic discrepancy between sight and verbal description that keys reports on the Martian invasion—become the tools of Welles's artifice. And the same formal acuity resurfaces in the newsreel sequence of *Citizen Kane*.

Finally, part of what made the Mercury Theater an experimental enterprise stemmed from its transposition of "cinematic" practices. Not only did Welles attempt to inscribe film sequences in individual productions, as in *Too Much Johnson* and *Around the World in 80 Days*, his approach to issues of pacing, optical scale, and style appeared to utilize properties of camera vision and editing inimical to the theater. *Horse Eats Hat* derived its madcap rhythms from Réné Clair's *The Italian Straw Hat* and possibly from Clair's dadaist farce *Entr'Acte*, which along with *Un Chien Andalou* and *The Cabinet of Dr. Caligari* were clearly parodic targets of *Hearts of Age*, Welles's schoolboy initiation into cinema. Several critics discerned "movielike techniques" in the mobility of settings in *Five Kings* and one commentator surmised that the clever use of a variable proscenium for the 1940 adaptation of *Native Son* evoked the endlessly flexible framing of motion picture editing.[15]

In François Truffaut's view, edging toward a transition from theater to film in 1939 naturally engaged Welles in figuring out the "differences and common points between the various media."[16] Considerably after the fact, however, Welles himself would decide that film and theater "are not in intimate rapport," that "technical solutions are so different for each of them that . . . I establish absolutely no relationship" between them.[17] Yet as is often the case, it pays to trust the tale rather than the teller. And the tale of *Citizen Kane* reveals, among many other designs and propositions, a rather thorough investigation of exactly the arena of technical solutions where film intersects, and poses radical alternatives to, an intractable condition of theater: the manipulation of an *illusion* of depth.

II

The great art historian Erwin Panofsky, writing in 1934 in support of film as a valid and independent art form, employs a tactic common to that period of film theory; he distinguishes "unique and specific possibilities" of the medium in contrast to those of other creative modes. Film is defined by its *"dynamization of space* and, accordingly, *spatialization of time."*[18] Panofsky develops this idea by opposing theater's "static" relation of the viewer to spectacle with the camera eye's "permanent motion." Without in any way suggesting that Welles was aware of this theoretical line of inquiry, his first encounters with the cinematic apparatus are everywhere etched with the ambition to transport the spectator through space in ways unimaginable, or impossible, in the theater.

The aborted plan for *Heart of Darkness* was to frame the narrative as a "journey" conveyed through a totally subjective camera optic, a technical problem whose solution proved overly costly and conceptually unwieldy.[19] Like his visionary mapping of the Conrad narrative, Welles discovers a perfect formal vehicle around which to organize the thematic tensions of Charlie Kane's life. Stated baldly, relations between public and private assessments of Kane's life—the "documentary" record against personal recollection—are limned and analogized by a constant fluctuation of image effects from absolute flatness to extreme spatial depth. Backward or forward movements within a shot or between shots, especially those involving two-dimensional objects (e.g., the page of a book or newspaper or legal document) and exaggerated interior perspectives (e.g., the reading room of the Thatcher Library) perform a multivalent function in *Citizen Kane*. Whereas the "flattest" views in *Kane* can remind us of the two-dimensional reality of the movie image, the "deepest" representations entice the eye with an unparalleled illusion of volumetric space. This modeling of an essentially social process by formal means is structurally reminiscent of the deployment of the border between Mexico and the United States in *Touch of Evil* and the elaboration of the trope of law-as-labyrinth in *The Trial*.[20]

From early theater production to late films, Welles has a proclivity for grounding moral or psychological or historical themes in an all-embracing, even reductive, stylistic device or visual motif. Because *Kane* is notorious in its encyclopedic passion, the repeated expansion-contraction of cinematic depth is but one of several key motifs; surely the jigsaw puzzle, glass paperweight, and hallway of mirrors have received ample attention as correlatives of Welles's *narrative* design. The play of flatness and deep space, however, is special insofar as its locus is not a single object or image and it can be mobilized through otherwise quite different formal gestures and narrative situations. There are at least twenty significant instances in which *Kane* engages the viewer in a choreographed reading of successive, at times mystifying or seemingly contradictory, fluctuations of cinematic depth.

The greater percentage occurs in the first half of the story, and the most striking and complicated examples are located in transitional segments—that is, where the narrational agency is neither a character's flashback memory nor the limited present-tense experience of journalist Thompson. Rather, the principal agent of knowledge is what Laura Mulvey refers to as the camera's autonomous "investigative drive," divorced from character perceptions and having the capacity to "materialise both the space of the film's enigma and the camera's privileged role in the film's subsequent unfolding of its enquiry into the enigma."[21] A primary function of the manipulation of depth is to install yet another, extradiegetic, source of knowledge (and commentary) within the roster of persons and other discursive entities—such as the newsreel—presenting facets of the Kane legend.

The opening sequence of *Citizen Kane* offers a protracted example of spatial compression, as if to cue the spectator to the formal roller coaster that follows. The flat, aspatial film title fades into a similarly flat close-up of a No Trespassing sign. A series of dissolves links fences and gates to a gradual movement across the fairytale grounds of Xanadu—presented in frozen long shots—to a lit gothic window. Richard Jameson comments that these initial shots "constitute an introduction to the most elemental language of the cinema."[22] More specifically, they introduce a range of surfaces, from the graphic flatness of the film's title to the hazy sign (whose message refers as much to the barrier of the movie screen as it does to the "life" depicted within it) to the unabashedly artificial Xanadu exteriors.

Several distinct methods of creating an impression of flatness are demonstrated: graphic two-dimensionality, camera proximity, and "deficient" rendering of a putatively expansive setting. The last method entails the perceptual paradox of a "long shot" that is recognized as flat due to the compositional quality of the image, as in the numerous newspaper photos of large-scale scenes that punctuate the body of the film.

Once the camera reaches the castle window—itself a barrier image—it magically transits from exterior to interior, and the sequence renews its inventory of spatial effects. A shallow field of snow, much like the previous fence surfaces, is followed by an image of a cabin, which a sharp backward movement reveals as the nostalgic paperweight. As we piece together what seems like a continuous spatial ensemble, the "exterior" long shot is transformed into an interior close-up. A moment later, following the huge mouth that shapes the word "Rosebud," the "closest" we ever get to Mr. Kane, the nurse's image glimpsed in a shard of the broken paperweight fosters a further paradox of close-up and long shot. This opening gambit—a declaration of narrative, thematic, stylistic, and metastylistic principles that, like publisher Kane's declaration on the first night of production, will soon be overturned—is brought to completion and we are given a new title card, "News on the March," and with it a new spatial terrain.[23]

If the newsreel sequence advances an investigation of the cinematic illusion of depth, it does so mostly through the technique of rapid editing, and thus is not as conducive to the measured contemplation of material underpinnings as other early sections. In the breakneck idiom of 1930s "infotainment," intertitles are blended with other graphic images—animated maps, photos, newspaper headlines—and with a wide variety of "archival" footage. Cut for maximum visual dynamics, spatial transpositions are accomplished by wipes, by sudden camera movements and object movements. For instance, a title card, "In its humble beginnings," introduces the development of the Kane press empire. In the next shot, an *Inquirer* truck races across the extreme foreground; as it passes the camera it exposes a deep view of the original newspaper building. A cut returns us to the flat image of a map with blinking lights to designate corporate growth. We then see a long shot of a grocery store that is interrupted by a passing car, this time compressing the space of the image. In the following shot in a papermill a roll of paper is thrust right at the camera from the extreme background.

Without belaboring the point, there is a concerted effort in this sequence to activate the viewer's capacity to assimilate and respond kinesthetically to rapid alterations in represented depth. In a sort of ragtime version of the variations orchestrated by Welles in later sequences, the newsreel sets up a dense counterpoint of proximate and distant, wielding spatial illusion like a musical instrument—a trombone perhaps or the bellows of an accordion.

The transition to the screening room editorial conference, itself depicted as a cave of moving shadows projected against a blank white surface, uses a blatantly reflexive gesture of material foregrounding. To detach the film-within-a-film from its enveloping dramatic context, the end title is shown first as an aspatial image coincident with the frame. Then it is shown from the side as a vignette within an interior space, forcing us to revise its original status and "remap" our orientation to the film's perspective. Two additional, rather ambiguous shots of the lighted projection booth window contribute to a developing motif of seeing certain images first as three-dimensional then as flat objects, or vice versa—or, improbably, as both flat and deep simultaneously (a good example is the reverse tracking shot from the window of the Kane family cabin that collapses a long shot of Charlie on his sled into a flattened screenlike square at the far end of the interior space).[24]

The segues into two succeeding sequences are marked by spectacular displays of spatial flexing amid the continuity of long takes—or more precisely, *pseudo–long takes*. Thompson's first visit to Susan in Atlantic City opens on a close-up of a rain-swept poster. A craning movement up the wall of the nightclub recalls the "scaling" of the Xanadu fences in the film's prelude. Depth suddenly expands as the camera reaches the roof and then tracks in toward the El Rancho sign, gliding through it and titling down until it reaches a close-up of the glass pane of a skylight. A tricky process shot allows an impression of continuous movement as the camera penetrates the interior of the club and descends to the floor, discovering Susan slouched over a table in the background. The trajectory here condenses several global themes and formal operations. It evolves from a flat representation—which is, nonetheless, ironized by the "tears" of rain that run down Susan's face[25]—to the person represented, yet withholds her emotional state by remaining in long shot. The exchange between flat and deep is mediated not once but twice: by "language" (the flat letters of the neon sign) and then by another screenlike rectangle containing a separate, disjunct image (the club interior seen through the window).

Turned away by Susan without a clue, Thompson arrives at the Thatcher Library where the camera again makes its own investigation whose object is space rather than Rosebud. A different medium of representation, a memorial sculpture, is featured as we see a close low-angle view of stony-faced Thatcher. A tilt down past the plinth provides a glimpse of a name plaque before tracking back to a long shot of Thompson at the librarian's desk. Once again Welles strings together diverse signifiers of personal identity, from iconic picture (or sculpted figure) to symbolic name to indexical trace (the actual Susan, Thatcher's handwriting). The librarian stands and moves toward an inner room, drawing our eye into the depths of the foyer. The camera tracks forward behind Thompson, reaching the open doorway just as a security guard parades into and out of the murky recesses of this sepulchral chamber. Then the door is slammed in our collective face. A dissolve through this thick barrier reexpands the space and the camera tracks in on Thompson seated before the Thatcher manuscript. Another dissolve brings us smack up against the giant letters of a page, scanning the opening line of text until perhaps the most miraculous transition in the history of cinema replaces words describing young Charlie with his animated image (a "character") at play in the snowy expanse of a white frame.

Citizen Kane is scarcely fifteen minutes old and already it has made an intensive foray into the mysteries of filmic illusion. Unlike the bulky, corporeal exertions of theatrical blocking, lighting shifts, and changes of scenery, the space of cinema can be "effortlessly" bridged. Long shot and close-up can not only coexist in separate zones of a single composition, the effect André Bazin found so liberating, they can be played off in dynamic, "impossible" choreographies within the shot and, with the aid of photographic trickery, brought into alignment *between* shots. The tools at hand are many and, under the guidance of inspired and playful collaborators,[26] wondrous.

A simple special effect transforms a close-up photograph of a rival newspaper's staff into a live-action long shot of the same crew under the command of Mr. Kane. An almost imperceptibly slow tracking movement on Bernstein in his corporate office changes a somewhat cold long shot into an intimate medium close-up in the course of an interview. The combined resources of camera angle, offscreen sound, actor movement, and object movement make Kane's task of signing over control of his depression-weakened empire into an intricate ballet of power relations and social impotence. In a long take Bernstein in close-up lowers a document to reveal Thatcher in medium shot, then Kane's voice announces his entrance in long shot; his heavy walk into the extreme background and his return to the legal proceedings are timed to the antagonists' musings on "greatness."

A pattern that figures in several of the above examples, accounting as well for a number of less spellbinding moments, deserves special acknowledgment. As befitting the central narrative and theme of the media's deforming publicity, *Kane* is suffused with printed documents. And rarely does a flat piece of paper make, as one might expect, a static appearance. Instead, as if in direct fealty to Panofsky's exclamation of cinematic ontology, these "lifeless" channels of information are constantly galvanized by quick camera movements or by a mise-en-scène in which a character brandishes a document for the camera only to sweep it away, disclosing an unanticipated vista. Consider, for example, the section of Thatcher's flashback in which he gets increasingly agitated by the headline hijinks of his former ward; a series of inflammatory front pages are pulled aside to show the older man's comical expressions in a variety of telling locations.

In regard to the foregoing strategy of spatial manipulation, I find it especially curious that André Bazin's much-celebrated cel-

ebration of Welles's visual style is predicated on the idea of a fixed
frame—directed at a film where hardly anything is allowed to sit
still for an instant. Although several insights are derived from *The
Magnificent Ambersons*, Bazin clearly intends his remarks to apply to
Welles's work in general.[27] He is certainly correct in saying Welles
breaks with "the usual practice of construction," but is just as
certainly mistaken in privileging "static shots of vertiginous duration" (72). Fastening on a scene from *Ambersons* that has virtually
no counterpart in Welles's oeuvre, the kitchen dialogue between
Fanny and George, Bazin extols the virtues of a composition for
which the addition of "the slightest camera movement" would
have "broken this heavy spell which forces us to participate intimately in the action" (72). Elsewhere Bazin presses his case for
absolute dramatic unity by admiring Welles's *refusal* to use camera
movements or other forms of reframing an integral action (76).
The lasting achievement engendered by the Wellesian long take
is the restoration to objects and settings of their "existential density, the weight of their presence" (80).

Even if *Ambersons* conforms in some degree to Bazin's prescrip-
tion, the method and epistemological lesson of *Citizen Kane* is
roughly the opposite of what Bazin asserts. As the most articulate
and influential champion of the ideology of cinematic realism, he
must of necessity blind himself to Welles's modernist, anti-
illusionist leanings.[28] Although the director is in truth an ambivalent fellow traveler in the movement(s) of filmic demystification,
a sort of realist agnostic or magical anti-illusionist, *Kane*'s genius
resides in the meshing of material paradox—the 3-D illusion on
a 2-D support—with an exploration of personal identity in an
age of mass media.[29] Assigning itself the problem of uncovering
the hidden essence of a powerful figure whose life provided an
endless source of public fascination, the film responds not just by
plumbing the depths of private memory but by juxtaposing con-
fidential anecdotes with a stream of codified biographical material,
underscoring the almost seamless yet achingly imperfect passage
from experience to artifact, from the inner depths to the flatness
of external records—including, Welles would seem to acknowledge, the representation that is *Citizen Kane*.

The newsreel producer instructs his minion that "it isn't enough to tell us what a man did, you've got to tell us who he was." But how can these interpretive realms be distinguished? What order of "truth" will be gained by doing so? And which, or what type of, agent of knowledge should be entrusted with the task? These are conundrums which the film nonetheless cannot and has little real interest in solving.[30] It is enough (!) that such questions are elicited, for the ultimate justification of the Rosebud quest is contained in its ability to instruct, and in so doing entertain and amaze us with the fantastic visual contrivance of the cinematic instrument, in particular its manifold process of creating spatial illusion. The positing of a single authoritative explanation of the Kane personality—whether it is Rosebud, the corrupting effects of wealth, or American social history—may be beside the point. The vehicle through which that biographical legend is conveyed, including historical variations and untapped resources, can be made to yield a *material* truth that is neither ambiguous nor a reification. It is available in the first instance not to the reflective or unconscious mind but to the organs of visual perception. To push the internal dynamics of a medium into the foreground of spectator experience indicates a decidedly modernist aspiration.

III

It should be obvious that not all movements of aesthetic modernism have been invested with avant-garde desiderata; color field painting and pop art, for example, refine modernist insights without offering the "difficulty" or cultural resistance expected of radical art. By the same token not all avant-gardes are modernist in method or scope; neither figurative surrealism nor most factions of German expressionism are commonly hailed within the modernist pantheon. However, in the context of film history at least until the French New Wave of the late 1950s, modernism and avant-garde practices, including those of economic production and social consumption, have generally appeared in tandem.

The aesthetic ramifications for film of adopting a modernist program can be reduced to three interrelated issues and their strategies of mobilization: the photographic illusion of depth on a flat plane; the cinematic conversion of still into moving pictures; and the limitations of narrative as organizing principle. In keeping with the modernist thrust in other arenas, especially painting and sculpture, a concern with defining the quiddity and potentialities of film became harnessed to an intensified exploration of "ontological" properties. During the brief flowering of a European avant-garde in the 1920s the problematics of screen space and movement took clear precedence over the issue of narrative (except for surrealist and, depending on one's demarcation of the term avant-garde, Soviet film artists). A core group of films, made predominantly by painters, adhering to the quest for formal rigor would include Richter's *Rhythmus 21*, Eggeling's *Symphonie Diagonale*, Leger's *Ballet Mecanique*, Duchamp's *Anemic Cinema*, Man Ray's *Emak Bakia*, and Vertov's *Man with a Movie Camera*. In each case the material play of flatness and depth is central.

Although Welles seems to have been aware of this aspect of European avant-garde activity, he was, judging from interview references and filmic allusions, far more intrigued by the movement's dramatic and comedic sides as represented by the work of Clair, Cocteau, Buñuel, and Dali. Nevertheless, regardless of the path or paths by which he arrived at *Kane's* modernist confrontation with spatial illusion—kinship with European avant-garde practices, brash determination (and contractual freedom) to experiment with Hollywood's technological toy, theatrical precedents—Welles's widely recognized formalism was an important spark for the movement of American independent filmmaking initiated in 1943 with Maya Deren and Alexander Hammid's *Meshes of the Afternoon*. This pioneering trance film, in its convoluted time scheme and subjective perspectives, owes a clear and acknowledged debt to narrative and visual strategies in *Citizen Kane*.[31]

Deren's continued pursuit of a "poetic" cinema in films such as *At Land*, and the spate of avant-garde psychodramas produced in the late 1940s by Kenneth Anger, Curtis Harrington, and others exemplify an intricate dialogue conducted with Hollywood forms by noncommercial, anticonventional filmmakers. Welles, along with Sternberg and perhaps von Stroheim, occupies a pivotal position in this dialogue as an aesthetically adventurous director stifled by the studio system yet lacking the fierce autonomy that would allow him to work at the cultural margins. Ironically, following his expulsion from the Hollywood industry Welles would wind up hammering together a group of personal, piecemeal projects, which in method and, at times, reception resemble the more impoverished precincts of experimental cinema.[32]

There is neither space nor urgent need to provide a nuanced account of the convergence of *Citizen Kane* with the modernist underpinnings of the American avant-garde. But it would be unwise to conclude without reexamining, from a less empirical vantage, the assertion of Welles's high modernist leanings, and the belief that the formal dynamics of his first Hollywood venture—which despite its dedicated "rule breaking" is indisputably marked at every turn by the demands and expectations of a mass cultural commodity—is in some sense commensurate with the rarefied effects of abstract painting or serial music.

The argument has been made in the negative by theorists Noël Burch and Jorge Dana.[33] Establishing a historical "crestline" of resistance—*Caligari, Potemkin, M, Vampyr*, and so on—to what they claim to be ideologically repressive "institutional codes," Burch and Dana locate *Citizen Kane* in an intermediary category of films not transparently determined by and complicit with dominant values but that, "for want of being dialecticised," mask their complicity behind a foregrounded "stylistic" (47). *Kane* therefore operates on a formal level merely by "amplifying the codes, whose operation becomes so grossly overdetermined that they thereby appear original" (47). What passes as "innovatory" in Welles's film fails to produce ambiguity or reflexive insight but "tends, in a relentlessly unilateral way, to accredit a number of myths which are perfectly acceptable to the dominant ideology" (54).[34]

This assault on *Kane* as being essentially hollow in its pretense to modernist critique would remain an obscure footnote did it not recall the distinction made by the highly influential proponent of modernist painting Clement Greenberg in his seminal article "Avant-Garde and Kitsch." Written in 1939, just as the historical engine of advanced American painting was revving up for its conquest of Western art, Greenberg's article laments the dominance of cultural kitsch as a sign of bourgeois decline for which the comforting and "indifferent" products of popular entertainment industries could serve as exemplar.[35] From an institutional perspective, then—and, for some, a historical perspective—*Kane* would seem to be kitsch.

Noël Carroll has recently advanced a different view. In what amounts to the epilogue of "Interpreting *Citizen Kane*" Carroll invokes Greenberg's distinction and suggests that the film, in virtue of its competing and unresolvable pronouncements about the essence of identity, "represents the possibility of a middle road . . . that is neither kitsch nor avant-garde."[36] His contention is carefully measured and appealing yet I feel that it blunts the edge of Welles's achievement by underestimating a genuine affinity with avant-garde practices. To be sure, the evidence I cite is rather narrowly formalistic; it skirts institutional and economic determinations while hedging the issue of narrative convention as militating against a truly modernist reflexivity. Nonetheless, if I am accurate in my appraisal of the prevalence and organizing force of *Kane*'s spatial expansion-contraction trope, a connection to high modernism, and especially to advanced painting, becomes less tenuous.

In a later consolidation of his remarks on the efficacy of avant-garde formal resistance, Greenberg hones the self-critical tendency of modernism into the axiom that each art (including, it now appears, film) has the task of elucidating "through the operations peculiar to itself, the effects peculiar and exclusive to itself." And further, "The task of self-criticism became to eliminate from the effects of each art any and every effect that might conceivably be borrowed from or by the medium of any other art."[37] In the case of painting it emerged that "Flatness alone was unique and exclusive to that art" (6). Thus the formal method or style of a particular painter might revolve around an original and percipient approach to the demonstration of a flat support. Hans Hoffman, for instance, was known in his work and his theorizing for a compositional tension "created by the simultaneous assertion of the two-dimensional surface plane and that of three-dimensional depth," a technique rather famously referred to as "push-pull."[38] It requires no giant leap of faith to reframe *Kane*'s concerted attention to the filmic illusion of depth as a gesture toward medium specificity, the search for those properties "unique and exclusive" to cinema. Nor does it take much ingenuity to perceive Welles's manipulations of space as analogous to, say, Hoffman's "push-pull" of surfaces. In truth, Welles was not, even in his initial foray into Hollywood's belly of the beast, a cubist or abstract expressionist in movie magician's clothing. There is such a swirl of diffuse sources, styles, and materials in *Citizen Kane* that the idea that it might univocally be dedicated to the demonstration of any single doctrine is ludicrous. What has characterized this film, and made it an enduring object of critical attention, is that it tries to do everything, to satisfy many masters at once: encapsulate a range of film historical trends and formulas; instigate a reform of Hollywood's narrative conventions; reconcile the prerogatives of popular art and high culture; address the "great man" theory of history in an age of mass media celebrity. In this pluralistic crucible of ambitions, there is ample room for the modernist testing of material limits. Given the multitude of disguises adopted by Welles both before and after *Kane*, the role of strident avant-gardist would have demanded only nominal fakery.

Notes

1. Juan Cobos, Miguel Rubio, and J. A. Pruneda "A Trip to Quixoteland: Conversations with Orson Welles," trans. Rose Kaplin, reprinted in *Focus on Citizen Kane*, ed. Ronald Gottesman (Englewood Cliffs, NJ: Prentice-Hall, 1971), 9.

2. Cited in Margaret Small and William G. Simon, "Rediscovering Welles' Theatre Work," in *Orson Welles: Theater, Radio, Film—Exhibition Catalogue* (New York: William G. Simon and Orson Welles Research Project, 1988), n.p.

3. Anthony Bower, *"Citizen Kane,"* in *American Film Criticism*, ed.

Stanley Kauffmann (New York: Liveright, 1972), 409; and Gottesman, *Citizen Kane*, 55.

4. Gottesman, *Citizen Kane*, 51. James Naremore compiles other instances of this charge in *The Magic World of Orson Welles* (New York: Oxford University Press, 1978), 45–46. Andrew Sarris weighs in on the same topic in "*Citizen Kane*: The American Baroque," in Gottesman, *Citizen Kane*, 103.

5. Toland's 1941 article, the tone of which seems very much under the influence of director Welles, is reprinted in Gottesman, *Citizen Kane*, 73–77.

6. Truffaut, foreword to André Bazin, *Orson Welles* (New York: Harper Colophon, 1972), 3.

7. The references are by Tangye Lean, in Gottesman, *Citizen Kane*, 60; Bazin, *Orson Welles*, 80; and Jorge Luis Borges, "*Citizen Kane*," in Gottesman, *Citizen Kane*, 127.

8. See Arthur Knight, "*Citizen Kane* Revisited," in Gottesman, *Citizen Kane*, 121. Manny Farber makes a similar, if less sanguine, point in his 1951 essay "The Gimp," in *Movies* (New York: Hillstone, 1971), 82.

9. This somewhat tangential topic has been argued at length in the art historical sphere by Serge Guilbaut in *How New York Stole the Idea of Modern Art*, trans. Arthur Goldhammer (Chicago: University of Chicago Press, 1983). On the recruitment of American literature in the international culture wars of the 1940s, see Lawrence H. Schwartz, *Creating Faulkner's Reputation* (Knoxville: University of Tennessee Press, 1988).

10. See, respectively, Richard France, *The Theater of Orson Welles* (Lewisburg, PA: Bucknell University Press, 1977), 88 and 153; and *Exhibition Catalogue*, n.p. Both of these sources contain additional attributions by newspaper and magazine reviewers.

11. Naremore, *Magic World*, 39.

12. France, *Theater*, 14.

13. See Ibid., 146–51, for production details and testimony.

14. Ibid., 55.

15. See, respectively, France, *Theater*, 159–60; and Kim Kline, "*Native Son*," in *Exhibition Catalogue*, n.p. James Naremore draws some similar inferences from the production design of *Julius Caesar*, in *Magic World*, 42.

16. In Bazin, *Orson Welles*, 11.

17. Cobos, Rubio, and Pruneda, "Trip," 14.

18. Erwin Panofsky, "Style and Medium in the Motion Pictures," in *Film: An Anthology*, ed. Daniel Talbot (Berkeley: University of California

Press, 1967), 18. V. I. Pudovkin, Rudolf Arnheim, and Allardyce Nicoll are among the writers making contemporaneous excursions into the gap between theater and film. Eisenstein's personal reckoning, "Through Theater to Film," appeared the same year as Panofsky's essay.

19. A useful account of the Conrad project is found in Robert Carringer, *The Making of "Citizen Kane"* (Berkeley: University of California Press, 1985), 1–15. Welles would return to this problem, albeit in a more conventional register, in *The Lady from Shanghai*, another subjectivized telling of a psychogeographic voyage.

20. To this group could be added the architectural structure of the mansion in *The Magnificent Ambersons*, the clocktower in *The Stranger*, and the image conceit of "interference" or disjunction in *Othello*.

21. Laura Mulvey, *Citizen Kane* (London: British Film Institute, 1992), 24.

22. In Ronald Gottesman, *Focus on Orson Welles* (Englewood Cliffs, NJ: Prentice-Hall, 1976), 68.

23. I have discussed at length the significance of *Kane*'s multiple openings and endings in Paul Arthur, "Orson Welles, Beginning to End: Every Film an Epitaph," *Persistence of Vision* 7 (1989): 44–46.

24. It should be obvious that there are many instances of images framed by or reflected in flat surfaces that appear as metaphoric incarnations of the movie screen that frames our vision: the window reflection of Charlie dancing during the *Inquirer* party and the receding mirror images of Kane after the destruction of Susan's room are two prominent examples.

25. Welles seems to have enjoyed this graphic joke so much that he used it again, several times, in *Touch of Evil*, as when a bottle of acid misses its target and strikes a poster advertising a stripper, giving a corrosive twist to the phrase "steamy sex."

26. The persuasive thrust of Carringer's *Making of "Citizen Kane"* is that credit for its visual design must be shared among director, cinematographer, and set designer. See his discussion of the elaborate effects employed to create the impression of spatial continuity, 92–94.

27. Bazin, *Orson Welles*, 72 (hereafter cited in the text).

28. Naremore, in *Magic World*, and Carringer, in *Making of "Citizen Kane,"* register objections to Bazin's construction of Welles's style that are related to, and ostensibly compatible with, my own; 49–51 and 83–85, respectively.

29. Peter Cowie offers an interesting reading of Kane as media-

sustained personality in "The Study of a Colossus," in Gottesman, *Citizen Kane*, 109–10.

30. Scott Bukatman makes a clever and engaging case for Welles as a practicing postmodernist whose late films *F for Fake* and *Filming Othello* fulfill the promise of earlier works such as *Kane* by gutting cinematic conventions, producing an absence of meaning in a "systematic refusal to totalize signification"; "Incompletion, Simulation, and the Refusal of the Real: The Last Films of Orson Welles," *Persistence of Vision* 7 (1989): 83–92.

31. P. Adams Sitney, *Visionary Film* (New York: Oxford University Press, 1974), 15. Sitney's discussion of the trance film in the book's opening chapter underscores further structural and thematic correspondences between Welles and the American postwar avant-garde. I analyze Welles's split function as actor and director and the psychodramatic undertow of *The Lady from Shanghai* in *On the Brink: Film Noir and Cold War America* (forthcoming).

32. While I am in disagreement with much of his argument, David Ehrenstein "promotes" Welles to the ranks of the avant-garde in *Film: The Front Line, 1984* (Denver, CO: Arden, 1984), 153–69. I have found no evidence to suggest that Welles knew of the growing network of independent filmmaking or that, if he had known, such a course was plausible for him. There have been occasional instances of avant-garde "upward mobility"—Harrington and John Cassavetes are two—but no *long-term* migrations from Hollywood to the avant-garde.

33. Noël Burch and Jorge Dana, "Propositions," *Afterimage* (U.K.) 5 (Spring 1974): 40–65 (hereafter cited in the text).

34. Stripped of its impenetrable locutions, the Burch-Dana argument parallels the complaints of Manny Farber in "The Gimp" and "White Elephant Art vs. Termite Art," in *Movies*, and those of Parker Tyler in "Orson Welles and the *Big* Experimental Film Cult," in *Film Culture Reader*, ed. P. Adams Sitney (New York: Praeger, 1970), 376–86. Where newspaper reviewers criticized the film for being narratively and visually "difficult" to assimilate, critics aligned with radical political or aesthetic agendas rebuked *Kane* for being too superficial and unreflective.

35. Art historian T. J. Clark summarizes Greenberg's conception of kitsch as "a culture of instant assimilation, of abject reconciliation to the everyday, of avoidance of difficulty, pretence [*sic*] to indifference, equality before the image of capital"; see "More on the Differences between Comrade Greenberg and Ourselves," in *Modernism and Modernity*, ed.

Benjamin H. D. Buchloh, Serge Guilbaut, and David Solkin (Halifax, Nova Scotia: Nova Scotia College of Art and Design, 1983), 177. Clark's brilliant reading of "Avant-Garde and Kitsch" has helped considerably in my formulation of Welles's radical impulse, and I wish to thank Scott Bukatman for suggesting its application.

36. It had never occurred to me to deploy the Greenberg argument on the cultural status of *Kane* until I heard Carroll deliver the paper published as "Interpreting *Citizen Kane*," *Persistence of Vision* 7 (1989): 51–62. At the time I told him that this line of inquiry was a critical dead end. Now, however, I want to turn Carroll's argument back on itself, or possibly around the bend, by claiming for *Kane* neither the purgatory of kitsch nor the honorable "middle road" but a solid contribution to the ongoing cinematic project of modernist demystification.

37. Clement Greenberg, "Modernist Painting," *Art and Literature* 4 (Spring 1965), reprinted in *Modern Art and Modernism*, ed. Francis Frascina and Charles Harrison (New York: Harper and Row, 1982), 5–6.

38. Barbara Rose, *American Art since 1900* (New York: Praeger, 1975), 129. Rose's review of modernist painting largely conforms to the Greenbergian model.

Suggested Reading

◆　◆　◆

In addition to the items listed below, there are several Web sites devoted to Orson Welles and to *Citizen Kane*. The most serious and useful of these is http://www.Wellesnet.com.

Altman, Rick. "Deep-Focus Sound: *Citizen Kane* and the Radio Aesthetic." *Quarterly Review of Film and Video* 15 (1994): 1–33. Also in Gottesman, *Perspectives on* Citizen Kane.

Bates, Robin, with Scott Bates. "Fiery Speech in a World of Shadows: Rosebud's Impact on Early Audiences." *Cinema Journal* 26, no. 2 (Winter 1987): 3–26. Also in Gottesman, *Perspectives on* Citizen Kane.

Bazin, André. *Orson Welles: A Critical View.* Trans. Jonathan Rosenbaum. New York: Harper and Row, 1978.

Beja, Morris, ed. *Perspectives on Orson Welles.* New York: Hall, 1995.

————. " 'Where You Can't Get at Him': Orson Welles and the Attempt to Escape from Father." *Literature/Film Quarterly* 13, no. 1 (1985): 2–9.

Berthomé, Jean-Pierre, and François Thomas. *Citizen Kane.* Paris: Flammarion, 1992.

Bordwell, David. "*Citizen Kane.*" *Film Comment* 7, no. 2 (Summer 1971): 38–47. Also in Gottesman, *Focus on* Citizen Kane, and in Beja, *Perspectives on Orson Welles.*

Bordwell, David, and Kristin Thompson. "Style in *Citizen Kane*." In *Film Art: An Introduction*. 4th ed. New York: McGraw-Hill, 1993, pp. 60–69.

Brady, Frank. *Citizen Welles: A Biography of Orson Welles*. New York: Scribner's, 1989.

Burch, Noël, and Dana Jorge. "Propositions." *Afterimage* 5 (1974): 40–66.

Bywater, William. "The Desire for Embodiment in Welles's *Citizen Kane*." *Post Script* 7, no. 2 (Winter 1998): 43–57.

Callow, Simon. *The Road to Xanadu*. New York: Viking, 1995.

Carroll, Noel. "Interpreting *Citizen Kane*." *Persistence of Vision* 7 (1989): 51–62. Also in Gottesman, *Perspectives on* Citizen Kane.

Carringer, Robert L. "*Citizen Kane*." *Journal of Aesthetic Education* 9 (April 1975): 32–49.

————. "*Citizen Kane, The Great Gatsby*, and Some Conventions of American Narrative." *Critical Inquiry* 2, no. 2 (1975): 307–25.

————. *The Making of* Citizen Kane. Berkeley: University of California Press, 1985.

————. "Rosebud Dead or Alive: Narrative and Symbolic Structure in *Citizen Kane*." *PMLA* 91, no. 4 (November 1976): 383–87.

Clipper, Lawrence J. "Art and Nature in Welles's Xanadu." *Film Criticism* 5, no. 3 (1981): 12–20.

Cohen, Hubert. "The Heart of Darkness in *Citizen Kane*." *Cinema Journal* 12, no. 1 (Fall 1972): 11–25.

Cook, David. *A History of Narrative Film*. 3d ed. New York: Norton, 1996.

Cowie, Peter. *A Ribbon of Dreams: The Cinema of Orson Welles*. New York: Barnes, 1973.

Damico, James. "News Marches in Place: Kane's Newsreel as a Cutting Critique." *Cinema Journal* 16, no. 2 (1977): 51–58.

Gilling, Ted. Interview with George Colouris and Bernard Herrmann on *The* Citizen Kane *Book*. *Sight and Sound* 41, no. 2 (Spring 1972): 71–3.

Gottesman, Ronald, ed. *Focus on* Citizen Kane. Englewood Cliffs, N.J.: Prentice-Hall, 1971.

————. *Focus on Orson Welles*. Englewood Cliffs, N.J.: Prentice-Hall, 1976.

————. *Perspectives on* Citizen Kane. New York: Hall, 1996.

Higham, Charles. *The Films of Orson Welles*. Berkeley: University of California Press, 1970.

Houseman, John. *Run-Through: A Memoir*. New York: Simon and Schuster, 1972.

Ishaghpour, Youssef. *Orson Welles: Cinéaste Une Caméra Visible*. 3 vols. Paris: Editions de la Difference, 2001.

Jaffe, Ira. "Film as the Narration of Space: *Citizen Kane.*" *Literature/Film Quarterly* 7, no. 2 (1979): 99–111. Also in Gottesman, *Perspectives on Citizen Kane.*

Kael, Pauline. "Raising Kane." Introduction to *The Citizen Kane Book.* Boston: Little, Brown, 1971.

Leaming, Barbara. *Orson Welles: A Biography.* New York: Viking, 1985.

Leff, Leonard J. "Reading Kane." *Film Quarterly* 39 (Fall 1985): 10–20. Also in Gottesman, *Perspectives on* Citizen Kane.

McBride, Joseph. *Orson Welles.* Rev. ed. New York: Da Capo, 1996.

Mulvey, Laura. *Citizen Kane.* London: British Film Institute, 1992.

Pipolo, Tony. "Screen Memories in *Citizen Kane.*" *Persistence of Vision* 10 (1993): 54–101. Also in Gottesman, *Perspectives on* Citizen Kane.

Rosenbaum, Jonathan. "Orson Welles as Ideological Challenge." In *Movie Wars: How Hollywood and the Media Conspire to Limit What Films We Can See.* Chicago, Ill.: A Capella Books, 2000, pp. 175–96.

Simon, William G., ed. *Persistence of Vision,* 7 (1989). Special issue on Welles.

Speidel, Sara, and Robert Brinkley. "Narrative Mimicry: *Citizen Kane* and the Function of the Gaze." *New Orleans Review* 14, no. 2 (1987): 72–83. Also in Gottesman, *Perspectives on* Citizen Kane.

Thomson, David. *America in the Dark.* New York: Morrow, 1997.

Tomasulo, Frank P. "Narrate *and* Describe? Point of View and Narrative Voice in *Citizen Kane*'s Thatcher Sequence." *Wide Angle* 8, nos. 3–4 (1986): 45–52. Also in Gottesman, *Perspectives on* Citizen Kane.

Trosman, Harry. "*Citizen Kane* and the Return of the Lost Object." In *Contemporary Psychoanalysis and Masterworks of Art and Film.* New York: New York University Press, 1996, pp. 138–56.

Wood, Bret. *Orson Welles: A Bio-Bibliography.* New York: Greenwood, 1990.

Production Credits

❖ ❖ ❖

PRODUCTION COMPANY: A Mercury Production for RKO Radio Pictures

PRODUCTION DATES: 29 June–23 October 1940

FIRST PUBLIC SCREENING: Palace Theater, New York City, 1 May 1941

U.S. PREMIERE: El Capitan Theater, Los Angeles, 8 May 1941

RUNNING TIME: 119 minutes

DIRECTOR: Orson Welles

PRODUCER: Orson Welles

ASSOCIATE PRODUCER: Richard Baer

ASSISTANT PRODUCERS: William Alland, Richard Wilson

SCREENPLAY: Herman J. Mankiewicz, Orson Welles, and (uncredited) John Houseman

PHOTOGRAPHY: Gregg Toland

CAMERA OPERATOR: Bert Shipman

ASSISTANT CAMERAMAN: Eddie Garvin

GAFFER: Bill McClellan

GRIP: Ralph Hoge

MUSIC: Bernard Herrmann

ART DIRECTOR: Perry Ferguson (Van Nest Polglase listed as department head)

ASSISTANT ART DIRECTOR: Hilyard Brown

SKETCH ARTIST: Charles Ohmann

SKETCHES AND GRAPHICS: Al Abbott, Claude Gillingwater, Jr., Albert Pyke, Maurice Zuberano

SET DECORATION: Darrell Silvera

ASSISTANT SET DECORATOR: Al Fields

PROP MANAGER: Charles Sayers

MAKEUP: Maurice Seiderman

ASSISTANT MAKEUP ARTIST: Layne Britton

COSTUME DESIGN: Edward Stevenson

WARDROBE: Earl Leas, Margaret Van Horn

SPECIAL EFFECTS: Vernon L. Walker (department head)

OPTICAL PRINTING: Linwood G. Dunn

EFFECTS CAMERAMAN: Russell Cully

MONTAGE EFFECTS: Douglas Travers

MATTE ARTIST: Mario Larrinaga

EDITOR: Robert Wise

ASSISTANT EDITOR: Mark Robson

SOUND: John Aalberg (department head)

MIXER: Bailey Fesler

BOOM: Jimmy Thompson

RERECORDING: James G. Stewart

SOUND EFFECTS: Harry Essman

DANCE CHOREOGRAPHY: Arthur Appel

CAST: Orson Welles (*Charles Foster Kane*), Joseph Cotten (*Jedediah Leland*), Dorothy Comingore (*Susan Alexander*), Agnes Moorehead (*Mary Kane*), Ruth Warrick (*Emily Norton*), Ray Collins (*"Boss" Jim Gettys*), Erskine Sanford (*Carter*), Everett Sloane (*Bernstein*), William Alland (*Thompson*), Paul Stewart (*Raymond*), George Coulouris (*Thatcher*), Fortunio Bonanova (*Matiste*), Gus Schilling (*Headwaiter*), Philip Van Zandt (*Mr. Rawlston*), Georgia Backus (*Miss Anderson*), Harry Shannon (*Jim Kane*), Sonny Bupp (*Kane, Jr.*), Buddy Swan (*Kane, age eight*), Al Eben (*Solly*), Ellen Lowe (*Miss Townsend*), Charles Bennett (*Entertainer*), Alan Ladd, Louise

Currie, Eddie Coke, Walter Sande, Arthur O'Connell, Richard Wilson, Katherine Trosper, Milt Kibbe (*Reporters*), Tom Curran (*Teddy Roosevelt*), Irving Mitchell (*Dr. Corey*), Edith Evanston (*Nurse*), Arthur Kay (*Orchestra Conductor*), Gino Corrado (*Gino, the Waiter*), Robert Dudley (*Photographer*)